ACADEMIC PRACTICE

Developing as a Professional in Higher Education

SAGE was founded in 1965 by Sara Miller McCune to support the dissemination of usable knowledge by publishing innovative and high-quality research and teaching content. Today, we publish more than 850 journals, including those of more than 300 learned societies, more than 800 new books per year, and a growing range of library products including archives, data, case studies, reports, and video. SAGE remains majority-owned by our founder, and after Sara's lifetime will become owned by a charitable trust that secures our continued independence.

Los Angeles | London | New Delhi | Singapore | Washington DC

ACADEMIC PRACTICE

Developing as a Professional in Higher Education

SARANNE WELLER

Los Angeles | London | New Delhi
Singapore | Washington DC

Los Angeles | London | New Delhi
Singapore | Washington DC

SAGE Publications Ltd
1 Oliver's Yard
55 City Road
London EC1Y 1SP

SAGE Publications Inc.
2455 Teller Road
Thousand Oaks, California 91320

SAGE Publications India Pvt Ltd
B 1/I 1 Mohan Cooperative Industrial Area
Mathura Road
New Delhi 110 044

SAGE Publications Asia-Pacific Pte Ltd
3 Church Street
#10-04 Samsung Hub
Singapore 049483

Editor: James Clark
Assistant editor: Rachael Plant
Production editor: Tom Bedford
Copyeditor: Joy Tucker
Proofreader: Caroline Stock
Indexer: Grace Rose
Marketing manager: Dilhara Attygalle
Cover design: Naomi Robinson
Typeset by: C&M Digitals (P) Ltd, Chennai, India
Printed and bound by CPI Group (UK) Ltd,
Croydon, CR0 4YY

© Saranne Weller 2016

First published 2016

Library of Congress Control Number: 2015935575

British Library Cataloguing in Publication data

A catalogue record for this book is available from
the British Library

ISBN 978-1-4462-7422-4
ISBN 978-1-4462-7423-1 (pbk)

This book is dedicated to my parents J. Elizabeth Weller and John Weller (1938–2010) and to Tim Julier.

CONTENTS

LIST OF FIGURES AND TABLES

Figures

Tables

ABOUT THE AUTHOR

Saranne Weller is Associate Dean Learning, Teaching and Enhancement at the University of the Arts London. Prior to taking up this role she was Assistant Director (Programmes) and Senior Lecturer in Higher Education at King's College London and previously Academic Development Adviser at the University of Surrey. She completed her PhD in English and Comparative Literary Studies at the University of Warwick in 2001. She has been teaching in higher education for 19 years, initially at undergraduate level and, subsequently, in academic development and higher education studies roles, at taught and research post-graduate level. She has previously published work on teaching observation, curriculum design, academic literacies and students as co-enquirers.

ACKNOWLEDGEMENTS

This book was written in part during research leave at both King's College London and the University of Arts London for which I am very grateful. I would also like to acknowledge the outstanding colleagues at both institutions and the many university teachers I have had the privilege to work with over the last 19 years. This book would never have been written without the incredible support and advice of James Clark and Rachael Plant at SAGE Publications. Finally, I would like to thank Tim Julier for his unfailing support.

SAGE would like to thank the following people whose valuable feedback helped to shape this book:

- Christopher Butcher, University of Leeds
- Clare Kell, Cardiff University
- Caroline Marcangelo, University of Cumbria
- Ruth Pilkington, University of Central Lancashire
- Pam Thompson, De Montfort University.

CHAPTER 1

BECOMING A TEACHER IN HIGHER EDUCATION

Introduction

This book is about being a teacher and a researcher in university. The routes into university teaching can be wide-ranging, teaching roles may differ and the formal research role of teachers may vary. Many teachers begin university teaching following doctoral or other higher degree study, but others are appointed on the basis of professional expertise, clinical or artistic practice experience or are undertaking teaching as PhD students while they themselves are also students. Teaching can be part of the role of lecturers alongside research commitments, but can equally be undertaken by teaching fellows, technicians, library or academic support staff or education technologists. For those with research roles, the need to maintain research and professional expertise alongside teaching may mean there is a tension between the demands and rewards for teaching or research. However, this book emerges out of what it might mean if we recognise the diversity of being a teacher and a researcher and see these as part of the multidimensional identity of those who are involved in teaching or the support of student learning in universities. Learning lies at the heart of research, professional or industry practice and teaching. To research or practise is to enquire, explore and recognise gaps in our understanding and to pose and answer questions. Likewise, teaching enables us to extend, test and explore our understanding of our disciplines with our students, as well as to enquire into the process of learning itself.

This book starts from the position that becoming a teacher in higher education, therefore, is first and foremost concerned with recognising ourselves as learners. We may have qualifications, expertise, knowledge and publications, but in essence we are continually learning both when we research and when we practise in our professional field, as well as when we teach. In this book we will consider what it is to be a teacher in contemporary higher education and how we might construct a meaningful multidimensional professional identity and role as a teacher in a complex and demanding sector undergoing tremendous change. This involves acknowledging that teaching is:

- reciprocal with learning – we cannot teach well if we do not recognise ourselves as learners in that process;
- a situated process that cannot be de-contextualised but takes place within a specific discipline, departmental and institutional setting;
- informed by the identity of a teacher and their values and beliefs about teaching, research and the role of the university.

These propositions all play out in the context of a sector that has increased student numbers, the participation of students from socio-demographic groups previously excluded from universities, different expectations about the outcomes of university study in relation to employment and the uses of knowledge in society as well as an increasingly global and technologically connected personal and professional world. In this chapter we will begin by exploring the implications of these propositions for new teachers. We will then explain the rationale for this book and how it will support you to engage with the ongoing questions about who we are as teachers, who we teach, to what purpose and how.

Understanding teacher identity in higher education

The traditional model of teaching has been described in transactional terms that position the teacher as authority and possessor of knowledge and teaching as an 'act of depositing' that knowledge into the minds of our students (Freire, 1970: 53). For many teachers, teaching is concerned with the presentation, transmission and retention of knowledge and this is manifested in the traditional didactic lecture, a monologue delivered to a student audience. An alternative position to this model, however, suggests a more emancipatory, democratic and transgressive conception of the relationship between student, teacher and knowledge. As a counter to a 'banking' model of education, Freire argues that 'in problem-posing education, people develop their power to perceive critically *the way they exist* in the world [...] they come to see the world not as a static reality, but as reality in process, in transformation' (p. 64, emphasis original). From this perspective teaching and learning are liberating, enabling us to interact with others to develop our mutual understanding in personal, collective and situated ways. Significantly, a conception of a teaching as either concerned with transformation or transmission has been found to relate to the approach that students then adopt to their learning: 'university teachers who focus on their students and their students' learning tend to have students who focus on meaning and understanding [...] while university teachers who focus on themselves and what they are doing tend to have students who focus on reproduction' of knowledge (Prosser and Trigwell, 1999: 142). What we think the purpose of learning and teaching is will influence what our students think the purpose of learning and teaching is.

The benefit of a student-rather than teacher-centred approach to teaching is that we reject a homogeneous 'rote, assembly-line approach to learning' and instead 'approach students with the will and desire to respond to our unique beings' and foster 'a relationship based on mutual recognition' (hooks, 1994: 13). This way of understanding the relationship between teachers and students as one of 'mutual recognition' and our knowledge of the world as a 'reality in process' enables us to acknowledge, first, our own ongoing learning experience as researchers or professionals who are also teachers and the impact our orientations to teaching will have on our students' learning. From this perspective we can understand learning and teaching as a 'partnership' in which 'staff and students [are] learning and working together to foster engaged student learning and engaging learning and teaching enhancement' (Healey *et al.*, 2014: 7).

The ambiguity of this academic identity as a process that is relational, situated and in partnership with students can be a valuable insight for new teachers. 'Becoming' a teacher in higher education involves a complex socialisation into the sometimes opaque culture of teaching and researching in a department or university (Smith, 2010). As Clegg (2008) argues, 'universities and academia are imaginary spaces as well as lived and experienced ones' (p. 339). Archer (2008) suggests teachers can experience feelings of 'inauthenticity' as a result of the juxtaposition of their gender, class, ethnicity, age or academic status as it relates with their imagined idea of the authoritative academic or teacher in university. New teachers may not feel they have the expertise, gravitas or status that is required to be an academic when they enter the academy. While the projected image of meritocratic university is often unquestioned, universities are social spaces that inevitably reflect the values, assumptions and histories of wider society including limiting constructions of race, gender, class and worth (ibid.). Understanding that academic identity is socially constructed means it is not something that we have or do not have, but is a process always in action that is an outcome of our individual agency, the personal values, aims and experiences as we teach or research as it relates to the social structures of institutional, disciplinary or professional contexts. Our academic identities are profoundly contextual and our practices are 'simultaneously about the individual *and* the group […] created socially, strongly influenced by the communities with which we identify and to which we feel a sense of belonging' (McAlpine and Åkerlind, 2010: 4).

Many disciplines and institutions have robust sets of values, traditions, narratives and histories that define, and are in turn shaped by, teachers' and researchers' identities. The process of becoming a teacher, therefore, involves exploring these collective values of the discipline with our students and how they interact with our own personal beliefs. This includes how the discipline generates new knowledge, how it validates or sanctions that knowledge, how it is communicated and used and how it should be taught. Yet it also means negotiating sometimes tacit assumptions about who has the right to engage in higher education or in a specific discipline and what are appropriate academic behaviours or practices. Being a teacher in higher education, therefore, involves understanding teaching as a social practice that is defined by the individual in relationship with their institution, department, discipline, peers and students.

The idea of the 'academic', therefore, is not a stable one and has changed significantly over a number of decades. While many teachers become teachers as a result of completing doctoral study, the data for 2012–13 reveals that only 53 per cent of academic staff in UK higher education hold a doctorate as the highest qualification with the remaining proportion having a range of higher degree postgraduate or undergraduate qualifications (UUK, 2014). In many fields, such as law, management, healthcare, engineering, education and creative arts, it is professional expertise and experience that are important prerequisites for a teaching role in university. At the same time, the conventional idea of an holistic 'tripartite role of academics in teaching, research and service activities' has also become increasingly 'unbundled' with the rise of the specialisation of research, teaching, leadership and support roles and activities. This has seen the rise of the 'para-academic' roles that include specialist researchers, teachers, student support advisers and library staff, technicians and learning technologists (Macfarlane, 2010: 59). In this context, traditional terminology such as 'academic' or 'lecturer' excludes the many individuals and roles that support student learning in universities. Teaching is also an unstable and shifting concept. It may involve one-to-one study support, laboratory and studio teaching as well as lectures and seminars. This shifting definition of teaching is exemplified in the more recent recognition of research supervision as teaching as well as research. Working with research students not only promotes the research objectives of a supervisor, but also involves the development of students as they learn to be researchers through the process of 'becoming a peer' within the research community their supervisor belongs to (Bruce and Stoodley, 2013; Boud and Lee, 2005: 511). Teaching, therefore, is not a set of transferable skills or strategies but is a dynamic, complex and situated process that requires teachers to interpret and make ongoing critical judgements about the identities, relationships and practices of all those involved. Layered over this are sector and institutional demands for teachers to respond to new policy agendas such as employability, inclusivity, internationalisation, digital technologies and student engagement. The aim of this book is to support teachers to navigate and respond to these debates in their practice.

Rationale and structure of this book

The understanding of teaching in higher education articulated above has determined the structure of this book. This model of teaching practice emphasises the reciprocity and mutuality of the learning of teachers and students at all levels in the university. We begin by considering the ways in which disciplines are socially constructed to define what knowledge is, how we create it, who sanctions and regulates it and how it is shared. For many new teachers, their initial identity is framed by the disciplinary and professional communities to which they previously belonged as postgraduate researchers or professional experts. Part I of the book, therefore, supports the process of translating this understanding of the discipline into meaningful learning experiences for students through the curriculum as we develop from disciplinary and professional expert to teacher of the discipline. The social practices approach to learning and teaching accentuates how we engage our students as valuable members of the disciplinary and university community and how we seek to integrate the sometimes separate priorities of teaching and research within our curricula. Through Part I, we develop an awareness of our beliefs, values and assumptions about the subjects we teach and how we and our students make meaning as we engage with the subject matter.

For many teachers, the demands of teaching their discipline are framed by wider institutional strategies that emphasise the employability, inclusivity and international relevance of their degrees, as well as different ways in which we might teach and learn virtually and collaboratively. While professional development for new teachers can focus on the different genres of teaching such as small group teaching, lecturing, assessment, curriculum design, e-learning or feedback, these institutional priorities enable us to think about teaching thematically in ways that help us to interrogate the purpose of university and what we are trying to achieve before we think about how we do that. In Part II we will look at this context and how we can respond and develop our teaching through our understanding of the purpose of higher education study. We will explore critically the policies, debates and research that inform these agendas, but also how we can respond as teachers to these priorities in practical and meaningful ways that helps us to extend our practice.

Being a member of the university community ultimately means learning to become a disciplinary or professional expert, translating that expertise into learning experiences that engage our students and becoming a researcher into the practices of teaching to continuously improve the student learning experience as the context changes. Teachers have to learn how to engage their students, how to reframe complex ideas through language and learning experiences that help a diverse student cohort make personal meaning rather than just rehearse what we tell them in lectures and, lastly how to make professional judgements about learning and teaching that are based on interpreting evidence and planning for change. In Part III we explore some of the ways in which becoming a professional means having the capacity as educators to make decisions about our teaching and drawing informed conclusions that in turn will challenge, enhance and develop our own disciplinary and pedagogic understanding.

In each chapter we will explore the research that has been undertaken into higher education learning and teaching and how we can use these ideas to inform our teaching practice. The language of educational research and academic development can be obfuscating, unpersuasive or disheartening for many new teachers who are unfamiliar with the specific methodologies, concepts and ways of communicating in educational research (Weller, 2011). The aim here is to engage with the complexities and debates without being reductive and finding practical ways to enact these ideas in practice. The case studies, 'Focus on practice' activities and further reading in each chapter are all designed to help that process of reflecting critically on our personal values and the context within which we teach as the basis for developing our practice. The case studies, in particular, have been selected on the basis that they are examples of teachers responding to questions they have about their own teaching in a range of disciplines, at different levels and in different types of institutions across the four nations of the UK. While reading from the beginning to the end of the book chronologically maps the trajectory of our development as a professional educator from disciplinary expert to scholarly teacher, equally each chapter can be read as a standalone introduction for those interested in exploring a specific topic or finding a solution to a particular challenge in practice. Ultimately, no book can be comprehensive and is only ever a starting point for the professional process of asking our own questions about why and how we teach. It is these questions that enable us to explore what we believe teaching and learning are, what it is to practise our discipline or profession, how we learn throughout our careers and how we can share this with our students as the basis for enhancing their own learning journeys.

PART I

FROM DISCIPLINARY EXPERT TO TEACHER

CHAPTER 2

DEVELOPING DISCIPLINARY UNDERSTANDING

Learning objectives

This chapter will support you to:

- Reflect critically on the characteristics of disciplines and the distinctive 'ways of thinking and practising' as experts in your field;
- Explore how these disciplinary 'ways of thinking and practising' can be made visible to students in teaching and supervisory practice;
- Introduce learning experiences into your practice that will help students develop their expertise and participate as new members of your discipline community.

Introduction

For many new teachers in higher education the progression to a teaching role is likely to have evolved out of a prolonged engagement with their discipline through postgraduate study, research or professional practice and applied experience. As an expert, you will have developed a depth of understanding of the discipline, how to think and practise as, for example, a physicist, economist, historian, artist, dentist or engineer, using commonly agreed concepts and methodologies to generate new knowledge through research or practice. You will also understand how to validate that knowledge and communicate it to others in a language that is meaningful to your academic or professional community. While this depth of understanding and expertise is a prerequisite for higher education teaching, however, as educators we need to appreciate how the discipline as it is taught differs from the discipline as it is defined by this research or practice experience. As researchers, practitioners or professionals that are also university teachers, when we attempt to introduce students to the concepts, practices and traditions of the discipline we need to find ways to make the structures, values and communication conventions of different disciplines visible and accessible to our students. The transition from disciplinary expert to disciplinary teacher, therefore, is an important process of developing our self-awareness of what it means to belong to a disciplinary community, the behaviours, values and what Meyer and Land (2003) describe as the 'ways of thinking and practising', as the basis for making the discipline meaningful for students.

In thinking about how to teach in the different disciplines, it is helpful to distinguish between the content or the body of knowledge in terms of the topics and themes of the subject from the different ways we generate, interpret, critique and evaluate that knowledge (Kreber, 2009). The idea of a subject is 'reassuringly concrete' because it can be defined as 'packages of knowledge and skills' that are 'taught, learned and delivered'. Lecture themes or chapters in textbooks often reflect this breakdown of the discipline into agreed topics that all students will need to master if they are to become disciplinary experts. We can, however, look at the idea of the discipline in a different way and consider that 'to be engaged in a discipline is to shape, and be shaped by, the subject, to be part of a scholarly community, to engage with fellow students – to become "disciplined"' (Parker, 2002: 374). This distinction between a passive subject knowledge base and the more fluid idea of becoming part of a disciplinary community is valuable because it helps us to think about the complex behaviours, practices, values, assumptions and attitudes we hold as disciplinary specialists and how we enable or deny access to our disciplinary community through the way we work and communicate. From this perspective, while the subject matter is what 'we look at', the modes of thinking and practising in the discipline can be understood as the 'disciplinary lens that we look with and through' (Kreber, 2009: 11). As new teachers we may be tempted to focus on including as much of the disciplinary body of knowledge in the curriculum as possible. But in doing so we significantly overlook how our students learn to generate, develop, apply and appraise that body of knowledge as new members of our discipline.

From this perspective, teaching in the disciplines is not about transmitting a discrete and ever-increasing subject matter but about connecting students to an academic, professional or research disciplinary community and helping them to perceive and participate in the 'ways of thinking and practising' that this community uses to make sense of the world.

The capacity to be aware of our distinctive behaviours and language means we can also recognise and distinguish the behaviours and languages of those working in other disciplines. This is valuable because, ultimately, we can then see how the same subject matter might be looked at through different disciplinary lenses and recognise the potential of interdisciplinary perspectives for solving real-world problems. For example, engineering students might look at the challenges of providing infrastructure systems for a new 'ecotown' development. This same topic, however, could also be looked at from the perspective of human geographers, economists, sociologists, architects or by individuals studying politics, media and communications or public relations. Each disciplinary perspective might draw on different theoretical concepts, identify different priorities or concerns and apply different methods for collecting and analysing data to understand the concept of an 'ecotown'. They will also use different ways to communicate the outcomes of the analysis and identify and speak to different stakeholders and audiences. Each perspective has validity and will generate knowledge outcomes that are rich and complex. Yet looking at the same topic from multiple disciplinary perspectives might also reveal the limitations or bias that a single perspective can bring to understanding a concept or problem. Understanding a discipline is also about understanding how the 'ways of thinking and practising' can differ from other disciplines. We will look at how we can exploit interdisciplinary thinking to enhance disciplinary thinking as well as to solve problems and foster criticality and creativity in Chapter 3.

The primary challenge for many new teachers is that, as disciplinary experts who become teachers, we can be so proficient in using one particular disciplinary lens that we find it difficult to articulate the intuitive assumptions and decision-making processes that we use when we analyse, select or reject and synthesise complex information about the world around us. This can be the case whether we are teaching an introductory module in the first year of undergraduate study or supervising a doctoral student. It can also mean that we do not take account of the other ways a particular topic could be looked at or how combining one or more perspectives might give greater insight and new understandings. Teaching the subject matter without explaining its parameters and assumptions or failing to contextualise it within the often tacit ways of working within a discipline means our students may appear to have achieved an appropriate level of mastery of key content, facts or information because they can correctly repeat back the subject matter to us at the end of a module. Yet they may, in reality, lack the genuine ability to critically interrogate, reflect on or modify that subject matter in new situations. In our teaching, curriculum design and supervisory practice, therefore, we need to find ways to verbalise and demonstrate our expert disciplinary practices, whether that be, for example, a clinical procedure, a critical evaluation of sources, communicating knowledge to others or constructing a legal argument. If we are able to articulate how we interpret the world in our discipline, we can then help students to adopt these 'ways of thinking and practising' and become critically aware of the disciplinary lens through which they are looking at a particular topic.

Translating the discipline as research into the discipline as taught is a process that Bernstein (2000) describes as the 'pedagogising of knowledge' whereby intellectual and practical discipline knowledge is transformed into a form that we can teach and students can learn. This means translating the disciplinary practices into specific teaching and learning practices, or pedagogies, that we use in education contexts. In this chapter we will begin by thinking about how we define the nature of the discipline. For example, are disciplines primarily the result of distinct and fixed ways in which knowledge exists or are different disciplines more fluid concepts that are the outcome of long histories and narratives that bind members of a group together? Inevitably, the discipline we are aligned to may well determine how we think about the nature of disciplinarity itself. What then are the implications for learning and teaching if we think about the nature of disciplines in these different ways? We will look at how we might introduce students to the discipline and how we make that process visible to ourselves and to our students as part of the way we plan the curriculum. We will look specifically at how we support our students to learn and be reflective about the disciplinary lens they are using to see, define and interpret data through which to understand the world.

How do we define disciplines?

There are two main ways we might approach the idea of the discipline:

- an epistemological perspective that is concerned with the nature of knowledge and differentiates between disciplines on the basis of inherent and distinctive ways in which that knowledge is structured and organised;
- a social perspective that defines disciplines in terms of how they reproduce existing social structures or are enacted collectively through distinctive disciplinary ways of behaving and their practices, as well as the histories, narratives and shared meanings of the individuals who undertake research and teaching within the discipline (Chettiparamb, 2007; Trowler, 2012).

The epistemological perspective is based on the principle that there is a defined and discrete form and structure of knowledge that is essential to the nature of, for example, physics or history. From this position, a discipline has distinctive characteristics: a body of knowledge, specific methods to carry out enquiry, and validate that knowledge base, and a specialist language to communicate the outcomes of enquiry that are inherently related to the form of knowledge. Biglan's (1973) influential classification of disciplines proposed that departments in universities and the individuals who work within them are organised and act in characteristic ways as a direct outcome of the fundamental differences in the essential structure of different disciplines. Subsequently it has been argued that approaches to the curriculum and the learning, teaching and assessment methods that are used by teachers will also reflect these traits (Neumann *et al.*, 2002).

Based on this conception of knowledge, Biglan (1973) differentiated disciplines in terms of where they can be plotted along two dimensions. First, disciplines could be plotted along a continuum from 'hard' to 'soft'. In a hard discipline there is likely to be consensus among researchers and educators about the content and methods of enquiry that are used, there are universal laws and the outcomes of enquiry are deemed to be generalisable. In contrast, 'soft' disciplines have less clearly defined theories, the content and methods used can be 'idiosyncratic' and reflect changing attitudes and values. 'Soft' disciplines can also have loosely defined parameters. Second, Biglan suggested that disciplines can be categorised along another continuum on the basis of their interest or not in the practical application of disciplinary knowledge to solving problems. Pure disciplines do not generate knowledge that can be directly applied to real-world problems or have immediate professional implications. Applied disciplines, however, have direct relevancy to the professions or seek to solve specific social or policy problems. Within this classification, natural sciences such as physics or chemistry and mathematics are described as both 'hard' and 'pure' disciplines. Medicine and engineering are described as 'hard' and 'applied' disciplines. In contrast, history and philosophy and some social sciences, such as sociology, are categorised as 'soft' and 'pure' disciplines while law and education are described as 'soft' and 'applied' disciplines.

From this perspective, different disciplines are seen to inevitably result in the selection and use of teaching, learning and assessment methods that reflect the structure and ways of developing knowledge in each discipline. For example, because 'hard', 'pure' disciplines such as physics are seen to have a hierarchical and cumulative knowledge structure, the curriculum is likely to be organised in a hierarchical and linear way. In a physics degree, therefore, you may learn foundational mechanics and mathematics in your first year before you progress to electromagnetism or quantum mechanics in subsequent years. You essentially need to learn some principles and concepts before you learn more advanced concepts. As the subject matter is considered propositional or factual in nature, with little need to debate or discuss ideas, teaching methods are more likely to be based on teaching in large group lectures supplemented by smaller, focused problem classes and laboratories. Assessment also aims for objective assessment judgements using multiple choice or short answer examination. In contrast, in 'soft', 'applied' disciplines such as, for example, education the subject matter is seen as more holistic and reiterative. Teaching methods are likely to be based around small group discussion and group work with opportunities to apply theory to practice and gain practical experience in professional contexts. Similarly, assessment is likely to be through essays, coursework and open-ended problem-solving (Trowler, 2012).

At face value it can appear intuitive and justifiable to presume that the way we organise a topic or topics in the curriculum, the teaching practices we adopt and the assessment choices we make all derive from the innate, unchangeable characteristics of each discipline. Yet this perspective on disciplinary difference can also be limiting and ignore the 'dynamism that disciplines display: growing, morphing and splitting' (Trowler, 2014: 1721). It also closes down options for disciplinary teachers to explore the ways teachers in other disciplines might organise the curriculum and precludes experimentation with different learning experiences influenced by other disciplines. It also means, if we assume the way we teach is profoundly and inescapably connected to what we teach, we cannot explore with our students both their, and our, own personal ways of working in the disciplines. The question this raises is: are these decisions we make about teaching inevitably the result of the subject matter, or a result of the traditions and preferences of researchers and teachers in those disciplines, or a combination of these factors? As teachers we can be influenced by the teachers, learning and teaching practices we experienced, where we studied and the types of teaching we personally preferred or disliked. What this reveals is the possibility that the way we organise learning and teaching might have more to do with the cultural customs, language and personalities of those who study a discipline than the innate qualities of the subject matter itself. This includes 'particular understandings, forms of discourse, values or ways of acting' that form the basis for 'what it might mean to be part of a particular disciplinary community' (McCune and Hounsell, 2005: 257). This second perspective on disciplines takes into account the actions of individual teachers, the learning and teaching context and the narratives, histories, values and beliefs that inform the structure of knowledge and how it is passed on to others. This means 'the stories faculty tell each other about disciplines and subdisciplines are very significant and help create a kind of reality themselves' (Trowler, 2012: 185).

One outcome of this alternative way of thinking about the discipline is that we do not focus on the subject matter as 'content to be transmitted' but view it as 'in dynamic relationship with the practices that are implicated in its creation, interpretation and use' or the methods for generating and evaluating new knowledge. This places an emphasis on the '*performance* of disciplinary ways of thinking and practising in relation to subject knowledge' or how we 'do' the subject. Over time, disciplines and the way we teach them can change and both teachers and students have an 'active and interpretive role' in the formation and enacting of disciplinary knowledge (Anderson and Hounsell, 2007: 475, emphasis original). As teachers and learners we are not constrained by the predetermined structure of a discipline but can explore, experiment and introduce new ways of learning and teaching or understanding knowledge alongside or instead of traditional, tried and tested methods we experienced as students. An important outcome of this mutual active role for teachers and students is that assumptions about who legitimately creates new knowledge through research are challenged. We will explore this relationship between research and teaching in Chapter 6.

Identifying disciplinary ways of thinking and practising

The advantage of identifying and exploring the disciplinary 'ways of thinking and practising' in a discipline with teaching colleagues as well as students is that it can be a way for disciplinary experts to understand how students learn the subject matter. Anderson and Hounsell (ibid.) suggest that, from this standpoint, 'rather than seeing their encounter with a discipline in terms of an all-or-nothing acquisition of an "object"' (p. 467) we can look at where students might experience critical or challenging moments or struggle to understand the language we use. The way we engage as experts in critical thinking, problem-posing, problem-solving and communicating in our disciplines, however, is likely to be mostly tacit. Students are also unlikely to fully master these ways of organising their thinking or working within the discipline simply by immersion or acculturation. If we think critically as disciplinary experts about the moments when students experience difficulties, however, as disciplinary teachers, we can begin to identify and introduce learning and teaching interventions that support students to see and develop their disciplinary thinking and practice. One way for teachers to do this is to 'decode the disciplines' (Middendorf and Pace, 2004) for students by looking at those moments in the curriculum that might block student learning. You can then think through how you and your peers undertake these tasks as experts and break down these particular skills into more manageable and explicit steps for your students. You then create opportunities for students to practise and get feedback on their attempts to perform these 'ways of thinking and practising'. Focusing on the subject matter in this way is about making explicit those things that are often hidden to new members of the disciplinary community. These can be 'bottlenecks' or 'obstacles' where many students stall or struggle to understand the subject matter. Sometimes these 'bottlenecks' can be significant 'threshold concepts' or '"conceptual gateways" or "portals" in a discipline that lead to a previously inaccessible, and initially perhaps "troublesome" way of thinking about something' (Meyer and Land, 2005: 373). The work on 'decoding the disciplines' in the USA and the 'ways of thinking and practising' in the UK emerged concurrently during the early 2000s and reflect a wider interest in defining disciplines in more social and collective ways. There are some differences between the two approaches and how they can be used to help educators plan for learning and teaching. One notable difference is that not all 'bottlenecks' in learning will be significant 'threshold concepts'. It is also recognised that not all students will struggle to grasp new ideas or new ways of thinking at the same time or in the same way. Interrogating where these critical moments might occur for some of our students and exploring how we can help these students to push past these obstacles, however, is a powerful way to translate our disciplinary expertise into meaningful pedagogic practice.

It is useful to define what makes a threshold concept within the curriculum. Meyer and Land (2003, 2005) argue that threshold concepts are likely to be:

- transformative: because 'we are what we know' (Cousin, 2006: 4), when we successfully apprehend a new concept we inevitably change our perspective in ways that can lead to transformation of who we are as a person. Understanding some concepts can mean that you not only change how you see the world, but also change your values, how you feel and who you are as a person;
- irreversible: once a new concept is understood it is almost impossible to unlearn it and this is why it can be very difficult for experts to recall how it felt before they crossed through this conceptual gateway;
- integrative: acquiring one concept opens up the possibility that learners will make connections with other concepts and reveal the potential networked nature of knowledge that was previously unavailable to them;
- troublesome: those aspects of the discipline that are threshold concepts are likely to involve what has been described as 'troublesome knowledge', or ways of knowing that can, for example, seem inconsistent or paradoxical and alien in the sense that they emerge out of a different perspective or language (Perkins, 1999, in Meyer and Land, 2003);
- discursive: crossing a conceptual threshold also involves changing or extending a learner's language or communicative repertoire. The specific demands of academic writing and the negotiation of the terminology and specialist language typical of experts or of practitioner communities mean that mastering new concepts will also mean mastering new ways of speaking.

Ultimately, it is unlikely that there will be consensus among discipline experts about the 'bottlenecks' or 'threshold concepts' in all disciplines or in all contexts. The important point is that we can use the idea of problem moments for those new to a discipline to shift our focus from thinking about teaching for the acquisition of disciplinary content to paying more attention to teaching students how to use the 'disciplinary lens that we look with and through'. Identifying 'threshold concepts' in a discipline can help us define the nature of that disciplinary lens. We can think about these concepts as the 'jewels in the curriculum' (Cousin, 2006: 5) which represent key moments in a student's learning experience. The process of investigating these moments of struggle also means that, as a discipline expert, we need to listen deeply to our students to try to hear where and how these moments are experienced as obstructive or challenging as it happens. As with any skill that we have mastered, remembering why something is challenging or empathising with a beginner's confusion or limitations of viewpoint is demanding. If 'threshold concepts' are transformative and change us as a person, looking back across them means remembering how the world looked from the perspective of someone we are no longer. We cannot forget this new knowledge once we hold it: it is irreversible.

While the idea of 'threshold concepts' is valuable in helping us to think about the fundamental ideas in a discipline and how they might relate to each other, the challenge is how we turn this knowledge into learning and teaching opportunities. The idea of 'decoding the disciplines' is useful because it embeds pedagogic decisions into the process of identifying, exploring and defining for students the points of a curriculum where they might struggle. Decoding a discipline requires a staged process to help break down composite and complex ways of thinking or practising into individual and incremental steps. Once we identify a disciplinary process that students struggle with, disciplinary specialists must critically reflect on and demonstrate to students how an expert might carry out each process and create opportunities for students to practise and get feedback on the elements of the task. Finally, assessments are designed to test students' mastery of these steps of understanding or practising as a whole. The six stages of the process and the questions that can help unpack the complex stages of the disciplinary practices are summarised in Figure 2.1. Middendorf and Pace (2004) include a seventh step focused on sharing with others what you have learnt from this process of enquiry into the curriculum. This commitment to making public your investigations into learning and teaching in your discipline and in your context is an important part of ensuring you are explicit and can explain your ideas to someone else. We will return to this in Chapter 12, when we look at ways we can engage in learning and teaching as scholarly teachers.

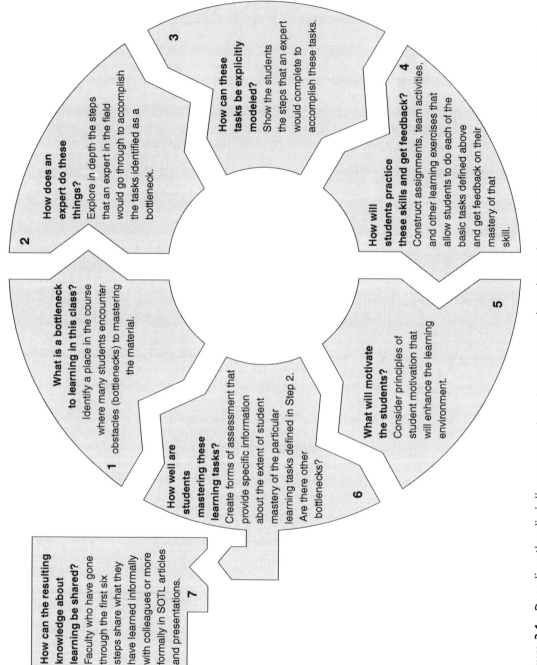

Figure 2.1 Decoding the disciplines: seven steps to overcome obstacles to learning (Reproduced with permission from Middendorf and Pace, 2004)

1 **What is a bottleneck to learning in this class?** Identify a place in the course where many students encounter obstacles (bottlenecks) to mastering the material.

2 **How does an expert do these things?** Explore in depth the steps that an expert in the field would go through to accomplish the tasks identified as a bottleneck.

3 **How can these tasks be explicitly modeled?** Show the students the steps that an expert would complete to accomplish these tasks.

4 **How will students practice these skills and get feedback?** Construct assignments, team activities, and other learning exercises that allow students to do each of the basic tasks defined above and get feedback on their mastery of that skill.

5 **What will motivate the students?** Consider principles of student motivation that will enhance the learning environment.

6 **How well are students mastering these learning tasks?** Create forms of assessment that provide specific information about the extent of student mastery of the particular learning tasks defined in Step 2. Are there other bottlenecks?

7 **How can the resulting knowledge about learning be shared?** Faculty who have gone through the first six steps share what they have learned informally with colleagues or more formally in SOTL articles and presentations.

For Middendorf and Pace (ibid.) there are a number of ways you can undertake the decoding process. They use face-to-face interviewing by someone outside the discipline with prompt questions to probe and help to elicit expert practices and they also suggest disciplinary experts write and discuss assessment rubrics that articulate precisely what they are looking for in the performance of disciplinary practices. Concept mapping is also useful for exploring the 'networks of knowledge' that form the expert knowledge of researchers and professionals and make it available to others. Hay *et al.* (2008) warn that large group teaching in particular can encourage superficial rote learning because 'lecturing requires that teachers convert complex scholarly networks of knowledge to simple and linear chains' (p. 306). Concept maps are made up of specific ideas (or concepts) that are joined together by labelled links to make short statements. They can be constructed by hand on paper, using drawing tools within word-processing software or open-source digital mapping software. It is a valuable teaching tool because 'it facilitates the declaration of understanding' (p. 302). Concept mapping also can be used by several teachers in preparation for teaching to share their understanding of the topic and identify agreed 'threshold concepts' or anticipated 'bottlenecks' for student learning. Sharing an expert map with student maps on the same topic and comparing differences can also help to reveal the 'bottlenecks' students have experienced in practice. Exploring the critical moments in a disciplinary curriculum with colleagues and students in these ways can be the beginning of a process of explaining the nature of the discipline and exploring the fundamental 'ways of thinking and practising' that define the disciplinary lens we want our students to adopt.

Focus on practice

With a colleague from a different discipline or with members of your programme or module team, use the question prompts in Figure 2.1 to help 'decode the discipline' for someone new to the discipline.

- If you are sharing this with a colleague from another discipline, does this reveal differences in language use or the nature of similar concepts across disciplines?
- If you are working with colleagues in your own discipline, do you agree on the likely 'bottlenecks' for students? Are any of these 'threshold concepts'?
- How do you introduce expert modelling and student experiences of the 'ways of thinking and practising' you identify in your curriculum?

Helping students to participate in disciplinary practices

One of the fundamental ways in which students learn how to participate fully in a chosen field is by accessing, using and critically reflecting on the specialist language and ways of communicating (or discourse) of that disciplinary community. Developing students' capacity to read and write texts within the discipline is profoundly linked to their development of the capacity to think critically within the discipline (Hammer and Green, 2011). All disciplines have distinctive textual, notational and numerical, as well as oral and visual, ways of representing knowledge and sharing it with others. In particular, these specialist ways of communicating are different to the familiar ways in which we communicate in our everyday interactions. Students, as new members of a disciplinary community, will need help to participate fully and credibly within these new communicative practices (Northedge, 2003). These discourses can include discipline-specific terminology or concepts but have a much wider dimension. A useful comparison is the experience of learning a second language where learning the vocabulary and grammar is only part of a much deeper acculturation into the ways people communicate in that language. The discursive practices of a discipline are similarly social acts of communication that go beyond mastery of the terminology and represent the ways in which individuals who are members of the group communicate with each other. These disciplinary literacy practices facilitate the sharing of ideas and complex knowledge effectively to others who are familiar with that language and the social codes and conventions it articulates. This can mean significant differences in the genre or form that oral and written communications in different disciplines take. For example, texts in different disciplinary and professional contexts might typically use a first-person 'I' or subjective voice or a third-person or objective voice, as well as construct an argument and use, validate and interpret evidence in distinct ways. Different types of communication even within a single discipline can also have distinctive demands. For example, in addition to a traditional academic assignment such as an essay or report, students may also be expected to write reflective, personal accounts such as a research journal or a reflective narrative in a workplace portfolio. Again, at another point in their studies, they may need to write using a professional voice, sometimes addressed to a reader who may not necessarily be familiar with the specialist discourses of the discipline: for example, a letter, poster, newsletter or a newspaper article. Each type of writing has particular demands and students are expected to develop the facility to write in different voices about the subject matter.

These conventions are not superficial or purely textual but reflect important disciplinary social and epistemological assumptions about how critical thinking is enacted and the identities and relationships between individuals within a disciplinary field. Academic literacy practices in different disciplines tacitly convey beliefs about what counts as valid knowledge in a specific context. The implications of this understanding of academic writing are that it is not a generic or transferable skill that can be taught outside the disciplinary curriculum but is central to what it means to think in disciplinary ways. As such, learning these communication practices is not just about students mastering appropriate ways to represent their learning to others when writing an essay, presentation, poster or laboratory report. Nor is it about being sufficiently skilful to be able to mimic the textual features or language practices of disciplinary or professional experts. Plagiarism or poor citation practices are examples where understanding the fundamental thinking practices embedded in writing is replaced by inauthentic mimicry of the communication practices of the discipline. Learning to recognise and use the disciplinary discourse is essential for a student to be able to understand the ways of thinking and practising in that discipline. Communicating in a discipline is about 'learning to take up disciplinary positions', to see with and through a specific 'disciplinary lens' in speaking, writing or visualising the subject matter. The position students take in their writing 'cannot be fully or richly understood without a discipline-internal awareness of what counts as knowledge and what counts as an authoritative disciplinary position' (Baynham, 2000: 18).

Significantly these practices are context-specific and students can often struggle to 'switch practices between one setting and another [and] to deploy a repertoire of linguistic practices appropriate to each setting' (Lea and Street, 2000: 35). This can make moving between different writing tasks and between different disciplines in modular multidisciplinary programmes highly charged for students and, as we will explore in Chapter 3, make interdisciplinary collaborations challenging. During assessment and giving feedback, academic staff also have significant authority in upholding appropriate literacy practices as 'a marker of difference and sustainer of boundaries' within the disciplines (p. 44). Reinforcing the specific academic literacy practices of the discipline through assessment enacts a level of authority and power on all students. The impact is most significant, however, on those coming from a broader range of social or educational backgrounds than have been traditionally engaged in higher education in previous decades. This makes academic writing a prime activity for thinking critically about the accessibility and inclusivity of higher education. We will consider this aspect in more detail in Chapter 8 when we reflect on the norms of academic discourses and explore how we might also critique our disciplinary 'ways of thinking and practising' by legitimating other, inclusive ways of making and expressing meaning.

Helping students to become more critically aware of the disciplinary 'ways of thinking and practising' through academic writing means that teachers are explicit about the ways an expert carries them out and create opportunities for students to internalise them through practice. Northedge (2003) argues that teachers have three specific roles in enabling students to participate in the discipline. They can:

- 'lend' students the ability to speak and make meaning within disciplinary discourses by introducing situations in which they work with students to create meaning together;
- lead 'excursions from familiar discourse into specialist discourse' to extend students' literacies in disciplinary contexts (p. 174);
- create spaces for students to 'speak and write in the "presence" of a competent speaker who can [...] help to shape their usage' through feedback and dialogue (p. 178).

In practice, this means planning opportunities for students to see disciplinary critical thinking explicitly modelled by their teachers and other experts. Then teachers need to scaffold student development and articulation of their own critical thinking processes. Students can do this by engaging in low-stakes learning tasks that enable them to practice and get feedback on their capacity to use writing as a way of thinking critically in the discipline. Traditional teaching methods such as lecture (modelling), seminar (discussion) and writing tasks (practising and feedback) may facilitate critical thinking in the discipline. Yet these approaches can sometimes insufficiently focus on making visible the 'disciplinary lens' students need to develop and instead focus more on 'what we look at' in terms of presenting the subject content. Additionally, for many teachers, even though they are 'insiders of the discourse community', their long socialisation into the discipline or profession can mean that their disciplinary practices can be invisible to them and difficult to explain to others (Wingate *et al.*, 2011: 70).

There a number of ways students can explore and practice what it means to think critically in the discipline if we explicate the academic literacy practices of our disciplinary community. Drawing on Northedge's (2003) and Anderson and Hounsell's (2007) definitions of the roles that teachers play in enabling participation in the discipline, we need to consider when and how we:

- define explicitly and make visible to students the features of disciplinary thinking;
- consciously model them for students as an expert 'insider';
- scaffold student attempts to adopt these practices;
- create opportunities for students to engage in independent practice and get feedback on their performance of disciplinary thinking.

These are considerations not only for first-year modules and students, but also for students as they make progress through a programme and develop increasing levels of expertise as well as content knowledge. In Chapter 8, case studies 8.1 and 8.2 provide examples of ways in which the specific conventions of disciplinary academic writing can be deciphered and explored with students as part of their learning of the discipline. The prompts for 'decoding the disciplines' and working with colleagues as outlined in the 'Focus on practice' task above can also help to elicit and examine how we engage specific disciplinary 'ways of thinking and practising' as an expert and how we can model the constituent stages of these skills for students. How we support student journeys into the disciplinary terrain and how we create opportunities for them to practice and get feedback are important in developing their metacognition or awareness and understanding of how knowledge is created and how they learn in the discipline. The following activities can be adapted to different disciplinary contexts to support students to develop disciplinary understanding by scaffolding their academic communication skills and creating opportunities for feedback from an expert 'speaker' of the discipline.

Introduce critical reading exercises

Both UK and international students often lack confidence in their writing skills and, potentially more importantly, have not had an opportunity to consider how they read texts critically as the basis for their own thinking and writing. In higher education, as well as developing the skills to interpret specialist language, students will need to learn how to adopt a critical position in their reading. They need to evaluate and make judgements about the quality of an argument, assess evidence and synthesise complex, sometimes contradictory data or positions. Students' understanding of these demands of critical reading, however, may actually be quite undeveloped even at later stages in their programme and they can have very different expectations about how to read, analyse and mine texts as readers (Weller, 2010). While textbooks and extracts in module readers can provide economical and useful introductions to the main concepts of a topic, Devereux and Wilson (2008) warn that they may also simplify the challenges of reading disciplinary academic and professional texts. Students therefore need to be encouraged to engage with texts that are academically and disciplinarily demanding. Supporting these encounters to help students approach the readings in critical ways, however, can make these experiences productive and elicit a better understanding of how expert readers respond to texts in the discipline.

You can introduce independent, structured reading into your module in a number of ways. One method is to set, or ask students to select, one or more relevant readings for the module such as journal articles, policy documents or book chapters as a preparatory reading task. Provide cues to encourage students to read and assess the text critically in terms of one or more features such as authorship, readership, construction of argument and their own approach to reading. Students can be asked to post their responses in the module virtual learning environment or share their answers with their peers via email before the class. Figure 2.2 summarises some of the questions you can pose students depending on the type of critical reading and thinking practices you want to develop. Questions about the provenance of the text are particularly useful in helping students to evaluate texts that they have sourced online. Questions about peer review and citations by other authors also help students to understand how they access and interpret editorial and citation data for journal articles that they might have previously ignored. Asking students to evaluate different readings encourages them to think about how knowledge is constructed in the discipline through debate, contestation and the evaluation of claims and evidence. Juxtaposing texts that have different ideological or methodological positions helps students to identify assumptions, values and beliefs that underpin knowledge claims. Case study 10.2 provides an example of how social bookmarking tools can be used to structure this type of activity.

Questions that prompt students to evaluate the author and critical stance	Questions that prompt students to analyse the quality of the argument
• Who is the author and why are they writing this text? • Who do you think the intended audience is for this text and why? • Is there evidence of the author's stance or bias? How does that affect their reasoning or conclusions? • Does the author's position support or contradict other texts you have read?	• What are the author's hypotheses or claims? • What is the data or evidence to support their claims? • How has data been collected and how valid is the method used to gather or synthesise the data? • Are the conclusions the author has reached legitimate and justified? Are there any inconsistencies? • Are there assumptions that have not been acknowledged?
Questions that prompt students to assess the validity and reliability of a text	**Questions that prompt students to reflect on their approach to reading a text**
• Where is the text published? • When was it published? Does that affect its relevancy and currency? • Has the text been peer reviewed and is it cited by others? • How does that impact on its credibility and quality as a text?	• What do you hope to learn from reading the text? • What specific question(s) do you bring to your reading? • How do you use any structural features of the text (e.g. title, headings, keywords, abstract) to help you read a text? • How do you take notes or annotate the text?

Figure 2.2 Prompts for scaffolding student critical reading of texts

Develop student writing by getting them to use different 'voices'

'Author's notes' (Fernsten and Reda, 2011) is an approach designed to help students to think about 'writing as a way of *thinking*' not just a way to represent learning. This strategy helps students to recognise 'writing as a process, the importance of self-awareness about the decisions and strategies one employs as a writer, and the socio-political realities of language use in the academy' (pp. 175, 177). Students are asked to submit, with a draft of their written work, responses to questions designed to help them reflect on the preparation of their writing before they receive feedback from their teacher. These 'author's notes' can include responses to questions on the experience of writing and decisions such as choice of topic and structure. They can also evaluate strengths and weaknesses of their argument or assumptions they have made about their reader's prior knowledge on the topic. Alternatively, prompts for the author's notes can support students to think about voice and can be helpful for students to reflect on their 'excursions from familiar to specialist discourse'. For example, students might consider how aspects of their voice (such as language, sentence structure or tone) might differ if they were discussing the topic in a conversation with friends or family members who do not have specialist knowledge of the topic. They can be asked to identify how writing an essay is similar or different to the other forms of writing they engage with everyday such as email, messaging, online postings, diaries or creative outputs. This helps students to articulate how they conceptualise an 'academic' voice and how it relates to their sense of their own voice in other contexts. We all slip between voices in different situations and it can be helpful to explore this experience as the basis for helping students see themselves as legitimate speakers with a disciplinary academic voice. Comparative use of a range of communication tasks (lecture notes, book reviews, commentary, podcasts, postings in discussion forums, professional journal articles or blogs) creates opportunities for students to consider the different demands of these forms of writing.

You might also consider including opportunities for students to write on a single topic from different or multiple positions. Students often do not revisit the same subject matter from different viewpoints and can struggle to relate and synthesise articles on a topic that have markedly different ideological, methodological or conceptual positions. One way to help students navigate key texts in a reading list is to ask them to annotate a bibliography, write short pieces as an advocate or critic of a new initiative or write on a topic from, for example, different political or methodological positions using relevant sources to support their arguments. This can help them to identify and organise different articles or chapters and recognise how the position of the author will affect the evidence they draw on and the conclusions they reach. Compiling together writings in which students are deliberately using different 'voices' required by the format, intended audience or position of the author enables them to reflect on the ways in which writing is implicated in the 'disciplinary lens' applied to the subject matter.

Use argument mapping to help analyse academic arguments

Visualising an argument is another method for helping students to analyse how an author has constructed their position. This process helps students to break down the stages of critical thinking and identify the premises and the types of evidence that underpin how knowledge is created and validated in the discipline. While concept maps are relational and highlight causal relationships between claims, the purpose of an argument map is to represent graphically the 'inferential structure of arguments' that links propositions, conclusions and the grounds that support them (Davies, 2011: 286). Diagramming an argument when reading a text can help students to distinguish between hypotheses and data or reveal limitations or faulty arguments. It can also be used to help students make explicit their claims and the evidence they are drawing upon when drafting an essay. Figure 2.3 is an example of a basic argument map on the topic of the introduction of student fees in UK higher education. An argument map is structured hierarchically or in tiers. At the top of the map will be the 'contention' of the argument. In the example this is the proposition 'Student fees are the only viable option for expanding student participation in higher education in the UK'. The second tier of the argument map will provide claims or 'reasons' that support this contention, as well as objections. Further claims and rebuttals are in turn provided for each of the second-tier reasons or objections. Each strand of the argument terminates with reference to evidence to support the claim such as empirical data or statistics, a quotation or reference to the literature. There is a range of software that enables students to quickly build up and manipulate an argument using colour and shape to clarify the different components of the argument: for example, the open-source Argumentative (www.argumentative.sourceforge.net/index.html) and Argunet (www.argunet.org) or the licensed software Rationale (www.rationale.austhink.com). Freehand mapping on paper, however, can be just as effective in supporting analysis and evaluation of arguments. Argument mapping has been used in a number of disciplines; one example comes from Carrington *et al.* (2011), who introduced argument mapping into a large cohort Financial Accounting module. This involved introducing the students to the chosen mapping software, weekly modelling of argument maps for questions in tutorials and a group essay assignment that included an argument map to demonstrate the structure of the argument and use of research evidence. With only minimal interventions, argument mapping was found to improve students' argumentation skills as the basis for enhanced critical thinking in the discipline.

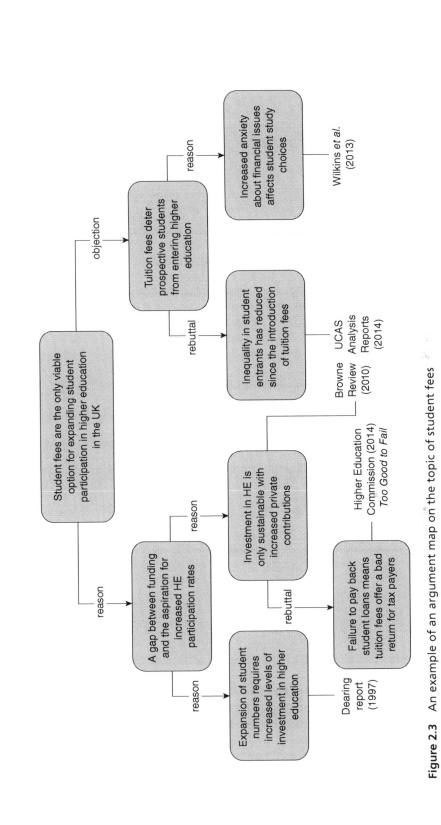

Figure 2.3 An example of an argument map on the topic of student fees

Focus on practice

Choose one of the 'bottlenecks' or 'threshold concepts' you identified in the process of 'decoding the discipline'. Revisit this concept and consider how well you:

- define the processes involved in this way of thinking or practising;
- model how you undertake this process as an expert;
- scaffold opportunities for students to carry out these ways of thinking or practising;
- create opportunities for feedback on their performance of disciplinary thinking.

How might you improve these stages in helping students to understand and overcome these bottlenecks in their learning?

Conclusion

In this chapter we have begun the process of translating your complex, disciplinary knowledge as an expert into a form that can be taught and learnt at university. For many new lecturers in higher education this can be the most challenging aspect of becoming a teacher. As experts in academic or professional contexts, the 'ways of thinking and practising' that constitute a discipline can be so well integrated that they can be imperceptible and difficult to explain to others. Yet they can also represent fundamental blockages or 'bottlenecks' for student learning that can halt meaningful engagement with the subject. When the 'disciplinary lens' through which we look at and interpret the world is invisible we can overly focus on the subject matter itself, assume that this represents the discipline and pack this into our curriculum without explaining what we expect students to 'do' with this content. Thinking about our disciplinary knowledge in performative terms, or what it means to be 'doing the discipline', is a powerful way to approach our academic practice. The most important principle to remember in planning teaching is that effective learning is not acquisitive but is active. 'Decoding' our subject matter with colleagues and with students enables us to focus on this active dimension of the discipline. Through this process we are not identifying concepts, facts or ideas but the ways we and our students engage with these concepts as disciplinary practitioners. The literacy practices of a discipline are an integral manifestation of these thinking skills and not just ways to represent learning after it has happened. Now we have started the process of defining what it means to 'do the discipline', we will look, in the next two chapters, at how we work in interdisciplinary contexts and how we transform disciplinary and interdisciplinary knowledge into a module or programme curriculum.

Further reading

'Disciplinary Thinking' (http://disciplinarythinking.wordpress.com)
This website, hosted by the University of Bath, includes a range of open educational resources for teachers including resource lists, presentations, tasks and hand-outs for developing disciplinary understanding in relation to, for example, feedback, textual practices, threshold concepts and values.

Middendorf, Joan and Pace, David (2004) 'Decoding the disciplines: a model for helping students learn disciplinary ways of thinking', *New Directions for Teaching and Learning*, 98: 1–12.
A key text introducing the 'decoding the disciplines' approach and introducing a special issue, with US examples of 'decoding' in, for example, biology, history, professional subjects and astronomy.

'Thinking Writing' (http://www.thinkingwriting.qmul.ac.uk)
Thinking Writing is based at Queen Mary University of London; this website has practical ideas for supporting student writing in the disciplinary curriculum such as developing reasoning and argument or critical engagement. It also includes disciplinary examples of some of these ideas in practice.

'Threshold Concepts' (http://www.ee.ucl.ac.uk/~mflanaga/thresholds.html)
This website, compiled by Dr Mick Flanagan in the Department of Electronic Engineering at University College London, brings together a regularly updated bibliography of key texts on threshold concepts, including videos and podcasts of presentations. There is a useful subject index of presentations and papers in many disciplines in relation to threshold concepts.

CHAPTER 3

LEARNING AND TEACHING FOR INTERDISCIPLINARITY

Learning objectives

This chapter will support you to:

- Develop a critical understanding of the concept of interdisciplinarity and its relationship to disciplines;
- Plan learning, teaching and assessment tasks that enable students to develop effective interdisciplinary knowledge and skills;
- Explore how interdisciplinarity can be used to solve real-world problems through the example of education for sustainability.

Introduction

In Chapter 2 we reflected on the distinctive nature of different disciplines and how we make this visible to students through the curriculum. Articulating the distinctive disciplinary 'ways of thinking and practising' (Meyer and Land, 2003), which we innately understand as researchers, practitioners or professional experts, is the first, fundamental step in becoming a teacher in university.

The reason it is not the final step in learning to teach, however, is the recognition, first, that mastery of disciplinary specialisms may not sufficiently prepare our students for their future careers after university. As Nutbeam (2013) argues, 'in the future most people's careers are unlikely to be defined by a single discipline [...] the conventional career ladder once they graduate is likely to be replaced by a career "lattice" which may involve moving upward or laterally [...] Inventiveness, flexibility and adaptability will be essential attributes.' Second, it is evident in many disciplines that the nature of knowledge, how it is created, used, shared and stored, has been transformed by new technologies and new challenges. Increasingly, we are also recognising that, in a globalised, interdependent world, single disciplinary approaches may not provide adequate answers to contemporary issues such as health pandemics, climate change, the political, technical and ethical implications of new communication technologies or national security questions. Interdisciplinarity, the combining of different disciplinary lenses to the same problem by multidisciplinary teams, is advocated as one way to respond to these multifaceted problems.

Enabling learning in interdisciplinary contexts, however, is a significant challenge for many universities. One difficulty is that universities are often organised socially, economically and physically using narrowly defined research and teaching identities based around disciplinary groupings. Faculties, departments and research centres frequently work with the grain of traditional disciplinary structures, making interdisciplinary collaborations for research and teaching problematic. Moving students or teachers between programmes or developing specific interdisciplinary modules can be difficult to achieve even at the simplest level because of practical considerations such as incompatible timetabling or funding models across departments. As we explored in the previous chapter, disciplines have ways of verifying or communicating knowledge that exclude non-specialists and this can be as problematic for teachers from outside a discipline as it is for their students. There are also several caveats for wholesale interdisciplinary transformation of the curriculum. Introducing interdisciplinary options into a programme might arguably be seen to dilute the disciplinary knowledge students need to gain as well as threatening disciplinary cultures. Likewise, introducing interdisciplinary modules into the curriculum can be seen as a choice between enabling breadth and sacrificing depth of study (Woods, 2007; Kandiko and Blackmore, 2012b). It is argued that students must have sufficient exposure to a 'parent' discipline so they learn disciplinary principles and methodologies before moving 'outside' their discipline to participate meaningfully in interdisciplinary encounters (Davies and Devlin, 2007: 6). Barnett (1997) argues that 'interdisciplinarity is necessarily *critical interdisciplinarity*' (p. 19, emphasis original) because it enables a critique of disciplinary perspectives that can help move disciplines forward. Nevertheless, while the applied nature of interdisciplinarity is its strength, there is a danger that 'pushing research towards a problem-solving mode [...] directs it away from critiquing the status quo, making it inherently more conservative' (Trowler, 2012: 14). The interdisciplinary turn of university curricula, therefore, is neither straightforward nor a failsafe method for developing critical and flexible thinkers of the future.

Despite these concerns, interdisciplinary modes of thinking are increasingly being integrated into university provision. In this chapter we will consider how interdisciplinarity can be defined and how it relates to other forms of cross-disciplinary affiliations and collaborations. We will then explore the content of interdisciplinary curricula and how we develop learning, teaching and assessment in ways that ensure interdisciplinary experiences enrich student outcomes. Interdisciplinary modes of thinking are particularly aligned to understanding and solving problems that draw on tentative, incomplete and multidisciplinary data. As such we will specifically focus on the role of interdisciplinarity for understanding and responding to complicated, whole system issues using the example of education for sustainable development (ESD).

Introducing interdisciplinarity into the university curriculum

Over the last decade there have been high-profile examples of international research-intensive universities undertaking major undergraduate curriculum reform as a response to the perceived need for different types of graduates and knowledge. This includes Harvard University's curriculum renewal, Hong Kong University's response to national university curriculum reforms and the University of Melbourne's implementation of the Melbourne Curriculum (originally known as the Melbourne Model). These major reviews of the curriculum identified the need to introduce opportunities to develop students' global citizenship, their ability to undertake research and their capacity to solve new and thorny interdisciplinary problems. For example, the Melbourne Curriculum reduced the number of degree programmes across the university but increased the emphasis on breadth as a way to encourage learners to choose personal, interdisciplinary pathways through the curriculum. Several UK universities have engaged in similar all-curriculum reviews and looked at ways in which they can increase the interdisciplinary experiences within or alongside the curriculum. Through the Curriculum Innovation Programme, for example, the University of Southampton gives students flexibility to choose modules that will broaden their studies beyond their chosen discipline. Alternatively, students in the humanities, social sciences, education, physics and geography can choose to study a minor subject alongside their major degree programme (www.southampton.ac.uk/cip).

Other UK institutions have adopted different approaches to creating interdisciplinary experiences for their students. Following a university-wide review, the University of Manchester established the University College for Interdisciplinary Learning in 2011. The College offers modules taught by teachers from across the university that allow students to enhance their specialism by taking specific interdisciplinary modules outside their department. These include modules such as 'Future Cities', which explores the challenges confronting urban spaces, or 'Science, the Media and the Public', which considers the role of science in society and how to communicate complex scientific information to the public (www.college.manchester.ac.uk). Likewise, the University of Aberdeen initiated a major Curriculum Reform (CRef) Project in 2010 leading to the declaration of the 'Aberdeen Difference'. This includes a commitment to an enhanced undergraduate experience through increased disciplinary breadth. Five centuries after it was first founded, Aberdeen introduced a portfolio of cross-disciplinary 'Sixth Century Courses'. These modules are designed to draw on cross-disciplinary expertise to encourage students to consider topics critically and use different approaches to knowledge. Examples of these modules include 'Digital Society', which examines how the digital world and digital divide impact on individuals and society, or 'Oceans and Society', which considers the relationship between humans and the ocean through time by looking at, for instance, ecology, geography and seafaring (www.abdn.ac.uk/study/about/the-difference.php).

These different approaches to whole curriculum reform reflect the alternative ways we might understand interdisciplinarity and interdisciplinary working in universities. These examples demonstrate that broadening the curriculum might constitute increased module choice across cognate disciplines or even modules from across a wider range of disciplines. The option for major and minor degrees with requirements to complete a specified number of credits within each discipline enables students to formalise these multidisciplinary choices in their final qualification. While increasing choice and enabling breadth, this approach, however, might not always include direction in how students and teachers are expected to connect different modules together. If the elective modules are offered to students in the 'home' discipline as well as students from 'outside' the discipline, it is also important, on the one hand, to consider how students new to the 'ways of thinking and practising' in the chosen elective collaborate with students who are more familiar with these modes. On the other hand, designing and teaching new, deliberately integrative interdisciplinary modules in new contexts make other demands on teachers and students to develop practices, modified methodologies and discourses for communicating the outcomes of interdisciplinary study. Defining and understanding the difference between these forms of collaboration across disciplines is, therefore, important for recognising the challenges of broadening the curriculum.

In Chapter 2 we considered what we mean when we adopt a 'disciplinary lens' to understand the world and how we communicate these specific 'ways of thinking and practising' to others in our own disciplinary community and beyond. Universities have traditionally been organised around disciplines in terms of teaching and research, but, increasingly, we are coming to rethink the classification and compartmentalisation of knowledge in this specialist way. Instead, 'knowledge today is depicted as a network or a web with multiple nodes of connection and a dynamic system' (Klein, 2004: 3). This is relevant because graduates will often work in environments where multi-professional team-working is required, so the capacity to collaborate effectively with disciplinary specialists is essential. Many of the problems that students will face in their future careers are also multidimensional and open-ended. These 'wicked' or 'messy' problems 'resist being tamed, bounded or managed by classical problem-solving approaches' defined through single disciplines. Such problems can only be addressed through 'cross-fertilization of multiple methods and perspectives' (ibid.: 4, 6). Yet the benefits of interdisciplinary working are not only concerned with future working. Viewing a discipline from another perspective can also inform critical thinking by developing students' awareness of the assumptions, communication practices and limitations of their ways of thinking and practising in mono-disciplinary contexts (Woods, 2007).

Despite the potential benefits of working across disciplines, defining and implementing interdisciplinarity remains contentious. For some, interdisciplinarity is seen as a progression from discipline-based learning and teaching, 'a kind of epistemological evolutionary step' in knowledge creation, while for others interdisciplinarity is only possible as a result of prior disciplinary knowledge (Blake *et al.*, 2013). From this perspective, interdisciplinarity is, therefore, only appropriate or achievable in final-year undergraduate capstone projects or postgraduate study. Yet the capacity for developing 'boundary-crossing skills' such as synthesising knowledge and coping with complexity, as well as the potential for the 'cross-fertilization' of knowledge remain powerful drivers for introducing interdisciplinarity earlier in the undergraduate curriculum (Spelt *et al.*, 2009). In creating possibilities for students to extend their studies outside of a single subject, it is valuable to distinguish between the different intentions and strategies for connecting and working with and across disciplines.

There is an expansive terminology for describing these encounters but in recent years these have narrowed to three different types of cross-disciplinary engagement: multidisciplinarity, interdisciplinarity and transdisciplinarity (Klein, 2010). Many joint degree programmes or flexible curricula that allow students to choose, sometimes with little guidance, option modules outside the 'home' department or lectures by disciplinary specialists on a single topic are more likely to result in multidisciplinary learning experiences. The principal characteristic of multidisciplinarity is 'encyclopaedic' or 'additive', where several disciplinary modules are juxtaposed together but little attempt is made explicitly to connect the learning in each module (Klein, 2010: 17; Spelt *et al.*, 2009: 366). Multidisciplinary teaching can involve little difference from teaching a module in a mono-disciplinary context or may involve specialists from a range of disciplines teaching individual topics within a single multidisciplinary module. Multidisciplinary opportunities broaden a student's knowledge base and the range of methods they may draw on to understand problems. Yet the distinctive disciplines involved in multidisciplinary experiences remain separate. For many educators, the multidisciplinary approach is arguably more attainable in the undergraduate curriculum given the dominance of the prevailing disciplinary structures of universities (Kandiko and Blackmore, 2012b).

Unlike multidisciplinarity, interdisciplinarity is concerned not only with broadening perspectives, but also with emphasising the 'integration and synthesis' of knowledge from different disciplines (Klein, 2004: 2). Interdisciplinarity therefore requires teachers to think through the experience for learners when they encounter new perspectives, questions or problems that require disciplinary 'boundary crossing'. Interdisciplinary experiences demand new ways of thinking that are unlikely to happen within each of the individual disciplines alone and are more than the sum of the individual parts. Interdisciplinary thinking includes communicating across disciplinary differences, collaborative interaction and working towards effective problem-solving (Spelt *et al.*, 2009). As Trowler (2012) notes, interdisciplinarity can take an instrumental approach that is narrowly focused towards preparing students to meet the present needs of society and employment. Yet it can also take a more open and critical approach that 'interrogates the dominant structures of knowledge and education with the aim of transforming them, raising questions of value and purpose' (Klein, 2010: 23). Transdisciplinarity is emerging from this critical end of interdisciplinarity and is defined by notions of transcending, transgressing and transforming existing disciplines. Transdisciplinarity does not seek to integrate existing ways of thinking but to foster new approaches to understanding that will generate paradigm-shifting perspectives not possible within existing mono-disciplinary or interdisciplinary contexts.

While whole institution curriculum rejuvenation can embed multidisciplinary, interdisciplinary or even transdisciplinary practices into the student experience, in the absence of such comprehensive reform there is still scope to consider smaller interdisciplinary interventions into existing disciplinary-based contexts (Pharo *et al.*, 2012). Implementing short-term interdisciplinary interventions, however, means thinking through what is taught (content) as well as how it is taught (pedagogy) and how it can be assessed in creative and collaborative ways. Working in interdisciplinary ways requires teachers and students to:

- identify why and when different disciplines might be brought together to promote interdisciplinary thinking;
- recognise and negotiate differences in language use and how they communicate findings to an interdisciplinary or non-specialist audience;
- develop a disciplinary 'meta-perspective' that enables them to see and describe the different disciplines and 'situate [...] disciplines in a wider "map" of knowledge' (Parker, 2010: 331);
- embrace opportunities for creative thinking, experimentation and active enquiry within an environment that encourages risk-taking, open-mindedness and autonomy free from the constraints of disciplinary structures (Livingstone, 2010);
- explore real-world problems experientially through fieldwork or work-placements that demonstrate the relevance of systems-thinking and importance of interdisciplinarity for future study and employment (Davies and Devlin, 2007);
- participate in multidisciplinary and multi-professional teams and find ways to collaborate and manage team-work to effectively integrate all perspectives.

Teaching for interdisciplinarity therefore means taking account of these desirable practices to create learning environments that will stimulate creative and critically reflective learning. There are a number of different ways in which you can facilitate these learning experiences in practice.

Interdisciplinary content

Nikitina (2006) proposes three different ways in which interdisciplinary content can be generated: contextualising, conceptualising and problem-centring. These different strategies provide a useful structure for planning interdisciplinary experiences and help educators to articulate the purpose of their interdisciplinary collaborations. A contextualising approach to interdisciplinarity uses knowledge from one discipline to situate and understand disciplinary 'ways of thinking and practising' culturally and historically. Examples of this type of interdisciplinarity include programmes such as history of science and technology, science and society or history of medicine programmes which draw on historical, literary or sociological perspectives to generate new understandings of knowledge creation and communication in science, technology or healthcare disciplines. For instance, in mathematics, where content is often 'presented ready-made', the introduction of brief background material to contextualise mathematical topics such as complex numbers, Fibonacci or non-Euclidean geometry reveals the 'false-starts, misattributions, confusions and dead-ends' that have led to the fundamental concepts of the discipline (McCartney *et al.*, 2011: 14).

Alternatively, a conceptualising approach to interdisciplinarity connects disciplines around a shared core concept or theme. This enables students to encounter and negotiate different disciplinary perspectives and methodologies focused on a single topic. Examples of this type of interdisciplinarity include women's studies or area studies, such as American, Middle Eastern or Chinese studies. Another strategy for generating interdisciplinary content is a problem-centring approach which involves bringing together disciplines such as biology, sociology, philosophy, law and economics to examine real-world problems that are complicated, open-ended and will need to draw on multiple perspectives to be understood or solved. Education for sustainable development is a widely cited example and we will look at this in more detail later on in this chapter. Other forms of this problem-centring approach to interdisciplinarity include medical law and ethics or international development.

Although the majority of these examples represent whole-programme interdisciplinary experiences, they establish a framework for thinking about the type of interdisciplinary experimentation possible at the module or individual topic level: for example, introducing different types of data or sources of evidence such as a literary text or artwork to reflect on the cultural impact of a scientific discovery. Alternatively, starting from a problem that has technical, economic, social and environmental dimensions can act as the basis for introducing a new concept within one of these disciplines. If interdisciplinary student groups are not possible, inviting colleagues from other disciplines to contribute to a discipline-based lecture or including online specialist lectures or multidisciplinary resources will help to locate the concept in wider disciplinary debates.

Interdisciplinary communication

Developing students' awareness of their communication strategies and how they are shaped by the disciplinary contexts within which they work is an important first step in introducing them to interdisciplinary working. Effective cross-disciplinary working is only possible when students and teachers from different disciplines have developed a 'collective understanding' (Yocom *et al.*, 2012: 20) from their diverse perspectives. The critical reading and writing strategies suggested in Chapter 2 are one way to make the disciplinary communication methods explicit and make them visible to non-specialists in interdisciplinary groups. As part of their induction into interdisciplinary collaboration, students can develop glossaries of relevant disciplinary terminology, disciplinary 'bluffers' guides' or critically compare their own discipline-based journal abstracts or articles to surface and explore these different ways of describing and conveying knowledge (Woods, 2007; Davies and Devlin, 2007). While higher education often privileges textual forms of communication, initiating interdisciplinarity communication can be supported by using visual or performative methods to express experiences in interdisciplinary groups. Drawing, collaging, making models or role-playing in response to stimuli facilitate understanding between individuals who may struggle to communicate across disciplines. For example, James (2013) has used Lego Serious Play, a process of model-building using Lego, to develop student metacognition and enhance reflection. Such visual methods encourage creativity and experimentation in an environment that is safe and allows students freedom to make, attribute and share meaning individually and collaboratively in the absence of a shared disciplinary language or expertise.

Disciplinary 'meta-perspectives'

As students and their teachers engage in exploring interdisciplinary problems or questions and evolving effective interdisciplinary communication strategies, they can begin to develop an awareness of the nature of the disciplines and how they relate to each other. Critically analysing the disciplinary 'ways of thinking and practising' will also provide teachers with insight into where it might be necessary to bridge disciplinary knowledge to enable interdisciplinary participation. Engaging both teachers and students in 'decoding the disciplines' or developing concept maps of key topics or questions, as described in Chapter 2, may serve as the basis for subsequently developing an interdisciplinary map together. Through 'decoding' it is possible to see where concepts traverse different disciplines and compare and contrast use of terminology and concepts. Emerging disciplinary 'meta-perspectives' are supported by embedding reflective strategies into interdisciplinary teaching and learning. Reflective journaling may support students to reflect on their experience of working with others from different disciplines and the impact these encounters have emotionally, as well as cognitively. Even if students ultimately return to their 'home' discipline, working with other disciplines can stimulate 'the ability to evaluate, critically [...] perspectives, practices and products in one's own and other disciplinary cultures' (Woods, 2007: 862).

Storytelling is a powerful way to facilitate the expression of these multiple perspectives on a topic as well as providing space to explore scenarios and capture the holistic nature of complex and uncertain situations. In particular, creating opportunities for telling and retelling narratives together from different perspectives enables students to identify the assumptions and bias inherent in single-discipline viewpoints. In this context, stories might be fictional but, equally, they might take the more factual form of a newspaper story. Creative rather than traditional academic student writing tasks can liberate thinking outside the conventions of their original discipline. Similarly, responding to 'what if' prompts can generate imaginative or hypothetical solutions to authentic problems that reveal and transgress the constraints of disciplinary frameworks (Moon, 2010). One tool for generating stories that articulate multiple perspectives in relation to real-world, interdisciplinary questions is a strategy called 'news stories' (adapted from McDrury and Alterio, 2002: 67). This task involves giving students a series of recent, potentially provocative, newspaper or online news headlines. Students choose one headline and write a short news story from a specific disciplinary or practitioner perspective. A keyword search of news websites can quickly generate examples of relevant headlines for the topic such as:

- 'Google Glass user treated for internet addiction caused by the device' (*Guardian*, 14 October 2014);
- 'World on course for warmest year' (BBC News, 4 December 2014);
- '"Girlification" of engineering has failed, says expert' (*The Times Higher Education Supplement*, 5 October 2014);
- 'Small businesses need more than money to survive and grow' (*The Times*, 1 October 2014).

In an interdisciplinary group context, students respond to these headlines in discipline-specific ways and then share these with students from other disciplinary backgrounds to discuss the concepts, biases and assumptions underpinning their engagement with the topic. For example, in response to the first headline above, how might a computer scientist, a psychologist, a sociologist or an engineer describe the relationship between humans and technology in different ways? Or in responding to the story on attempts to encourage more women to study engineering, how might an historian, literary studies, business or law student respond to the idea of 'girlification' or the role of women in engineering that this headline provokes?

Creative thinking and interdisciplinary enquiry

Building on the creative exploration of disciplinary 'meta-perspectives', interdisciplinary learning is based on the opportunity for 'rigorous forms of experimentation' that are developed through creative thinking and enquiry. Interdisciplinary collaboration creates opportunities to investigate and engage in 'iteratively evaluating and adjusting the framing and response to a problem' based on testing out different disciplinary approaches and methods (Yocom *et al.*, 2012: 19). For Robinson (2001), 'creativity involves a dynamic interplay between generating ideas and making judgements about them' (p. 133). In this sense, creative thinking involves the freedom to experiment and take risks, but is not an indulgent or trivial mode of enquiry. Creative thinking in the context of interdisciplinarity is concerned with finding ways to escape habitual modes of thinking and to generate alternatives to conventional solutions. Yet it is also concerned with evaluating these new solutions to determine what works and what does not. It is this balance between facilitating 'generative thinking' and 'critical appraisal' that makes creativity a valuable addition to the processes of research and enquiry in higher education (Robinson, 2001: 136). Baillie (2006) suggests that the process of creative thinking comprises divergent and convergent stages of question formulation and reformulation, idea generation and development followed by the clustering of ideas and evaluation.

Creative thinking can be stimulated by responding to questions or challenges through open thinking techniques such as brainstorming or buzz groups, where students are given time to discuss and record all ideas or responses to a prompt or question individually or in small groups. Drawing tasks such as mind-mapping, collage or posters also help students to explore the topic in ways that allow free association and lateral thinking. Yet once ideas have been generated it is essential that the ideas are tested and evaluated to determine how they might provide solutions to a problem: for example, using evaluative prompt questions such as 'Will it solve the problem?', 'Is this idea viable technically, economically or ethically in this context?' or 'Would this solution generate other unanticipated outcomes?' Involving students in interdisciplinary thinking also means creating opportunities for them to undertake enquiry that allows them to experiment with new methodologies, new tools and gain insight into new perspectives that might not be available to them through mono-disciplinary study. Fundamental to making this happen is finding ways to connect learning and teaching with the practices of research and enquiry; we will look at this further in Chapter 6. Research tasks for students can be disciplinarily focused or, as in case study 3.1, involve interdisciplinary collaboration between students and researchers.

Case study 3.1   Student participation in extracurricular interdisciplinary research (Barnett and Smith, 2013)

At the University of Westminster, 40 undergraduate students and six researchers have been involved, since 2010, in an interdisciplinary, extracurricular research project called 'Broad Vision: The Art and Science of Looking'. Since 2012 this has also included a credit-bearing module. The project has brought together researchers and students from photographic art, imaging science, illustration, computer science, psychology and life sciences to investigate vision and perception of microscopic worlds from both art and science perspectives. The first phase of the project involved disciplinary exchange whereby students from different disciplines became familiar with the language and methodologies of other disciplines through taster experiences such as experiments or demonstrations. The second phase emphasised the importance of collaboration by supporting student researchers to work together with staff to focus on interdisciplinary research themes in smaller research groups. The final phase involved making public the research process and outcomes through innovative strategies such as art exhibitions. The project team used collaborative and active learning approaches to create a safe and exploratory space for learners and researchers to work across disciplines and test ideas. The project also helped students to assume roles as disciplinary experts and interdisciplinary researchers. A project website (http://broad-vision.info) contributes to the wider dissemination of the collaborations.

Working on interdisciplinary problems to develop expertise

Involving students in active research projects is one strategy for demonstrating the legitimate value of interdisciplinarity and its relevancy for future working in multidisciplinary and multi-professional teams. Focusing on multidimensional problems relevant to workplace or societal contexts enables students to combine theory and activism in ways that break down the boundaries not only between disciplines, but also between the university and the wider community. Yet for many students and teachers 'it may well feel counter-cultural to trespass too far into those dimensions not usually identified as falling with the framework of reference of the discipline' (Selby, 2006: 57). Interdisciplinary working can provoke what Tremonte (2011), when talking about the experience of teachers starting to explore their academic disciplinary practice from an unfamiliar educational perspective, describes as a 'fear of "novice-stry"'. Tremonte's solution to this anxiety is to engage in the practice of disciplinary '*window shopping*: to try on (and try out) various methodological masks and guises; to dress in other disciplines' and inter-disciplines' clothes'. This is done with the intention to 'experiment […] without the expectation of extra-disciplinary expertise. But it does so with an expectation of building a knowledge base and repertoire relevant to the local context' (pp. 2–3, emphasis original). This idea of window shopping allows for playful, provisional and recursive experimentation in trying out different discipline perspectives without the need for mastery of discipline-specific knowledge or the permanent inhabiting of new disciplinary identities.

Working on everyday scenarios can also challenge assumptions about the relationship between knowledge generated within universities and knowledge created in other contexts. Undertaking tasks such as collecting data from a range of sources requires students to recognise that 'knowledge is no longer dependent solely on academic research but involves learning from multiple public spaces, ranging from lay to professional knowledge' (Miles and Rainbird, 2014: 12). This, in turn, legitimises and values students learning from their own experiences (for example, from extracurricular employment or community-engagement activities) alongside the development of academic disciplinary knowledge. Building students' sense of the academic expertise they already bring to the study of new problems helps them to overcome the fear of trespassing into unfamiliar disciplinary modes.

One learning strategy recommended to support this is the 'jigsaw' technique (Woods, 2007; Brookfield and Preskill, 1999). Students prepare for interdisciplinary seminars or lectures by completing relevant readings, collecting and analysing data or compiling briefings in response to the topic from within their more familiar 'home' discipline before taking it in turns to share this for the benefit of all members of the multidisciplinary group. Individual students or peer groups of students each hold one piece of the 'jigsaw' that makes up the body of knowledge they might need to draw on to solve the problem. This means all students begin from a position of expertise before venturing into more uncertain disciplinary or interdisciplinary contexts. It enables all students to engage in 'window shopping' by individually and collectively selecting different, potentially useful theories, methodologies or methods from other disciplines to solve interdisciplinary problems. Ultimately, this strategy might achieve multidisciplinary rather than interdisciplinary outcomes, but it is a first step to achieving a more integrated and systemic understanding of multifaceted questions.

Working collaboratively in interdisciplinary groups

In addition to thinking through how students can become critically reflexive about their own disciplinary lens and how content from different disciplines might be brought together, facilitating team-working is an essential component for introducing students to interdisciplinary practice. In Chapter 2 we began to explore the shift from understanding teaching as the transmission of disciplinary content to a process of engaging students as participants in a disciplinary community. Working in interdisciplinary contexts will require ongoing support to foster student autonomy as learners. Building students' confidence in their own disciplinary and interdisciplinary expertise is a crucial part of shifting the focus away from the view of teacher as expert, instead framing learning as a dynamic partnership between teachers and students. The complexities of team-work in interdisciplinary groups, when both students and teachers may feel unsure about their expertise or skills, demand an explicit introduction to team-building and collaborative processes (Yocom *et al.*, 2012). Introducing tasks that are student- rather than teacher-led also helps to promote student engagement and empower them to take responsibility for their and their peers' learning. Case study 3.2 provides an example of facilitating team-working in interdisciplinary groups.

 Case study 3.2   The interdisciplinary design studio for Masters students (Blair, 2011)

The MA in Design with Learning and Teaching in Higher Education at Kingston University was designed to equip graduating students for working in an interdisciplinary and multidisciplinary professional environment. Students on the MA are professional designers with a minimum of two years' professional experience. To meet the needs of users, designers increasingly need to take into account a range of disciplinary perspectives including ideas drawn from economics, bioengineering, religion and cultural identity. Within the Masters programme, students undertake 60 credits in studio-based interdisciplinary design groups. They work with students on MA programmes such as Fashion, Graphic Design and Design with the Creative Industries. Students also take 60 credits from modules in the Postgraduate Certificate in Learning and Teaching alongside new academic staff from across a range of disciplines including healthcare, science, law and the humanities. The final 60 credits are completed by individual project. The aim is for the interdisciplinary groupings to reflect collaboration within professional practice as well as the demands of many contemporary briefs that call on the expertise of different disciplines. Benefits for students working in interdisciplinary groups included challenging formulaic ways of thinking in design, developing analytic skills and aligning academic study and professional practice. It was also found, however, that differences in language and terminology and the need to focus different disciplinary ideas to reach a single solution could make interdisciplinary working challenging for group members. Careful teacher support and guidance for managing group work was one solution to supporting effective outcomes for the interdisciplinary learning.

We will explore further some of the strategies for supporting collaborative learning in Chapter 11 that are relevant to disciplinary as well as interdisciplinary contexts. Importantly, however, authentic collaborative assessment tasks such as practical work, project work and work-placements will demonstrate the significance of group processes. These are often undervalued in higher education but are a central component of effective interdisciplinary working (Stefani, 2008). The inclusion of reflective journals, peer- and self-review as part of learning and assessment tasks helps students to recognise the importance of their role in group working and critically evaluate the experience of collaboration. One example of this approach developed by Miles and Rainbird (2014) involves reflecting on interdisciplinary and interprofessional team-work in an event-based assessment task. Students organised a symposium to showcase their collaborative work as an outcome of working in interdisciplinary teams. They developed team projects to examine the relationship between art and society in the context of a social problem or issue, which could be presented as an exhibition or artefact, film, written paper or oral performance. Students also submitted a text-based or visual journal of their experience of group work during the project as well as peer and self-assessment of their contribution. This assessment approach ensured that the group interactions including the challenges and opportunities of interdisciplinary collaboration were recognised as an important part of student learning.

Focus on practice

Identify where you might authentically introduce interdisciplinary learning experiences into a module you contribute to. Consider how you might implement one or more of the six aspects of interdisciplinary learning above into you practice: multi- and interdisciplinary content, communication, disciplinary 'meta-perspectives', creativity and enquiry, solving real-world problems or team-working. What are the benefits and challenges of introducing interdisciplinary learning in your context?

Interdisciplinarity and education for sustainable development (ESD)

One of the primary drivers for more interdisciplinary approaches to knowledge creation and understanding over the last decade has been the sustainable development agenda and the role education at all levels will play in it (Blake *et al.*, 2013). ESD therefore provides a useful example of how interdisciplinarity can be developed within the curriculum. Sustainable development has been defined by the United Nations as 'development that meets the needs of the present without compromising the ability of future generations to meet their own needs' (United Nations, 1987, cited in UNESCO, 2014: 20). Sustainability 'represents a condition, or set of conditions, whereby human and natural systems can continue indefinitely in a state of mutual well-being, security and survival' (Blake *et al.*, 2013). While it might often be considered synonymous, or solely occupied, with ecological conservation, sustainable development is also concerned with wider social, economic and cultural values such as social justice, global citizenship and the promotion of sustainable futures-thinking, as well as environmental steward-ship (QAA, 2014a: 5). What is evident from this broader definition of sustainable development is that, while it is possible to understand social and ecological systems from single disciplinary perspectives, a holistic and integrative approach will discover valuable interrelationships between different methodological and conceptual positions (Jones et al., 2010). Interdisciplinary rather than mono-disciplinary approaches to research and ESD are therefore more likely to yield successful solutions to the complex and fuzzy interdisciplinary challenges posed by sustainable development.

Introducing sustainable development into the curriculum is inevitably con-tentious. When the Higher Education Funding Council for England (HEFCE) published its first ESD strategy for higher education in 2005, Knight (2005) challenged the principle that sustainable development should be an integral part of all university curricula. He argued that 'It is not the job of universities to promote a particular political orthodoxy. It is their role to educate students to examine critically policies, ideas, concepts and systems, then to make up their own mind.' Passing over the challengeable assumption that existing university curricula are inherently politically neutral, it is important to recognise the nor-mative dimension of ESD (Blake et al., 2013). In implementing ESD in universi-ties it is fundamental 'not to "indoctrinate" students in a counter ideology' but encourage them 'to explore the values and assumptions that inform decision-making processes' (Stubbs and Schapper, 2011: 262).

Critical approaches to ESD nevertheless offer the potential for engaging stu-dents in debate about controversial issues as well as challenging universities to model sustainable practices in terms of, for example, their corporate social responsibilities. This means that ESD has the capacity to contribute to whole learning experiences that foster what Barnett (1997) describes as 'critical being' in the world. For Barnett, critical being is not about having disciplinary competence but about being able to critique disciplinary knowledge and the social and politi-cal powers that have shaped it, to be critically self-reflective and, importantly, to make critical interventions in the world. Interdisciplinary enquiry, and the practi-cal problems it is applied to, demand not just the creation of knowledge and cri-tique of how that knowledge has been generated but also critical action to effect change in the world. When universities are held to account by their students for their waste management strategies, differential retention and achievement of eth-nic minority students or fair pay, students are engaging in critical action that is at the heart of this wider conception of interdisciplinary 'critical being'.

There are a number of perceived obstacles for introducing ESD into the cur-riculum including the perception of an already-packed curriculum and uncer-tainty about the relevancy of sustainability for disciplines outside geography or environmental studies (Cotton et al., 2009). These arguments may reflect overly narrow definitions of sustainable development but many teachers feel 'ill-equipped' to respond to the conceptual and pedagogic demands of implementing interdisciplinary learning experiences relevant to ESD in their practice (Selby, 2006: 57). A survey by the Higher Education Academy (HEA) and the National Union of Students (NUS), however, indicates that over 60 per cent of UK students want to learn more about sustainable development. They also expressed a preference for sustainability content to be embedded in the existing content of their programme rather than in specialised modules (Drayson *et al.*, 2014). The United Nations final report to mark the end of the 'Decade of Education for Sustainable Development' advocates that a commitment to ESD is not framed as an add-on but fundamentally requires a 'reorientation of education systems and structures', including the curriculum; this means enabling 'systems-thinking' and applied learning through participatory and collaborative learning and teaching practices (UNESCO, 2014: 20). We will explore further how to support active and collaborative learning in Chapter 11, but we will consider here what implementing ESD means at the curriculum level. Selby (2006) identifies three ways in which ESD can be embedded into the curriculum: infusionist, interdisciplinary and transdisciplinary approaches. An infusionist approach involves taking advantage of points in an existing disciplinary curriculum to introduce sustainability issues. Examples might include social, environmental, ethical, health and economic questions in relation to the use of pesticides (in chemistry or agriculture), location of a new garment factory (in business studies or fashion), water-born parasites (in biology or medicine) or the building of a hydropower dam (in geography or international development). While this approach enriches the disciplinary curriculum, relevancy in all disciplines can be difficult to articulate. In contrast, interdisciplinary approaches – whereby multiple disciplines are brought together in sustainability modules or whole programmes or transdisciplinary approaches, which are neither constrained by individual disciplines or their integration through interdisciplinarity – arguably create opportunities for developing thinking that challenges the way students and their teachers see the world.

In reality, in the face of structures and prior knowledge based on disciplines, the infusionist approach might be the more achievable strategy for individual teachers to drive forwards a sustainable development perspective or, more generally, interdisciplinarity in practice. Indeed, Cotton *et al.* (2009) urge patience for 'changes that are within the reach of individuals' as a preferable 'second-best' alternative for radical ESD approaches: 'a need to look not for revolution but evolution' (p. 732). This can be initiated within your own practice, often without the need to revise or rewrite the curriculum, by introducing learning experiences that encourage interconnected and applied thinking. Possible activities that support problem-solving, holistic and applied learning include:

- Case studies: students can be introduced to sustainability using authentic case examples of sustainable development in practice either within a single discipline or as part of interdisciplinary group work. Input from teachers or visiting experts from different disciplinary or professional contexts and interdisciplinary collaboration in small groups can help elicit multiple perspectives to better understand the case (Selby, 2006).
- Problem-based learning (PBL): PBL is an approach that involves responding to a set problem using a trigger such as a factual scenario. PBL is not a teacher-led pedagogy but instead involves students in active problem-identification and problem-solving. Students determine the aspects of the problem they want to investigate, research the topic and define a solution or solutions with the teacher providing further information or data as the topic is investigated (QAA, 2014a).
- Systems-thinking: a key principle of sustainable development is the recognition of the need for interconnected solutions to authentic problems. We often seek and accept 'mono-causal explanations' for outcomes rather than explore more holistic, multiple factors. Systems-thinking can be developed using multiple cause diagrams in which students draw and connect the multiple complex ecological, economic, social and ethical factors that are implicated in a complex problem. Students could also develop impact evaluation reports or management plans for global issues such as population growth, fair trade or water supply that recognises both 'victims' and 'beneficiaries' of particular decisions (Morris and Martin, 2009).

 Case study 3.3   Interdisciplinary group design exercises in an MEng programme (Grant et al., 2010)

Colleagues at the University of Edinburgh recognised that engineering degrees often operate within a single discipline model leading to the development of graduates as specialists. Yet in the workplace students will be expected to join multidisciplinary teams in industry or, if working in small and medium enterprises, may need to span disciplinary roles. To respond to this challenge, they worked in collaboration with visiting professors in the Integrated Design Systems scheme of the Royal Academy of Engineering, to improve alignment between the teaching of engineering design and practice in the context of the MEng degree programme. They introduced interdisciplinary design exercises that integrated electrical, mechanical, civil and chemical engineering specialisms based around three

(Continued)

(Continued)

themes: hydropower system design, potable water supply design and miniature accelerometer design. These themes were linked to the expertise of the visiting professors. The different exercises required students to work in small teams to investigate technical, economic, legal and environmental impact considerations to design systems solutions for clients. Students could indicate their preferred design exercise but all teams were allocated on the basis of mixed disciplinary expertise. The design exercises were completed within a 20-credit module run over a ten-week period. The module website included reading lists, guidance, contacts and tutorial presentations. In addition, a single day was timetabled for students from across all the disciplinary degrees to meet. Relevant lectures and 'surgery' hours with the visiting professors were also in place to support the student groups. Assessment was undertaken using key project milestones: a planning document, interim progress briefing and final report with oral presentation to a multidisciplinary panel. These staged assessments reflect the realities of keeping a client up to date on the progress of a project. The group mark was calculated from marks for each of the milestone assessments and individual student marks were calculated by combining the group mark with a peer marking exercise to peer assess contribution to the final design.

Case study 3.4   Facilitating interdisciplinary problem-based learning through education for sustainable development (Dobson and Tomkinson, 2012, 2013)

Interdisciplinary Sustainable Development (ISD) is an elective, cross-university ten-credit third-year module in the Manchester Business School at the University of Manchester. The module is designed around the completion of short, problem-based projects working in interdisciplinary teams. Student teams take on the role of sustainability consultants to focus on responding to problem 'triggers' that have multi-stakeholder views, span disciplinary boundaries and develop skills for solving open-ended, complex problems. Students work together in teams of six to ten that reflect the gender, nationality and discipline diversity of the wider group. Students start with a project brief that must be sufficiently difficult to have multiple potential outcomes as well as being 'live', unsolved global problems that have currency and do not have readily available prior solutions. Importantly, problem 'triggers' are 'discipline neutral' and projects are designed so that all students in the group have to understand the whole problem rather than a narrow disciplinary strand. Students should not break down projects into disciplinary aspects or participate only, for example, as engineering or economic specialists on multidisciplinary teams, but instead work in interdisciplinary ways. Example project briefs include 'Public consultation for siting a PVC recycling facility', 'Sustainable grocery supply for a proposed UK "ecotown"' and 'Assessing the feasibility of mainstream funeral company introducing innovative, less environmentally harmful, practices'. The problems require students to balance social, economic, regulatory and cultural concerns with environmental impact. They also need to develop skills for managing risk, facilitating stakeholder engagement and multi-criteria decision-making. Assessment is based on a team report, a quantitative peer assessment of individual contributions to the group work and an individual, reflective report.

Focus on practice

Review the examples above or relevant examples of ESD in Sterling (2012) or Roberts and Roberts (2010). How might you introduce content and pedagogies relevant for interdisciplinary thinking for sustainable development into your existing practice? What are the pros for implementing ESD in your curriculum? What are the constraints on successfully embedding this in practice?

Conclusion

In this chapter we have built on how greater awareness of disciplinary 'ways of thinking and practising' is a useful first step in working in multidisciplinary and interdisciplinary contexts that reflect the realities of working environments. Equally, multi- and interdisciplinary experiences can be used to stimulate 'meta-perspectives' and critique of mono-disciplinary approaches. The principles of ESD, as an example of interdisciplinarity in practice, are a response to the belief that mono-disciplinary and non-systemic thinking have ultimately contributed to global problems such as desertification, health pandemics and poverty. Interdisciplinarity offers the possibility for finding solutions to these challenges while establishing a new, integrative and non-dualistic future for knowledge generation. Thinking critically from disciplinary and interdisciplinary perspectives is an important step in translating knowledge and experience as a researcher or professional within a discipline or field into forms of knowledge and understanding that are accessible to students. Significantly, what we find is that developing students' criticality is based not upon the transmission of a body of knowledge but on establishing activities in which students engage in active learning such as writing, case studies, problem-based learning and working in groups. The idea of 'critical being' emphasises the importance not only of critical thinking, but also of critical action that connects theory and practice. While there may be examples of topics that are not amenable to interdisciplinary or applied perspectives, thinking through how students become participants in the disciplinary community and how they enact that disciplinary knowledge within and outside the university remain key questions for teachers, regardless of the discipline. The ideas we have explored in both this and the preceding chapter emphasise the following considerations in responding to these questions:

- knowledge as we frame it in the curriculum is not neutral but socially constructed and reflective of the power and interests of those who create and disseminate it;
- critical thinking means helping students to adopt 'meta-perspectives' about how knowledge is created, communicated and used;
- multi- and interdisciplinary thinking enables holistic, systems-thinking necessary for complex real-world challenges;
- learning to be critical involves opportunities for participatory, discursive and collaborative engagement and action.

Applied, interdisciplinary problems inevitably resist reductionist outcomes and are uncertain and open-ended. Yet, in teaching practice, the constraints of designing modules and programmes entail us to make decisions about the boundaries of the curriculum. In the next chapter we will, therefore, explore further how we 'make' a meaningful curriculum out of the expansive discipline or disciplines we teach.

Further reading

Klein, Julie (2010) 'A taxonomy of interdisciplinarity', in R. Frodeman and J.T. Klein (eds), *The Oxford Handbook of Interdisciplinarity*. New York: Oxford University Press. pp. 15–30.

Klein has been a leading researcher in the field of interdisciplinarity for over a decade and this short article provides a clear overview of the principles of multidisciplinarity, interdisciplinarity and transdisciplinarity.

Sterling, Stephen (2012) *The Future Fit Framework: An Introductory Guide to Teaching and Learning for Sustainability in HE*. York: HEA (http://www.heacademy.ac.uk/sites/default/files/Future_Fit_270412_1435.pdf).
This teacher guide provides an accessible dip-in resource on ESD, with suggestions on how to start and links to policy and disciplinary examples of ESD in practice.

CHAPTER 4

PROMOTING CRITICAL APPROACHES TO THE CURRICULUM

Learning objectives

This chapter will support you to:

- Explore how you conceptualise curriculum in your disciplinary and departmental context;
- Appraise different perspectives of curriculum and the implications these have for teachers and students;
- Engage critically with the processes of 'curriculum-making' in your context and teaching practice.

Introduction

The curriculum was, at least until recently, a neglected topic in both higher education policy and learning and teaching debates (Barnett and Coate, 2005). Although teaching methods were developed in the light of changing technologies and student demographics, the decisions about what should be included in university curricula and how a curriculum would be delivered were less likely to be scrutinised. Institutional competition in the global university marketplace and the role of universities in teaching graduates to fulfil the changing intellectual, economic and citizenship 'needs' of society, however, have prompted a renewed global interest in curriculum (Kandiko and Blackmore, 2012a). Institutions now place a premium on making their portfolio of programmes distinctive to attract students as well as fulfil employer demands for different sets of graduate skills. Two related factors have impacted on university teachers' engagement with curriculum decisions. The dominant way of understanding and describing the curriculum in contemporary UK higher education uses an outcomes-based or rational planning model. We will interrogate this model further later in this chapter but this approach is based on making explicit the organisation of the curriculum in advance of teaching, and stating specific student outcomes at the end of the module or programme. This way of organising curriculum facilitates modularisation by enabling universities to allocate numerical credit to units of study based on the level and scope of these outcomes. By focusing on the pre-statement of learning outcomes, this approach also prioritises the planned curriculum and diminishes the value of 'emergent' or 'unintended' learning experiences that occur during teaching (Knight, 2001). This emphasis on the planned curriculum can sideline the engagement of individual teachers, who may only have formal responsibility for teaching discrete elements of a module.

This chapter begins, however, from the principle that 'curricula live in and are subject to the interpretations and interventions of those conducting the activities that in part constitute a curriculum' (Barnett and Coate, 2005: 151). The week-on-week experience of a curriculum through teaching, learning and assessment cannot be separated from the planning and statement of a programme or module curriculum. Working with a curriculum before, in and after the classroom is a fundamental responsibility for all teachers involved in the teaching and assessment of a module or programme, not just for those who are responsible for designing a module or programme. This more holistic view of the curriculum distinguishes between several dimensions (Knight, 2001). All modules and programmes will comprise:

- the planned curriculum made explicit and public to students and colleagues through curriculum programme or module documentation;
- the 'real-time' curriculum or 'curriculum-in-action' as it happens in practice (Uchiyama and Radin, 2009: 272; Barnett and Coate, 2005: 45). This takes form only in the actual teaching and assessment activities of a module or programme and is the outcome of teacher and student interpretation of, and interactions with, the planned curriculum;

- the 'hidden' curriculum or the tacit assumptions and unintentional messages about what and how students should learn and how that learning is successfully demonstrated (Portelli, 1993). This dimension of the curriculum reflects the beliefs and values of individuals as well as the institutional and departmental context (Sharpe and Oliver, 2007).

For most teachers the planned curriculum (with clearly stated content and outcomes) can offer a concrete basis for the weekly selection of appropriate teaching materials and activities. The main objective of a planned curriculum is to 'deliver' the curriculum as designed as precisely as possible and to be able to replicate that curriculum experience each year. Teachers and students have a role in shaping, and subverting, this planned curriculum into the curriculum-in-action when it is taught and assessed, whether intentionally or inadvertently. This means that new teachers, even those without a current role in designing or leading a programme or module, still have a major stake in understanding and thinking critically about how the curricula they teach has been planned, how that is translated in practice and how it is experienced by students.

Curricula also articulate beliefs about what is appropriate knowledge or ways of interpreting a subject drawing an educator's conception of the discipline and their personal views about learning and teaching. However, entrenched in the traditions of a discipline or department, curricula are not natural or inevitable but are created in specific ways that reflect their context, their history and the people who work within them. For example, English studies curricula since the 1940s have successively reflected the different theoretical positions of feminist criticism, post-structuralism, post-colonialism and post-modernism. How a curriculum is designed and delivered is intertwined with our perception of the discipline and our collective ways of making meaning as part of a disciplinary community. They also reflect the tacit values and power relations that inform the social processes of creating a curriculum (Weller, 2012). The term 'curriculum-making', used by Knight (2001), with its emphasis on the creative experience of translating a carefully planned schematic into a living learning space, better captures the dynamic and concurrent relationship between the processes of design and delivery. The ideas explored in this chapter, therefore, are relevant if you have a module (a course or unit) or programme (undergraduate or postgraduate degree) leadership role or current responsibility for curriculum design. But they are also fundamental for understanding how the decisions you and others make as teachers are informed by the deliberate and unintentional ways in which you create the curriculum with your students every time you step into the lecture hall, studio or clinic or log on to a virtual learning environment.

What is the curriculum?

In the context of higher education there is recognition that the use of the term 'curriculum' can encode very different individual and collective beliefs about what knowledge is and how it relates to learning and teaching, as well as recognising the different perspectives that individuals bring to the process of curriculum-making. A curriculum is a social construction that is never apolitical but reflects different agenda (some intellectual and some strategic) and is designed to conform with, or to contest, the traditions of a subject or a department. All 'curricula, then are creatures of circumstance: they are influenced by national needs, histories and political investment as well as an institutional inertia' (Whalley *et al.*, 2011: 381). Individuals can also mean very different things when they talk about curricula. A curriculum can mean:

- a body of disciplinary knowledge and practices, the agreed texts, concepts and disciplinary protocols, of the subject;
- a means-to-an-end whereby specific and predetermined student learning outcomes are indicated;
- a critical engagement between teachers and their students about how learning happens in the discipline that is responsive to the students' needs and focuses on enabling student learning in the discipline;
- an iterative and dynamic process of teacher and student co-constructing of knowledge leading to mutual transformation of identity and perspective.

Fraser and Bosanquet (2006) categorise these different perspectives along a continuum, from product-focused conceptions, such as the curriculum as a body of knowledge or the curriculum as a means-to-an-end, which are concerned with consistency of outcomes for all students. Process-focused conceptions, such as a learning-centred curriculum or a curriculum as the co-construction of knowledge, however, are concerned with teachers developing rich learning environments with students. Each of these perspectives places a different emphasis on the three dimensions of a curriculum: the planned curriculum, the curriculum-in-action and the hidden curriculum. This categorisation provides a useful framework for critically reflecting on how we and our students understand the curriculum and our expectations about our different roles and responsibilities in curriculum-making. The different conceptions of the curriculum and the characteristic propositions that underpin these conceptions (Toohey, 1999; Short, 2002) are summarised in Table 4.1.

Table 4.1 Principles aligned to the different conceptions of curriculum

	Conception of curriculum	Principles
Product focus	Curriculum as a body of knowledge	• Knowledge exists independently of students and educators, amassed over a period of time and accessed in books, journals and other validated sources • The curriculum is organised on the basis of well-established structures of the discipline such as by genre, chronology, scope or complexity • Successful engagement with the curriculum is demonstrated by the extent of the breadth and depth of a student's assimilation of the curriculum content
	Curriculum as a means-to-an-end	• Knowledge is only discernible in the ways people behave, the disciplinary and practical skills they perform and the capacities they demonstrate • The curriculum begins with the precise statement of what a successful learner should be able to understand and do at the end of the period of study • Assessment tasks are chosen on the basis of how accurately they measure the quality of the student's performance of the stated outcomes
	Curriculum as learner-centred	• Knowledge is both personal (different people construct knowledge in different ways based on prior knowledge, experience and perception of relevance to their interests) and collective (there are specific ways of knowing as a scientist, a clinician or an historian) • The curriculum is organised on the basis of how it contributes to a student's understanding and development of key concepts and skills that can be applied to unseen and unforeseen real-world problems • Assessment tasks are selected to enable engagement in complex problem-solving and decision-making that applies discipline knowledge and skills to contextually bound questions
	Curriculum as co-construction of knowledge	• Knowledge construction is historically, socially and culturally bounded and is not disembodied from the person and is collaborative between the student and teacher as an outcome of the 'interaction of knowledges' (Fraser and Bosanquet, 2006: 276) • Curriculum content is negotiated, organised and mutually evaluated in ways that enable a critique of the privileging of certain knowledge claims over others and the assumptions students and teachers bring • Assessment tasks are developed for their relevancy to further the transformation of the discipline, the individual and society as an outcome of mutual engagement in learning
Process focus		

Focus on practice

- Which statements in Table 4.1 most closely reflect your understandings of the curriculum in your context?
- How is this understanding of the curriculum communicated to your colleagues and your students?
- In what ways do you think your discipline or institution, its history and traditions, are influential in terms of the perspective you and colleagues hold in relation to the curriculum?
- How could you rethink the curriculum of a module or programme you contribute to from a different perspective? What would change and what would be the same in terms of content, teaching and learning strategies and assessment?

Each of these different curriculum perspectives leads to different approaches to the design, development and implementation of the curriculum in practice. In each case, educators translating their understanding of the curriculum into practice will focus on the three dimensions of the curriculum in different ways.

Curriculum as a body of knowledge

If the curriculum is understood as a discrete body of knowledge then, in both design and teaching, educators will focus on the transmission of the planned curriculum over what happens when the curriculum is delivered. This idea of curriculum has been described as a 'shopping list' or 'recipe' approach (Barnett and Coate, 2005: 60; Kandiko and Blackmore, 2012a: 9). The teacher's knowledge and expertise enables them to select the essential components or define the agreed canon, the texts, concepts and theories, of a typical core module such as 'The Nineteenth Century British Novel' or 'Electromagnetism' or 'Principles of Accounting and Finance'. The selection and sequencing of content may be viewed as self-evident and not open to debate. The teacher's role is to ensure that each lecture, seminar or laboratory provides sufficient coverage of the specified content as effectively as possible. The student's role is relatively passive as a recipient of this content. Individual students' prior educational experiences, purposes in undertaking the module or their individual abilities are not significant in the design and delivery of the curriculum. From this perspective there is little concern that the planned curriculum will vary in form or intention during delivery in the classroom or assessment. There is also limited consideration of the possibility that there will be an implicit dimension that might convey helpful or unhelpful messages to some students: for example, that different students will interpret what a 'good' essay or report will include or determine whether memorisation or the application of knowledge is rewarded by assessors. From this perspective, there might be little attention given to how the planned curriculum is inevitably altered or subverted in practice: for example, by students misconstruing the relative importance or the relationships between concepts presented during a lecture because the most important topics were only introduced at the end. This conception of the curriculum articulates what Freire (1970: 53) has described as education as 'an act of depositing' between teacher and student. In this 'banking' model of education, the role of the student is to 'receive, memorise and repeat' the knowledge presented by their teachers.

Even within a curriculum-as-content approach, however, the selection of content by teachers is never the outcome of neutral decision-making. What is included and what is excluded can be inflected by a wide range of political, social and intellectual factors related to implicit and explicit beliefs about the topic, who should study it and the wider purpose of higher education. With all knowledge fields continuing to expand while the length of an undergraduate and postgraduate degree remains constant, decisions have to be made when new content is added about what will need to be removed or how new knowledge might require the reconfiguring of the module or programme to reflect the advances or changing priorities of the field. As case study 4.1 demonstrates, these decisions are articulated as part of a hidden curriculum that often reflects individual beliefs about what counts as knowledge and the influence of a teacher's interests, experience and expectations about what type of engagement with that knowledge leads to success in the module.

 Case study 4.1   Investigating the 'hidden curriculum' in higher education (Cotton *et al.*, 2013; Cotton *et al.*, 2009)

In the absence of a national curriculum or, in some disciplines, a professional body defining the curriculum content, how higher education curriculum designers select and prioritise topics and resources provides an important insight into the 'hidden curriculum' or the messages, values and practices that are tacit in the way we publically talk about the curriculum. The decisions teachers make about what is included and what is excluded in a curriculum are never more important than when considering if and how controversial topics are introduced. At Plymouth University, an online questionnaire and follow-up interviews were used to investigate teachers' beliefs about one of these contentious topics, sustainability, and their views about including sustainability in the curriculum. In total, 328 teachers responded to the questionnaire and 14 teachers from a range of disciplines were interviewed about their understanding of sustainable development and the extent to which they believed it should be included in the curriculum, as well as barriers and teaching methods. Results suggest that the perception of relevance of a topic such as sustainable development to the curriculum reflects the teacher's personal beliefs, values and context rather than an expected relevancy to some disciplines, such as geography, over others.

Focus on practice

- Talk to two or three colleagues about the rationale for how the content for the module or programme is selected and delivered and compare their answers. Is there a shared rationale for content selection? How is it communicated to students and colleagues?
- At the end of a lecture or seminar ask your students to complete a 'minute paper' to evaluate their learning by responding to two questions: 'What was the most important thing you learnt in class today?' and 'What question is unanswered?' (Stead, 2005: 119). Do all students agree about what is the most important concept, idea or skill they learnt? How do these answers compare with your own objectives for the session? If there are discrepancies, what might explain these differences?

Curriculum as a means-to-an-end

An alternative to the traditional content-focused perspective towards the curriculum is to be more explicit not only about the concepts and theories introduced, but also about what students should be able to understand and do at the end of a period of study. Where the curriculum-as-content begins from a list of topics, concepts or texts, an outcomes-based approach will elaborate on the type of understanding, skills and attitudes a student will be able to demonstrate in relation to this content. For example, to be able to explain a concept, apply the concept to a familiar problem or evaluate the validity of different concepts in relation to a new problem. Curriculum-making begins from the specification of the aims of the module or programme and the relevant learning outcomes or the graduate attributes that students will be able to demonstrate and the content they will engage with to achieve these outcomes. Further decisions are then made about the types of assessment tasks that will allow assessors to determine how well students have demonstrated the learning outcomes, and the necessary teaching and learning activities that will support students to develop and practice them. The learning outcomes and assessment are developed iteratively to ensure that the learning outcomes are measurable and will effectively enable educators to make unequivocal judgements about the quality of the performance. A final feature of the outcomes-based curriculum is evaluation to determine how the curriculum can be improved when it is next delivered (Moon, 2002). It must be possible, therefore, for every learning outcome to be demonstrated and assessable.

Outcomes-based curricula and national qualifications frameworks

The learning outcomes approach is embedded in the quality assurance mechanisms of UK higher education as a consequence of the recommendations of the 1997 report of the National Committee of Inquiry into Higher Education (the Dearing Report) and the report of its partner Scottish Committee (the Garrick Report). The aim of these committees was to make recommendations for the future of higher education. The reports resulted in two national standard qualifications frameworks recently revised as the *UK Quality Code for Higher Education* (QAA, 2014b) for all four nations of the UK. The code identifies five levels of undergraduate and postgraduate qualification descriptors from first-year undergraduate to doctoral degree in England, Wales and Northern Ireland and Scotland. Qualification descriptors specify what a student should be able to demonstrate to be awarded credit or a qualification at that level. The qualifications descriptors are generic but, in addition, subject benchmark statements at undergraduate and, in some subjects, postgraduate level have been developed that specify in detail the discipline-specific dimensions of the qualifications descriptors.

As well as enabling transparency and comparability across institutions in the UK, the framework also works within the wider context of an increasingly global higher education marketplace. The Bologna Declaration (1999) stated a shared commitment to increasing comparability and compatibility of the higher education systems across Europe. The subsequent implementation through the ongoing Bologna Process has sought to ensure that credit and qualifications have an agreed exchange value across European institutions. The *UK Quality Code* aligns with the qualifications framework of the European

Higher Education Area (http://www.ehea.info). The underpinning priorities of this process are 'mobility, employability and quality' (European Commission, 2013) to enable students to move across national higher education systems within Europe with relative equality between the credit and qualifications awarded. The *UK Quality Code* was developed to support institutions, teachers and students to articulate and understand the nature of programmes of study. This is defined in terms of knowledge and understanding, key practical skills including communication skills, information handling, cognitive skills such as critical analysis and subject-specific skills such as clinical or laboratory skills. The outcomes-based approach has therefore become the dominant approach for framing the curriculum in the UK. Anyone designing a programme or module needs to relate the provision to the appropriate descriptors for the level of study. Institutions must also ensure that these benchmarked learning outcomes are publicly available to students, teachers, employers and external assessors in the form of module and programme specifications.

There are a number of ways to categorise the types of learning that learning outcomes specify. Bloom's taxonomy (Bloom, 1956; Krathwohl, 2002) has been influential in the classification of different verbs in relation to knowledge and understanding, application, analysis, synthesis and evaluation outcomes. Biggs' five levels of the 'Structure of the Observed Learning Outcomes' (SOLO) taxonomy (Biggs and Tang, 2011) similarly demarcate the different levels of understanding within a hierarchical 'staircase' of increasing levels of complexity. Learning outcomes will include:

- knowledge and understanding: this is the conceptual or empirical body of knowledge of the subject described as propositional, 'declarative' knowledge (Biggs and Tang, 2011);
- cognitive (thinking) skills: these are critical thinking skills such as analysis, synthesis and problem-solving that enable students to make meaning and be able to communicate it to others in disciplinarily appropriate ways (Toohey, 1999);
- performance and practice skills: these are the skills related to performing or applying knowledge in ways that enable a student to put their understanding into practice taking into account the specific disciplinary or professional context;
- personal and enabling skills: these are the skills that relate to learner autonomy, self-reflection and self-evaluation drawing on individual experience (Toohey, 1999).

Each of these different types of learning can then in turn be demonstrated by students at different levels of desirable complexity that can be categorised as descriptive, integrative or critical. At a descriptive level, a learner will provide an account of a topic or concept, isolate key features and contextualise the topic. At an integrative level, a learner begins to make meaning of the topic, bringing different or conflicting concepts, perspectives or orientations together and considering the interrelationships between different positions or conceptions. At the critical level, a learner examines assumptions and makes evaluative decisions about the different perspectives or interrelationships as the basis for future critically informed action in potentially unforeseen contexts. Table 4.2 summarises the type and level of learning outcome using typical indicative verbs that are used in the writing of learning outcomes and assessment criteria. Learning outcomes will always include a verb to indicate the type of expected performance and an indication of the level of complexity of the performance needed to demonstrate the learning outcome at the pass mark (Moon and Gosling, 2002).

Table 4.2 Indicative learning outcome verbs at different levels of complexity

Type of learning outcome	Level of complexity		
	Descriptive	Integrative	Critical
Knowledge and understanding	Define, label, name, recognise, reproduce, state, memorise, record, list, identify, recall, observe, report, present, name, paraphrase	Classify, organise, convert, relate, arrange, order, explain, express, clarify, compare, contrast, distinguish, discuss, extrapolate, summarise	Select, restate, translate, estimate, extend, generalise, predict, review, infer, reorganise
Cognitive skills	Distinguish, analyse, calculate, collect, distil, differentiate, derive, investigate, examine, inspect, outline, discriminate	Assemble, organise, categorise, debate, appraise, synthesise, associate, compare, contrast, combine, manage, rearrange, experiment, relate, consider possibilities	Criticise, conceptualise, appraise, assess, question, construct, formulate, devise, modify, propose, hypothesise, evaluate, generate
Performance and practice	Practise, solve, apply, demonstrate, use, employ, operate, implement, recognise, measure, compute, give examples of	Interpret, choose, select, associate, manipulate	Propose, plan, create, formulate, adapt, evaluate, design, create
Personal and enabling skills	Communicate, present, illustrate, demonstrate, express	Argue, explain, summarise, debate, respond, defend, conclude	Reflect, appraise, question, justify, evaluate, adopt a position

Focus on practice

Take a module that you teach and review the learning outcomes in relation to Table 4.2:

- Are all the outcomes focused in one area – for example, in the descriptive level of knowledge and understanding?
- Do the types and levels of learning outcomes reflect your expectations about the level and content of the module? Are there any learning outcomes that need to be rewritten to better reflect the type and level of desired learning?
- Based on your recent experience of teaching the module, are there other desirable and relevant outcomes that have emerged in the day-to-day teaching that are not included in the pre-specified learning outcomes?

The outcomes-based approach seeks to unpack what student learning will look like. It also recognises the possibility that the planned curriculum may be reconstructed during learning and teaching as a curriculum-in-action. It is based on the assumption, however, that greater specificity in planning the curriculum can limit this by more carefully regulating the quality and consistency of the experience in the classroom. The evaluation of the outcomes at the end of the module can help to identify and rectify where there may be discrepancies between the planned curriculum and the curriculum-in-action. A further argument for an outcomes-based approach is that, in defining exactly what is expected of students and choosing learning opportunities and assessment that is designed to measure achievement of those specific outcomes, there is transparency for both teachers and students about the beliefs, values and aims of a module or programme. In this way, educators focus on greater specificity in the planned curriculum as a way to obviate the risks that the curriculum-in-action and the hidden curriculum pose for the original design and intentions of a module or programme. The main assumption within this approach is that the risks of the curriculum-in-action and hidden curriculum can be mitigated by careful planning. An outcomes-based curriculum is frequently described as a 'logical' or 'rational' curriculum with adjustments being made on the basis of 'objective' evaluation to ensure this 'systematic process' is improved each time it is delivered (Cowan and Harding, 1986: 106). This conveys a fundamental presumption about the learning and teaching experience because it is 'presented as a logical way of proceeding, redolent of scientific method' that 'assumes a determinate and linear universe in which the specialness of setting are irritants that science should rise above' (Knight, 2001: 372).

While attempting to expose the tacit convictions about discipline knowledge and the nature of disciplinary thinking, an outcomes-based approach asserts a strongly performative understanding of effective learning and teaching. Critical accounts of the outcomes-based approach, therefore, have questioned the feasibility of writing learning outcomes that are genuinely meaningful for the type of authentic and complex learning that higher education aims to foster. Well-written learning outcomes must be measurable to be assessed, but what is easily measurable is also potentially reductive and de-contextualised from the learner and their learning experience in the classroom or beyond (Hussey and Smith, 2002; Knight, 2001). More student-centred curriculum approaches are also inclined to be responsive to the interests and needs of students in ways that can reduce the likelihood that all the pre-specified outcomes will be achieved. A range of unpredicted outcomes could emerge as the curriculum happens in real-time that might be relevant and highly desirable, even if not anticipated in advance. Although ostensibly articulated in ways that suggest greater student control over their learning experience, outcomes-based approaches in practice potentially assert more not less teacher control over learning. If teachers maintain a strict adherence to the planned curriculum they can reduce the possibility of recognising and rewarding the unpredictable, open, unrepeatable and exciting outcomes of engaging with their students (Hussey and Smith, 2003). In addition, if we want our curricula to be interdisciplinary or more reflective of the workplace and the social challenges graduates will face in the future we also need to recognise that 'learning in real life situations tends to shift curriculum away from the pre-ordained and towards the emergent' (Selby, 2006: 57).

The contractual nature of the learning outcomes approach seeks to ensure that the learning system is auditable and that educators themselves are accountable for the effectiveness of the system and the efficiency of their delivery within that system. This intention to resolve the uncertainties of the curriculum-in-action through careful specification of the learning outcomes to empower students has, it is argued, replaced the hidden paradigm of the traditional curriculum with equally powerful 'ideological regulatory systems' that operate to control the curriculum and how its outputs are used (O'Brien and Brancaleone, 2011: 12). It is the emphasis on a depersonalised, objective student experience that has justified a modification of an outcomes-based approach to take into account how students learn as individuals to a greater degree.

Curriculum as learner-centred

Ensuring that learning outcomes and relevant assessment tasks and criteria are predetermined in advance of learning and teaching is also fundamental to a learning-centred approach to the curriculum. The distinction between this approach and an outcomes-based curriculum, however, is that it integrates a theory of student learning into curriculum planning and delivery decisions which takes account of how individual students process information differently. As with an outcomes-based approach, this approach to curriculum focuses on enabling student learning by emphasising the planned dimension of the curriculum with precise definition of learning outcomes. The learner-centred approach, however, is also informed by an understanding of the curriculum-in-action as a more complex interaction between teachers, students and content. From this perspective, learning is a result of a number of internal and external contextual factors: how individual students learn, the learning and teaching activities they engage in and the learning environment. In adopting this approach to the curriculum, educators therefore shift their perspective from viewing the curriculum as a definable product to conceptualising the curriculum as a process to support student learning. This way of curriculum-making is grounded in a psychological orientation to learning (Tennant *et al.*, 2010) that assumes that an individual student's learning is influenced by their prior knowledge, their motivations and their perception of learning and assessment tasks. Understanding is developed on the basis of a learner's active construction of knowledge in relation to their existing knowledge and understanding. This is a theory of learning known as constructivism. It challenges the belief that knowledge and understanding can be straightforwardly passed from the teacher to the student during a lecture and instead explains learning as the result of the processes of integration of new understanding into a student's existing knowledge frameworks. A curriculum that is based on a constructivist conception of how learning takes place is distinguished from other forms of curriculum-making by the shift to a learner-centred approach where the emphasis is on the opportunities that the curriculum provides for learners to create or construct their own knowledge. From this perspective, the curriculum is not concerned exclusively with an educator's decisions about what to teach, but also about how learning happens in ways that validate individual experience. Hence students are at the 'centre of a flexible curriculum process, and are able to explore with their teachers areas that suit their needs and motivations' (Fraser and Bosanquet, 2006: 274).

One of the most influential approaches to curriculum-making that aims to focus on student learning is Biggs' model of 'constructive alignment' (Biggs and Tang, 2011). While grounded in an outcomes-based approach, this model integrates a constructivist theory of learning into a rational approach so that learning outcomes and assessment criteria are defined and aligned to each other. Biggs configures the well-made curriculum as a 'balanced system in which all components support each other, as they do in an ecosystem' (Biggs, 2003: 26). Learning and teaching methods are selected to provide the best opportunities for students to create their own understanding. Assessment tasks and criteria are selected on the basis of their appropriateness to encourage students to adopt suitable approaches to learning and test the achievement of the outcomes. For example, using long answer questions, applied problem tasks, multiple choice exams and essays will all encourage different types of learning and test different learning outcomes. In an aligned curriculum no method is incorrect in itself as long as the learning, teaching and assessment methods are appropriate for the desired student outcomes and are in alignment with each other.

With its focus on the curriculum-in-action, a fundamental component of this approach is the relationship between new knowledge introduced during a module and a student's prior knowledge and individual experience. This prior knowledge can vary significantly across a cohort of students regardless of previous qualifications or the completion of prerequisite modules. Prior knowledge scaffolds how new knowledge is integrated and, where there are gaps or misconceptions, can significantly impact on student learning (Hay *et al.*, 2008). In implementing a curriculum that is learner-centred, therefore, it is essential to reflect on the knowledge and understanding that we can reasonably expect students to bring to a module or programme. It is also important to gather real-time information so that we can make decisions about students' existing understanding and how successfully they are integrating new knowledge into their personal knowledge schemas as the curriculum is enacted in practice.

Many of the strategies for collecting this data to inform our teaching are also useful tools for helping students to monitor their progress, reflect on how their knowledge and understanding is organised and revise new topics. The following list suggests some of the ways in which we can interrogate our students' prior knowledge and support the integration of new knowledge as part of a learner-centred approach to the curriculum:

- Be familiar with the learning outcomes and content for prerequisite modules and programmes or previous sessions that are relevant to the module or topic. Briefly revise or ask students to list key concepts at the beginning of the lecture, seminar or clinic and link them to the intended learning outcomes for the session or module.
- Instead of presenting a bullet point list of learning outcomes or content topics at the beginning of a lecture, think about how the lecture could be organised in relation to the overarching conceptual framework of the topic. Are there primary and subsidiary concepts and how do they relate to each other? Can the relationships between concepts be visualised and signposted for students? An advanced organiser presents general or abstract concepts to illustrate how the ideas introduced in the lecture relate to each other. Alternatively, it can be useful to start with a sample problem or concrete

example from which concepts are derived. Gurlitt *et al.* (2012) suggest that problems with 'a close correspondence to everyday experiences [...] increase the chance for learners to use their general world knowledge to complement' (p. 353) their lack of specific disciplinary knowledge.

- Evaluation techniques that assess prior knowledge such as 'Background Knowledge Probe' or 'Misconception/Preconception Check' can be introduced into learning. For the 'Background Knowledge Probe', plan two or three open-ended questions on key concepts that are necessary for understanding a new topic and ask students individually to write short responses. For the 'Misconception/Preconception Check', identify common mistakes or areas of difficulty related to the topic and use multiple choice or short-form questions to check areas of difficulty that may impact on future learning (Angelo and Cross, 1993: 121–5, 132–7). These rapid techniques can be carried out by show of hands, paper or electronic voting systems which use 'clickers' or apps on student smartphones. Reviewing the outcomes can help you to plan the starting point for the new topic and provide formative feedback to students on their understanding of the topic (see case studies 5.2 and 11.2 in later chapters for examples of this in practice).

While the student experience of learning is central to this approach, according to Biggs, a well-aligned curriculum will ensure that all 'students are "entrapped" in this web of consistency, optimizing the likelihood that they will engage the appropriate learning activities'. When 'teaching methods do not directly encourage the appropriate learning activities, students can easily "escape" by engaging in inappropriate learning activities' (Biggs and Tang, 2011: 99). This suggests that, although informed by a constructivist theory of learning that pays attention to the student experience, an aligned curriculum as defined by Biggs focuses on acknowledging but minimising the impact of the messy realities of the curriculum-in-action in the lecture or seminar.

The attempt to define and respond to student learning needs is also problematic because the construction of those needs, even by the students themselves, is not neutral but is embedded in current social and context-specific interpretations about the purpose of higher education or assumptions about the individual student's role and responsibilities (Clegg, 2011). For example, as the purpose of higher education has been explicitly allied to the needs of the economy and post-graduation employment, so the language of the outcomes-based approach has embodied the marketisation of the individual with the aim to produce 'a competent and efficacious person [...] who is critically aware of how their skills and attributes sit within the labour market – a kind of "entrepreneur of the self"' (Tennant *et al.*, 2010: 19–20). This is, Parker (2003) has argued, a 'commodification of the students' that 'militates against the subject areas and disciplines operating as communities of practice' (pp. 532–3). A fourth conception of the curriculum builds on the constructivist theory of how students learn but does so by arguing that learning is better understood as fundamentally social and that the 'individualised approaches to study obscure a sense of oneself as part of a social group of learners' (Ecclestone, 1999: 40). In this socially dynamic and collaborative conception of curriculum, students and their teachers become co-creators of subject knowledge that is not universal but situated and mutually transformative.

Curriculum as the co-construction of knowledge

For many teachers, inspiring university curricula are about the intellectual 'presence' of both students and teachers in creative and imaginative interaction with each other as they engage with what it means to know, think and do in their discipline. This is as opposed to the 'disembodied intelligence and objective manipulation of knowledge for precise and identifiable outcomes' (Anderson, 2010: 206) that is articulated through more technical approaches to curriculum-making. Barnett (2012) also warns that, in planning 'learning for an unknown future', a curriculum based around skills is a 'cul-de-sac' and the 'way forward lies in a construing and enacting a pedagogy for human being' (p. 65). Recognising the curriculum as a social, creative process values the curriculum-in-action, the interactions between students, teachers, the subject matter and the context, over the planned curriculum so that we develop our students' disciplinary understanding in ways that are situated and meaningful. In this approach, the values, assumptions and ideologies that shape the curriculum are deliberately and productively available to scrutiny and critique. As the curriculum is enacted in practice, 'what counts as knowledge, how knowledge is organised and transmitted, who has access to knowledge and whose interests are served by the current system' (Tennant *et al.*, 2010: 20) are central to the questions and problems students and teachers use in making meaning. As case study 4.2 demonstrates, curriculum co-design approaches that involve students in evaluating and planning curricula with their teachers can help to surface and critique these values and the power differentials they enact (Bovill and Bulley, 2011).

Case study 4.2   Engaging with students in the curriculum design process (Brooman *et al.*, 2014)

The module team for the European Law second-year module of the undergraduate law programme at Liverpool John Moores University wanted to respond to several ongoing concerns including low grades, poor student module feedback and attendance issues. The curriculum redesign process was initially teacher-led and a new module was developed based around a restructuring of lectures and seminars, the provision of more extensive resources in a module workbook and compulsory preparatory tasks. Student performance and module feedback, however, went down further following the curriculum redesign. The team therefore decided to undertake a second redesign exercise but this time work more closely with students to understand better their perception of the module and learning needs. Forty-four students registered on the module participated in small focus groups with a researcher before the final assessment to explore their learning experience and suggest possible improvements to the module. Following changes made to the curriculum as an outcome of listening more fully to the student voice, student performance, attendance and module feedback all improved. While the focus groups did not create an opportunity for co-design with students, exploring their experience with students challenged the teams' assumptions about the student learning experience, raised their awareness about the impact of the curriculum structure on student outcomes and re-engaged them with the curriculum research and evidence they use to inform their design decisions.

A curriculum based around the co-construction of knowledge is still aligned to fulfilling what Baxter-Magolda (2001) has defined as highly sought-after outcomes of higher education: to acquire knowledge and understand how to analyse it and reach conclusions. Yet it also supports the development of self-identity and values, engagement with others and shared responsibility for learning. As educators 'we expect [students] to integrate these ways of knowing, being and interacting with others into the capacity for self-authorship – the capacity to internally define their own beliefs, identity and relationships' (p. xvi). She argues that our responsibility as educators is to be 'good company' on that journey with our students. To achieve this, we need to pay attention to Baxter-Magolda's three educational principles as the basis for enabling student 'self-authorship':

- knowledge is socially constructed and the curriculum needs to validate learners as knowers alongside their teachers so that they understand how they can construct knowledge and make knowledge claims;
- sense of self or subjective experience cannot be separated from what and how it is to know. Learning involves our identity so the curriculum needs to provide opportunities to respect and situate knowledge in a student's own experience;
- expertise and authority are shared between a student, their peers and their teacher in the mutual construction of knowledge. The curriculum therefore needs to invite students to participate equally in knowledge construction (Baxter-Magolda, 2001).

Knowledge construction is the result of a shared and reciprocal process of structured investigation, with the curriculum supporting students to engage in disciplinary self-positioning in relation to the subject matter. It means being aware of what students bring to the curriculum, what their relationship is to the knowledge field and how it relates to their own experience.

Drawing on these principles of student 'self-authorship', throughout this book we will explore how practice can be oriented towards teacher and student co-construction of knowledge and critical understanding of the experience of learning. This form of curriculum will:

- encourage students to interact with each other and with their teachers in partnership to become active and critically engaged learners (Chapter 5);
- involve students in experiences of enquiry that enable them to develop an understanding of how they learn and how their knowledge is constructed (Chapter 6);
- create opportunities for learning experiences that are authentic to the real world of employment and citizenship (Chapter 7);
- provide opportunities for students to experience and value multiple and contrasting perspectives (Chapters 8 and 9);
- require students to work independently and collaboratively through, what Barnett (2009) describes as their real and virtual 'continued presence and commitment' (p. 438) in their learning (Chapters 10 and 11).

Conclusion

This chapter has worked from the premise that those who design and lead a curriculum and those who enact it in practice (both teachers and students) have an equal investment in understanding the values, beliefs and assumptions that underpin how a curriculum is made. While acknowledging the need to work within existing institutional frameworks that use an outcomes-based approach, this chapter has put forward alternative ways to engage with the curriculum. These alternative perspectives suggest that as educators we should seek to:

- understand the curriculum as a social process that reflects the beliefs, values and power relationships of the context within which they are designed and delivered;
- critically evaluate the curriculum as a process in which knowledge is co-constructed with our students;

- rethink the ways in which we interact with our students as new members of the academic community and bringing resources, perspectives and 'knowledges' (Fraser and Bosanquet, 2006: 276) that will enrich our own.

In undertaking the 'Focus on practice' tasks in this chapter, you will have already started to scope out the questions and challenges of the curriculum you are working with and how they operate in their context. These exercises have hopefully raised doubts about the validity of product-focused curriculum approaches by revealing that the experience of a curriculum is subjective and nuanced. No two students or teachers experience the curriculum in the same way. We can attempt to standardise these experiences as far as possible, but a more creative, sustainable and intellectually enriching approach is to embrace these experiences and use them to power both our own and our students learning in our fields. Over the next seven chapters we will look specifically at how we can work with our students to transform our curricula so that they can fulfil the desirable principles of co-construction and self-authorship.

Further reading

Bovill, Catherine (2014) 'An investigation of co-created curricula within higher education in the UK, Ireland and the USA', *Innovations in Education and Teaching International*, 51(4): 15–25.
This paper provides three examples of collaborating with students in the design of curricula in geography, education and environmental justice programmes and provides guidance for those wishing to undertake a process of co-design including what students are involved and what role they play in the process.

Fraser, Sharon P. and Bosanquet, Agnes M. (2006) 'The curriculum? That's just a unit outline, isn't it?', *Studies in Higher Education*, 31(3): 269–84.
This accessible article identifies educators' different conceptions of the curriculum and can be a useful prompt for reflecting on the values and assumptions that teachers bring to the design and implementation of curricula.

Knight, Peter T. (2001) 'Complexity and curriculum: a process approach to curriculum-making', *Teaching in Higher Education*, 6(3): 369–81.
In the context of more instrumental approaches to defining curricula outcomes and practices, this paper provides a meaningful account of the process of curriculum-making and -remaking in teaching that resonates for many new teachers.

CHAPTER 5

WORKING WITH STUDENTS: FROM ENGAGEMENT TO PARTNERSHIP

Learning objectives

This chapter will support you to:

- Reflect critically on the nature of student engagement and why students engage or disengage with their learning at university;
- Plan and facilitate learning experiences and environments that promote student engagement;
- Identify strategies for working with students as partners in the enhancement of learning and teaching.

Introduction

Substantive changes to the way UK universities are funded have resulted in undergraduate students taking more direct financial responsibility for their education than in previous generations. These changes in the fee regime across the sector have impacted on how the relationship between universities and their students is often described. The 'student-as-consumer' metaphor has been particularly dominant as a way to explain a perceived shift in the purpose of contemporary higher education and, in particular, the pedagogic relationship between teachers and their students (Molesworth *et al.*, 2009). This metaphor can imply that students have greater rights to question and influence the quality of their education as informed participants, and that universities are more accountable. Yet the allusion to the provision of a commodified educational product also lends itself to impoverished versions of the teacher–student and university–student relationship (McCulloch, 2009). Anecdotally, many teachers have perceived a parallel trend of student disengagement with the types of learning, such as independent learning or critical thinking, which higher education has customarily claimed to reward.

This student disengagement, or perhaps more appropriately student 'inertia' – which Krause (2005) argues better characterises the more passive absence of engagement, is demonstrated in:

- low student attendance at timetabled teaching and learning activities;
- lack of appropriate independent study and preparation for class;
- reluctance to participate in active face-to-face or online learning activities;
- failure to adopt meaningful approaches to learning;
- preference for transmission modes of teaching;
- an emphasis on individual credentialism and competition rather than collaboration as members of a learning community (Baron and Corbin, 2012; McCulloch, 2009).

Conversely, student engagement with the academic challenge of their university experience and their sense of belonging to their institution have been linked to improved retention and increased levels of persistence. Research suggests that student engagement also leads to the achievement of higher-level learning outcomes and increased student satisfaction with their educational experience (Bryson and Hand, 2008; Krause, 2005).

The potential for student engagement to impact on satisfaction with their university experience has ensured that it has become a significant issue for many university leaders in recent years, particularly in the context of the undergraduate National Student Survey (NSS). This annual survey of final-year students has been run across the UK since 2005 and the results are publically available as key information sets for all programmes. Postgraduate experience surveys for taught (PTES) and research postgraduates (PRES) are also now being used by many UK universities. Student engagement is therefore seen as an important focus for improving satisfaction survey results which can have significant international, political and economic implications for institutions. The focus on surveys to measure quality inevitably raises other questions.

In this highly politicised context, the student satisfaction agenda potentially focuses institutional attention on improving ratings rather than necessarily improving learning (Yorke, 2013). In addition, as Collini (2012) argues, satisfaction may not be the best measure of the quality of learning and teaching. In reality, educators may hope that their students 'come away with certain kinds of dissatisfaction' and that 'it matters more that they carry on wondering about the source of that dissatisfaction than whether they "liked" the course or not' (p. 185).

So how do we teach in ways that promote engagement with the academic challenge of study at university, discourage student 'inertia' and make student 'dissatisfaction' something that drives learning? In this chapter we will begin by looking at how we define student engagement as the basis for effective learning. We will then explore strategies that create learning experiences aligned to some key principles of student engagement in the context of a mass higher education system. We will focus specifically on how students can be encouraged to develop as active and independent learners in classroom contexts and how to develop their engagement with feedback on assessment as the basis for self-regulated learning. While traditional evaluation forms and student satisfaction surveys have dominated the ways in which educators listen to the student input, we will consider how participative approaches to the curriculum can enable staff and students to work in partnership to enhance learning and teaching.

What is student engagement?

The dominant definition of student engagement is that it involves student participation in purposeful learning activities inside and outside timetabled teaching. These activities should lead to desirable and emergent learning outcomes of university study. It therefore encompasses both the activities students engage in for learning and what educators and their institutions do to enable this to happen. For Kuh (2009), engagement is straightforward: the more students practise a subject and receive meaningful feedback on that practice, the more complex their levels of understanding. In contrast to the UK model of student satisfaction, the extent of student engagement has been used as the basis for measuring and enhancing the quality of the student university experience in other Western education systems. The National Survey of Student Engagement (NSSE) was first used in North America in 1999, drawing on over a decade of work on undergraduate education. The Australasian Survey of Student Engagement (AUSSE) developed out of the NSSE and has been used since 2007. The NSSE comprises five scales for measuring student perceptions of their engagement, with the AUSSE adding a sixth employability scale:

- perception of academic challenge;
- participation in active learning;
- involvement in student and staff interaction;
- participation in enriching educational experiences;
- experience of a supportive learning environment;
- opportunities for work-integrated learning (Hagel *et al.*, 2012).

As with the NSS, there is much debate over the validity of the scales within these national surveys and the activity-oriented focus of the questions which emphasise student and teaching behaviours (Kahu, 2013). Critiques of this definition of engagement suggest that these performative indicators focus too much on behaviour or activities at the expense of other, more critical dimensions of engagement such as student attitudes and values, as well as the social context of the university (Bryson and Hand, 2008; Kahu, 2013). In recent years student engagement has been increasingly defined as more holistic and multidimensional.

From a holistic perspective, student engagement is viewed as a social practice that takes account of the identity of teachers and their students situated in the context of the classroom, institution and wider society. This expanded definition of engagement recognises the mutual responsibility of both students and teachers for learning in the context of the university and the function of higher education within society. Student engagement is also better represented as a continuum between experiences of full participation and confident citizenship within the university and experiences of alienation or 'inertia' (Bryson and Hand, 2008). These two intersecting dimensions of student–teacher responsibility for learning and engagement–disengagement are summarised in Figure 5.1.

As a social practice, staff and student interaction is fundamental for fostering student engagement that leads to critical thinking, conceptual understanding and self-regulated learning. More recent definitions of student engagement highlight some important caveats to an uncritical adoption of a cross-disciplinary model for effective learning and teaching in higher education. Engagement is not a value-free concept. What we see from an educator's perspective as legitimate student engagement (for example, active oral participation or not in class or evidence of independent learning) can be a result of student compliance to other external disciplinary or cultural expectations rather than a demonstration

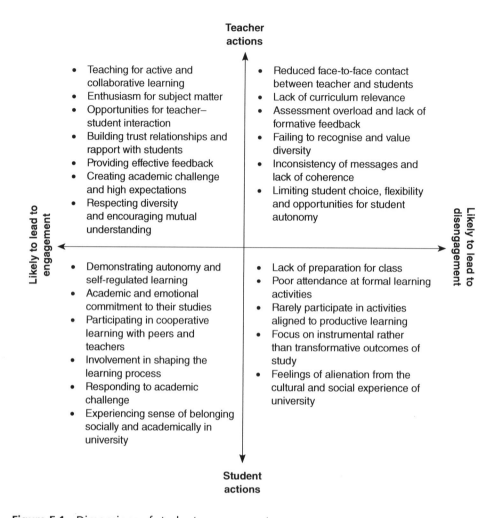

Figure 5.1 Dimensions of student engagement

of an individual student's commitment to study (Hagel *et al.*, 2012). There are a number of other factors that frame how staff and students define and enact engagement including:

- disciplinary differences in what counts as engagement;
- different perceptions of the purpose and desirable outcomes of higher education;
- student demographics such as year of study, gender, age, socio-economic background, culture and ethnicity;

- non-institutional factors such as family, friends, caring responsibilities and employment;
- expectations about sustained engagement across a module or programme versus short-term engagement with specific tasks.

As discussed in Chapter 2, teacher and student expectations about disciplinary pedagogy can shape the nature of engagement in different subjects, evidencing what Brint *et al.* (2008) describe as 'two distinct cultures of engagement' (p. 383) between the humanities and social sciences and natural sciences and engineering subjects. For example, the traditional culture of engagement in the humanities and social sciences can stress active participation in discussion, interaction and student responsibility for learning outside of restricted timetabled provision. Conversely, the culture of engagement in sciences and engineering can encourage collaborative problem-solving and technical competency with greater dependency on teachers to guide learning alongside student management of the workload of a more prescribed curricula. Cross-disciplinary definitions of student engagement as encompassing both participatory and discursive attributes and collaborative problem-solving for all students in all disciplines, therefore, may be difficult to achieve. The absence of one or more of these attributes in an individual student studying a degree in English Literature or Biochemistry may not necessarily indicate a lack of valid engagement in their studies. However, challenging humanities students to engage in collaborative problem-solving or science students to debate the ethical implications of science knowledge could also be powerful approaches to inducing additional forms of disciplinary criticality and engagement.

In some disciplines or parts of the sector we may also value perceived intrinsic motivations for study, 'learning for learning's sake', over more instrumental or vocational objectives. This can be reflected in how student engagement is characterised by teachers and institutions. Some of the typical indicators of student engagement in Figure 5.1, such as autonomous and self-regulated learning, are not neutral ways to account for quality learning but reflect specific assumptions about the purpose of a higher education. Students who do not share these assumptions or may be purposefully participating in higher education for extrinsic reasons such as employment can therefore engage with their learning in different but equally valid ways (Haggis, 2006; Kahu, 2013).

While engagement is often characterised by teachers in terms of the demonstration of abstract intellectual skills, students themselves also include emotional attributes when describing their experiences of engagement. Teaching for engagement, therefore, may need to take into account these affective dimensions of learning for students within the university (Solomonides and Martin,

2008). While there are many areas within an institution that influence student engagement in their studies, it is also recognised that university study does not exist in a vacuum and that there are a number of areas of students' lives that significantly impact on their engagement. Student employment during study has been explicitly connected to student disengagement (Baron and Corbin, 2012), but, for many full- and part-time students, the support from family and friends in terms of childcare or the creation of space for study are fundamental factors in determining their level of engagement (Leach and Zepke, 2011).

These variations in what student engagement means to different students and teachers underscore the need to understand student-engaged learning as fundamentally context-specific. Across the sector, different institutions have different educational missions, serve diverse communities and have different understandings of what constitutes effective learning and teaching (Hardy and Bryson, 2009). In planning for student-engaged learning we need to consider what engagement might look like in our own discipline across different student demographic groups and how engagement might change over the length of a degree or even across different modules or activities. This helps us to plan learning and teaching to promote engagement and communicate what engagement looks like to our students. Hagel *et al.* (2012) suggest that engagement may not be a stable and general state but can also be a short-term intense involvement in specific activities. Engaged students may not be invariably engaged in all their learning experiences regardless of the circumstances. Disengaged students can become more absorbed in their educational experience if certain conditions are in place. Engagement, then, 'is not merely the sum of useful and productive activities that students experience. Rather, engagement derives from the quality, nature and depth of these activities' (p. 477) within their disciplinary and institutional context. Table 5.1 summarises five different dimensions of engagement and the critical questions we can use to audit engagement in practice (Leach and Zepke, 2011; Kahu, 2013). These dimensions are:

- motivation: how individual student and teacher motivation, enthusiasm and sense of agency are integrated into the learning experience;
- relationships: how interactions and relationships between students and between students and their teachers are built and sustained;
- curriculum culture: how a culture of engagement and shared responsibility for successful learning is embedded in the curriculum;
- citizenship: how students are supported to develop informed viewpoints and behave ethically as active citizens within the university;
- socio-cultural context: how the relationship between the academy and its wider social, economic and cultural context is managed.

Table 5.1 A framework for evaluating and enabling student engagement in practice

Dimension of engagement	Critical questions	Examples of activities to foster engagement
Motivation	When do students have opportunities to make decisions about how and what they learn? When are students responsible for setting their own learning goals? How are student and teacher interests acknowledged and incorporated into the module?	• Provide opportunities for student peer instruction to recognise students as experts • Provide choice in assessment topics and tasks to enable students to decide how to demonstrate learning outcomes
Relationships	What opportunities are available for students to engage actively in group work? How are students prepared to work effectively in groups? When do students and teachers work collaboratively? How do students and teachers develop constructive feedback on learning throughout the module?	• Use creative group tasks at key points in large classes with opportunities for reflection • Introduce interactive feedback coversheets to support self-assessment • Use electronic voting systems in lectures to give instant feedback on learning
Curriculum culture	When are expectations about student and teacher responsibility for learning discussed? How is trust between students and teachers built and developed? How do teachers ensure students experience sufficient academic challenge during their studies? How are students involved in the enhancement of the curriculum?	• Students and teachers collaborate to develop ground rules for participation or the learning process • Engage students as partners in the evaluation of learning experiences to make recommendations for enhancing practice
Citizenship	When are students supported to develop a position on a topic based on independently collating and evaluating evidence? How do learning experiences enable students to be self-critical and respectful of a range of perspectives? What opportunities are possible for students to learn how to act in ways that are ethically and politically informed?	• Use enquiry-based and problem-solving tasks that require synthesis and evaluation of contradictory evidence • Introduce role play, debate or simulation tasks to encourage the adopting of different perspectives

(Continued)

Table 5.1 (Continued)

Dimension of engagement	Critical questions	Examples of activities to foster engagement
Socio-cultural context	How do students and teachers negotiate their power in the context of the module? How are students supported to manage their studies alongside employment, volunteering and family commitments? In what ways are students prepared to effect change in their communities inside and outside the university?	• Enable students to input into the criteria for assessment decisions to recalibrate assessor–student power relationships • Consider alternative assessment tools that recognise the different resources students bring to learning • Use case studies and applied examples or work placements that enable students to learn in personally meaningful ways

The decision to change the relationship between student and teacher roles through student engagement is, therefore, both an ideological and pedagogic one. Introducing more participatory methods into your practice places an emphasis on the university as an inclusive learning community with an active role to intervene in society to challenge traditional power structures in ways that are transformatory for students and their teachers.

Focus on practice

Using the critical questions in Table 5.1, reflect on your expectations about the types of engagement you want to foster in your students in a module you teach:

- Does your module adopt a student-engaged approach or are there elements that might, conversely, encourage student 'inertia'?
- What dimensions of engagement are well supported in the module and what areas could be developed further?
- What examples can you add to the third column of strategies that you use or could introduce into the module to enhance student engagement?

Putting student engagement into practice

Although student engagement in learning will be determined by both individual and contextual factors, we can draw some general principles from the research for fostering student engagement in practice (Coates, 2007; Zepke and Leach, 2010). These principles contribute to the development of enriching educational experiences that are academically challenging for students. A student-engaged approach will:

- encourage students to participate in active and collaborative learning experiences appropriate to the discipline and context;
- put student–teacher and peer formative dialogue and feedback at the centre of the learning experience;
- support students to develop their capacity to be independent and self-regulated learners;
- legitimate the resources (knowledge, experience, values) students bring to university and increase their sense of agency for their learning.

If introduced individually to enhance some aspects of practice or, ideally, as part of a re-engineering of the teacher–student relationship within a module, these principles facilitate a shift of perspective from teaching as transmission of information to teaching as the enabling of student understanding. There are many ways in which these principles can be enacted within the curriculum aligned to the discipline. In large enrolment classes, where high student numbers often make regular student–teacher contact and active participation in class challenging, there are significant benefits for learning if appropriate student engagement strategies are introduced. Using examples from different disciplines, we will focus on each of these principles in turn with suggestions for the types of activities that you can use to foster student engagement in your context.

Encourage students to participate in active and collaborative learning experiences

In disciplines traditionally based around smaller group seminar or tutorial teaching, active engagement is more typical and more straightforward to facilitate. Cooper and Robinson (2000a), however, advocate 'making large classes seem small' as the basis for creating better engagement opportunities within large enrolment modules. Despite the potential gains of promoting student engagement, for many educators a number of factors inhibit their use of active learning strategies in larger groups. With potentially limited contact hours with students, concerns about content coverage can be a disincentive to introducing other elements into the large group format and make lecturing seem the best option. Practical issues such as room layout in tiered lecture halls, fixed seating or poor acoustics also make short interactive tasks difficult to manage. Student and teacher discomfort with changes to the implied agreement that large group teaching in university only involves telling and listening can similarly lead to resistance on both sides to the introduction of activities that might threaten the 'comfort zone' of the traditional lecture (Huxham, 2005; Barnett, 2000: 159).

While not every topic is best served by involving students and teachers in discussion, therefore, teaching that aims to encourage individual engagement and critical thinking can benefit from the introduction of strategies that emphasise active learning in large and small groups. Ni Raghallaigh and Cunniffe (2013) have framed their student-engaged curriculum drawing on three components of active learning: doing, observing and reflecting. A curriculum that is underpinned by active learning creates experiences that include opportunities for students to enact what they are learning and observe others engaged in relevant activities. Yet without opportunities for reflection, students cannot make their learning personally meaningful. Therefore, there must also be space for students to reflect on both what and how they learn. The following case studies demonstrate some ways in which the experiential and reflective components can be put into practice.

 Case study 5.1   Collaborative learning using a jigsaw wiki in philosophy tutorials (Honeychurch, 2012)

A blended model of face-to-face small group tutorials and online discussion forum was used to support active learning for first-year philosophy students at the University of Glasgow. Each tutorial group was divided into three sub-topic groups and allocated a topic for the week's tutorial using an active learning strategy called the jigsaw technique (see Chapter 4 for a discussion of this technique). A wiki was set up for each sub-group in the virtual learning environment with prompt questions to support the enquiry. Students were encouraged to work collaboratively to contribute to the wiki and read the contributions of others prior to the seminar. At the beginning of the tutorial each sub-group convened for 20 minutes to discuss their answers before presenting on their topic to the rest of the group. All students were provided with hand-outs summarising all the questions and could annotate these during the sub-group presentations to build a full set of notes. Evaluation of the class indicated increased levels of participation by all students in class discussions, high levels of achievement in the final assessment and high student satisfaction.

Case study 5.2   Active learning using an electronic voting system in bioscience lectures (Efstathiou and Bailey, 2012)

An electronic voting system, also known as an audience response system, was introduced into bioscience lectures for first-year nursing students at the University of Birmingham. In traditional lectures students were failing to understand the material, focusing on specific detail rather than underpinning concepts. Voting technology enabled the teachers to ask a series of multiple choice questions and students to select an answer using a keypad. Responses were automatically collated and displayed by the software in the PowerPoint presentation. It allowed students to compare their own understanding of the content with the correct answers and their peers' responses, as well as helping the teacher to immediately identify gaps in student knowledge and misunderstandings and teach to these in the subsequent lecture. The electronic voting system was introduced into two optional bioscience lectures for 110 and 85 students respectively. It was used as a formative assessment similar in format and content to the final module assessment. It also aimed to increase student participation in class and to provide immediate feedback to students and teachers on comprehension of topics. Students were overwhelmingly positive about the opportunity to evaluate their own knowledge levels and the results enabled their teachers to provide focused teaching on areas of difficulty rather than revising topics that students had already grasped. The use of an electronic voting system also promoted peer discussion and participation in class.

These case studies demonstrate a number of shared principles for engaging students in active learning in both small and large group contexts. Active learning encourages students to take greater responsibility for knowledge acquisition, shifting the focus away from the transmission model of traditional lectures without necessarily sacrificing content coverage. Active learning also creates opportunities to put knowledge immediately into practice by getting students to do something with that new content: for example, synthesise arguments or solve problems. There are a range of other strategies that can be adapted to promote active learning within large or small group contexts with students working individually or in pairs (Cooper and Robinson, 2000b; Smith, 2000):

- set students real-world problems to work through their understanding of a new concept;
- introduce case studies or examples to illustrate a theory in practice or use examples as the basis for facilitating students to derive theoretical principles;

- ask students to paraphrase a newly presented concept or model to another student;
- use pair work to generate a range of perspectives or discuss an open-ended question;
- rather than immediately giving a complete and correct answer, provide opportunities for error spotting in a proof, identifying gaps in arguments or evaluating supporting evidence;
- ask students to predict the outcome of a test, argument or plan of action;
- pause a lecture to ask students to undertake a differential diagnosis or follow a protocol that has just been introduced and use show of hands or voting tools to collate the outcomes;
- use a 'minute paper' (see Chapter 4) at the end of a lecture and encourage students to reflect on the class by summarising key concepts or identifying gaps or questions.

These student-centred activities can be used to structure a whole session or follow on from ten- to 15-minute mini-lectures introducing key concepts. Individual activities to test understanding will provide immediate and ongoing feedback on student performance before formal assessment takes place later in a module. Likewise, collaborative activities in pairs promote social and emotional development by providing opportunities to practise teamwork and communication skills. They contribute to a curriculum culture in which responsibility for learning is mutual and collaborative peer relationships drive the learning experience.

Put student-teacher and peer formative dialogue and feedback at the centre of the learning experience

Over a number of years the NSS has suggested significant student dissatisfaction with their assessment and feedback experience at UK universities (Carless *et al.*, 2011; Boud and Molloy, 2013). In some cases this can be an outcome of insufficient and poor-quality assessor feedback. Yet it also reflects the perceived limited value of feedback on specific assessments within a modularised system if feedback does not provide suggestions that 'feed forward' into future learning and assessment. In this context, feedback can be considered to be principally summative, serving the sole, if unintended, purpose of explaining the assessor judgement that has been made on the work. There is also evidence that even when detailed developmental feedback is provided by teachers many students do not sufficiently recognise, understand or engage with the feedback they have received (Gibbs and Simpson, 2004).

For many students and their teachers, assessment has traditionally served the purpose of distinguishing and rewarding individual student achievement as an outcome of their time at university; it is assessment *of* their learning. As a critical driver for student learning, however, assessment can serve other, more formative functions by enhancing student engagement and setting up the opportunities for partnership in learning with students (Healey *et al.*, 2014). Assessment outcomes can be geared towards providing feedback to teachers, enabling them to monitor the ongoing learning needs of specific students or cohorts. Assessment can also provide opportunities for feedback from teachers to students to inform their learning; it is assessment *for* learning (Samball *et al.*, 2013). Going further, if students are actively involved as partners in assessment through self- and peer assessment, as well as participating in the design of assessment tasks and criteria, assessment *as* learning is achievable (Bloxham and Boyd, 2007).

The traditional notion of assessment of learning constructs the feedback process as the unidirectional transmission of information from expert teacher to novice student, often after a module is over. Assessment both for and as learning, however, can make the assessment and feedback process an extension of the everyday interaction between teachers and students. Prior to the expansion of higher education, lower student numbers meant that written assessment feedback to students was always only a part of ongoing student–teacher conversations about the subject in class. There were also more opportunities for redrafting and reviewing of assessed work as an outcome of those discussions before final submission. With increased student numbers and a higher student–teacher ratio, the feedback conversations are now often dislocated from the classroom experiences and relationships (Nicol, 2010). Building on the development of active, discursive and formative approaches within the student-engaged classroom, developing a dialogue-based approach to assessment and feedback is, therefore, the next component in fostering student engagement.

A student-engaged approach reconfigures the role of assessment and feedback from a predominantly teacher-led transmission of expert information to a participative and discursive activity. Through dialogue, academic standards, the meaning of feedback and how to translate feedback into action are collaboratively developed by teachers and their students (Price *et al.*, 2011; Boud and Molloy, 2013). This iterative approach, recognising the social interaction of producing and receiving feedback, is the basis for what has been advocated as 'sustainable feedback' (Carless *et al.*, 2011; Carless, 2013). Sustainable feedback is dialogue-based rather than transmission-oriented and is fundamental to developing students' autonomy as learners by:

- enabling teachers and students to interrogate assessment expectations and academic standards before and after assessment (Carless, 2013);
- developing students' capacity for self-evaluation as autonomous learners prepared not just to receive, but also to seek and use feedback from multiple

sources (teacher, peer and self) to improve their performance (Nicol and Macfarlane-Dick, 2006);

- encouraging students to be 'central and engaged partners in assessment praxis' (O'Donovan *et al.*, 2008: 210).

This means that feedback is not exclusively aimed at explaining a grade or supporting the instrumental passing of assessments, but develops students' abilities as lifelong learners who can make independent judgements about their work and how to improve it (Boud and Molloy, 2013). A fundamental objective in enhancing student engagement with assessment and feedback is to bring the dialogue about assessment into formal teaching contexts and not just after it has ended. For example, in many modules an explanation of the assessment (often in the form of one-way written feedback from teacher to student) happens only when students have completed a task rather than before (Hendry, 2013).

When assessment is geared around the generation of sustainable feedback, students are supported not only to become experts in the subject matter, but also to develop 'pedagogical intelligence' or an understanding of how learning happens and how to manage their own learning in the discipline using feedback (O'Donovan *et al.*, 2008). Giving students increased opportunities to 'emulate the behaviour of experts and take a more active role in constructing the assessment task' underpins a more student-engaged approach to learning (Nicol, 2010: 505). Although the dominant outcomes-based approach to curricula emphasises the explicit sharing of assessment standards with students in module handbooks, this is not sufficient to enable students to internalise a working understanding of assessment criteria. It is important that the criteria used to assess work is transparent, but for students to learn to self-evaluate their own work they also need to learn from experience and internalise an understanding of assessment expectations that may be difficult for teachers to articulate explicitly (Rust *et al.*, 2003).

Peer feedback between students is one strategy that significantly reframes feedback from primarily a teacher activity with students as passive recipients to one in which students play an active role. While student marking can be perceived as problematic for allocating final grades, embedding formative peer feedback develops students' capacity to self-assess and take a more active role in defining the types of feedback they seek from others. It increases opportunities for feedback on full drafts or plans when high student numbers make it impracticable for teachers to provide detailed feedback prior to summative assessment (Liu and Carless, 2006). There is also evidence that there is a correlation between the quality of feedback a student gives and the quality of their own work, regardless of the quality of peer feedback they receive themselves (Lan *et al.*, 2009).

There are several ways in which assessment tasks and feedback can be enhanced to include more discussion about the task and criteria in advance of the submission of work and encourage student engagement with feedback. In planning for assessment you can:

- Provide samples of work and get students to discuss the strengths and weaknesses of the examples in relation to assessment criteria (Hendry, 2013; Nicol, 2010).
- Use multistage tasks – for example, oral presentation and written report, or draft plans or submissions – rather than single, end-of-module assessments to provide occasions for formative feedback and development throughout a module (Carless *et al.*, 2011).
- Introduce peer review as a fundamental part of the learning process, enabling students to review multiple examples of peers' work. This can be managed by introducing short independent study tasks between timetabled teaching that entail students collating and evaluating evidence, assessing concepts or making claims. Students then appraise various examples from peers and discuss the process of reaching judgements about the quality of the work of others. In this way, assessment and mastery of subject content are not in tension: 'student engagement with the substance of the course takes place through a sequence of "produce and appraise" rather than "study and learn" activities' (Sadler, 2009: 60).
- Encourage students to take control of the feedback they want on their work rather than provide the same volume and type of feedback to all students. Students can be given the option to seek increasing levels of specific, individual feedback (see case study 12.3).
- Create spaces for students to reflect critically on feedback and what they need to do to action the feedback in future assessments. Quinton and Smallbone (2010) introduced reflection sheets to prompt students to reflect on the feedback they had received by asking them to answer the following questions: 'What do I feel about this feedback?'; 'What do I think about this feedback?'; and 'Based on this feedback what actions could I take to improve my work for another assignment?'. These prompts encourage students to actually read the feedback and engage with it emotionally and analytically. It also helps translate feedback into meaningful actions for future work.

Support students to develop their capacity to be independent and self-regulated learners

Introducing more interactive and dialogue-based learning into teaching and assessment works towards creating a climate that fosters student engagement, but high student numbers and limited contact hours can make introducing active learning difficult to accommodate. Content-based, didactic lectures are often used to serve the purpose of content coverage, with varying levels of effectiveness, supplemented by problem-solving and self-regulated learning as independent study tasks. A recent development in lecture pedagogy, emerging primarily in US school and now university education, however, is the proposal to 'flip' this relationship by reversing the activities of independent study and lectures. A flipped lecture approach brings together a number of features underpinning student engagement: a student-centred learning culture, active learning opportunities and peer instruction. What lecture flipping can enable, therefore, is a greater emphasis on students managing their own learning and having greater agency in planning and fulfilling their individual learning goals.

The wide availability of textbooks and online resources make the information transfer role of lectures increasingly redundant and digital technologies now make it possible for students to access videos or recorded lectures before meeting in face-to-face contexts. Flipped teaching begins from the fundamental question regarding what constitutes the most effective use of the limited contact hours we have with students. If students can access preparatory reading, podcasts or recorded lectures or undertake individual-group research (including tasks such as the jigsaw technique described above), then time in a room with the teacher and peers can be used for more active learning experiences (Baepler *et al.*, 2014). As such, the 'first exposure to content is student–text not student–instructor' (Davis and Minifie, 2013: 14), where 'text' can refer to a range of multimedia objects as well as the module textbook or readings. The more typical activities assigned to independent study after a lecture in a traditional learning and teaching approach are then undertaken in class with the teacher present to facilitate higher-level learning outcomes such as synthesis or evaluation, as well as to monitor and correct misconceptions. These active classes can include learning tasks such as problem-solving, working through examples and group project work, as well as student presentations, peer-assisted learning, discussion and teacher feedback. Flipped teaching is a fundamental revision of the traditional lecture format, particularly in traditionally content-heavy disciplines, and there are emerging examples in Physics (Bates and Galloway, 2012), Biology (Stone, 2012), Management (Davis and Minifie, 2013), Chemistry (Lancaster, 2013) and Computer Science (Largent, 2012).

These examples of lecture flipping utilise both high- and low-technology strategies to support student preparation outside of class, demanding varying levels of support. Without in-depth and sustained preparation on the part of students, face-to-face sessions can fail, so asking students to be autonomous as learners before class may leave teachers anxious that students may not gain sufficient content coverage. Kim *et al.* (2014) suggest there are a number of design principles to ensure flipped approaches will foster active student learning: students must have an incentive to prepare for the face-to-face session; mechanisms should be in place to enable students to assess their understanding; learning activities before and during face-to-face sessions should be well-defined and well-structured; students should have sufficient time to complete tasks in class; teachers need to pay attention to developing collaboration and there should be prompt and useful feedback on learning. Strategies for supporting student preparation include:

- Structured preparatory tasks: prior to each class, students prepare written answers to three to five questions about an assigned reading or other resource. Multiple choice or open-ended questions can include finding specific examples in the allocated materials of specific themes or concepts, paraphrasing the main arguments, identifying and analysing the thesis of a chapter or article and citing quotations to support their analysis. The aim of the preparatory task is to help focus student independent reading and to encourage them to come prepared for discussion. Students bring hard copies of their answers to the session or post in the virtual learning environment and correct their copy or supplement it with the ideas of their peers to inform their analysis during group work. These assignments provide an individualised resource for preparation for later assessments or revision (Davis and Minifie, 2013).
- Student question generation: an alternative to posing questions to students is to ask them to frame their own questions for class discussion or for assessment. Asking students to draft questions on a topic or module reveals what students think are the key concepts, the complexity of their understanding of the material and, if used as part of preparation for assessment, can develop their understanding of the format of upcoming assessments, criteria and academic standards. In advance of face-to-face sessions students submit two to three questions on a selected topic. The teacher can classify questions in terms of the types of understanding they are seeking (for example, knowledge, synthesis, analysis or evaluation) and allocate them to other students to answer in groups (Angelo and Cross, 1993).
- Quizzes: low-stakes quizzes on the preparatory materials available in the virtual learning environment or at the beginning of the face-to-face session motivate students to complete preparatory work, enable students to self-assess their understanding and provide feedback to the teacher on areas of difficulty (Lancaster, 2013). Warburton and Volet (2013) use 'content quiz group assignments' with first-year biology students working in groups to prepare five short answer or multiple choice questions for other students, based on a lecture topic. They must also provide correct answers and feedback on potential wrong answers. These are posted online as a self-test for the rest of the group two weeks after the relevant class.

Legitimate the resources students bring to the university and increase their sense of agency for their learning

Emphasising active learning and creating opportunities for students to interact with their teachers and their peers are fundamental to student ownership of their learning experience. A further dimension to embedding the principles of student engagement in practice, however, is through the active participation of students in co-creating the ways in which their learning is organised, evaluated and enhanced. Students can provide unique and powerful insights into the relevancy of curriculum content, how they are assessed and the usefulness of learning resources. Working in partnership with students to evaluate and identify ways to improve their own and others' learning and teaching experiences can also contribute to their sense of membership in the university community.

Student involvement in quality assurance processes and representation in university decision-making are demonstrated in recent commitments in the *UK Quality Code for Higher Education* (QAA, 2014b), the *Partnership for Higher Education in Wales* (HEFCW, 2014) and as an underpinning principle of the Enhancement Themes in Scotland. Yet while student engagement in formal quality assurance processes can ensure a more transparent institutional approach, partnerships with students in curriculum design and development, as we explored in Chapter 4, and in evaluation provide a further way to shift from a transmission-based pedagogic culture to one of shared understanding and responsibility for learning. The National Union of Students *A Manifesto for Partnership* (NUS, 2012) warns against 'seek[ing] to engage students merely in order to find out what they want and give it them'. In doing this 'we reproduce this dangerous narrative of consumerism and lose sight of the responsibility of educators to challenge and stretch students' (p. 5). Alternative models of working with students in curriculum design and programme evaluation, however, maximise the culture of shared responsibility for the quality of learning.

Levels of student participation in the process of curriculum design can be characterised as rungs of a ladder (Bovill and Bulley, 2011). On the bottom rung is traditional teacher-controlled curriculum decision-making where students have no input in the organisation of the curriculum 'delivered' to students. The next rung of the ladder still represents teacher-controlled curricula but involves recognition and response to student feedback. On the higher rungs, however, student–teacher partnership in curriculum design can involve students:

- selecting relevant content, identifying required readings or creating learning resources;
- planning an assessment project to fulfil module learning outcomes;
- using their workplace or professional experiences as the basis for the curriculum;

- participating as equal members in a curriculum design team in the development of curriculum;
- taking on active roles in evaluating the learning experience to identify how learning and teaching can be enhanced.

The involvement of students in the curriculum process in these different ways does not undermine or marginalise the disciplinary expertise of educators but recognises that students have expertise *as students* and that they can make a significant contribution to successful curriculum design. Partnership creates opportunities for students and teachers to share power in making the curriculum meaningful to those teaching and studying it and promotes greater levels of student ownership of the learning experience (Delpish *et al.*, 2010).

Case study 5.3 Formative student evaluation of teaching and learning to enhance student engagement (Bovill, 2011)

Taking the model of assessment *for* learning as the basis for developing a formative evaluation tool, Bovill sought to rethink evaluation *of* learning as evaluation *for* learning. Evaluation often focuses on getting student feedback on teaching quality, but less often on the students' role in the learning experience. Using an adapted version of the small-scale evaluation tool 'stop, start, continue', she introduced an alternative formative evaluation for postgraduate students at the University of Glasgow. In the evaluation, students indicate what they want their teacher to stop doing in class, what they want to see added to the teaching approach and what should continue without change to aid their learning. This was adapted to include a comparable set of prompts related to what a student should stop doing in order to improve their own and others' learning, what they should start doing to enhance their learning and what they would continue doing. This exercise promotes student critical reflection on their own contribution to the learning process and develops explicit actions for them to take increased responsibility for their learning.

Focus on practice

Review the suggested activities and case study examples in this chapter and identify one strategy that could be adapted to your context. What will be the challenges in implementing this in practice in terms of resources, learning culture or changes to student and teacher roles? What are the anticipated outcomes of implementing this in practice? How can you share these outcomes with your students and colleagues?

Conclusion

In this chapter we have explored the different dimensions of a student-engaged learning environment: introducing active and collaborative learning experiences, engaging students in dialogue, promoting student autonomy and legitimising the resources they bring to learning as equal partners in the university. It is possible to introduce a student-engaged approach into your classroom and assessment practices by adapting one or more of the suggestions outlined in this chapter. Teaching in ways that promote student engagement, however, can be pedagogically transformative for teacher–student relationships. Teaching for engagement is about recognising the whole student, their emotional, social and intellectual experience of learning, and finding ways to harness that within the curriculum. Engagement is also about contextualising learning so that students and teachers are explicit not only about the subject matter, but also about the shared process of learning. Bringing together the different elements of a student-engaged learning experience can change how students and their teachers collaborate across all the activities of universities. In Chapter 6 we will look at how this transformed relationship can be extended to create a research-led teaching climate in which undergraduates and postgraduates participate in an active departmental research culture.

Further reading

Barkley, Elizabeth F. (2010) *Student Engagement Techniques: A Handbook for College Faculty.* San Francisco: Jossey-Bass.
This US book updates Angelo and Cross (1993) 'classroom assessment techniques' with a range of different active learning techniques, disciplinary examples and ideas for adapting participatory and collaborative learning tasks to virtual environments.

Cooper, James L. and Robinson, Pamela (2000b) 'Getting started: informal small group strategies in large classes', *New Directions for Teaching and Learning*, 81: 17–24.
This short and accessible article provides practical strategies for introducing small group activities in lecture-based large classes.

'Enhancing Feedback' (http://www.enhancingfeedback.ed.ac.uk)
This extensive website at the University of Edinburgh has guidance on ways to increase and enhance feedback, including how to prepare students for feedback, how to involve them in feedback and how to design feedback-rich assessments.

CHAPTER 6

CONNECTING RESEARCH AND TEACHING IN PRACTICE

Learning objectives

This chapter will support you to:

- Reflect on the different ways in which the processes and outcomes of research can be understood in universities;
- Develop your understanding of how research and teaching activities can be connected in practice;
- Plan and enable authentic research and enquiry learning experiences for undergraduate and postgraduate students.

Introduction

For many academics and students, one of the unique characteristics of higher education is that those who teach are also likely to be actively advancing their disciplinary fields as researchers or are teaching in the context of an institutional or departmental culture of research (Neumann, 1992). Particularly at the post-graduate level, universities are also involved in preparing the next generation of academic and industry researchers. For many universities, unity between the 'dual economy' of research and teaching in higher education has been advocated on the basis that there is a mutually beneficial relationship between excellent research and excellent teaching (Scott, 2005: 56; Hughes, 2005). Despite claims for an active relationship between research and teaching, or what is often described as a research–teaching nexus, for many academics the experience is more divisive and demands of research and teaching can be divergent rather than complementary, with different and arguably unequal reward structures for research and teaching success. Empirical evidence of a positive relationship between high-quality research and teaching has also been elusive (Hattie and Marsh, 1996; Hughes, 2005). Teaching-only contracted staff or those within clinical, creative or professional disciplines may also feel excluded from such debates about how research and teaching can be integrated.

Yet though it might be difficult to find evidence of a past or even present relationship between the teaching and research activities of individuals and institutions, this does not mean that it is not possible to see future connections as highly desirable. Where research is complementary to teaching, educators are able to teach the most recent findings of fast-moving disciplines to ensure that curricula remain current and responsive (Pan et al., 2014). The research expertise and experience of educators can also inform the curriculum to enhance student critical thinking and problem-solving skills that are aligned to concrete academic, societal, environmental and business problems. At the same time, if teaching is conceptualised as discursive and exploratory rather than knowledge transmission, as teachers we engage in a process of 'transforming and extending' knowledge through teaching itself. This inclusive conception of a 'scholarship of teaching' means teaching is itself an act of scholarship, of mutual learning and knowledge-building through interaction with students (Boyer, 1990: 24).

If teaching can be an act of scholarship, it is also recognised that linking teaching to research is not a unidirectional relationship; involving students in current research activities can lead to reciprocal benefits for researchers. Engaging students in research can provide new insights into research problems and stimulate reflection about the sometimes uncontested assumptions of the discipline. Student participation can also be used to generate resources that input directly and potentially collaboratively into research (Visser-Wijnveen et al., 2010). For example, researchers are increasingly benefiting from 'citizen science' projects that involve 'amateur' researchers in the wider community in the collection or analysis of large volumes of data and resources or participation in problem-solving in ongoing research (Sabou et al., 2012). Public projects such as 'Galaxy Zoo' (www.galaxyzoo.org) and the 'Milky Way Project' (www.milkywayproject.org) have engaged the public in analysing and classifying galaxies in the thousands of telescope images that have been collected. In the UK a number of projects are drawing on 'citizen scientist' collaborators to analyse or verify data: for example, the Omega-Locate project, at Queen Mary University of London, asks participants to check coordinate data by mapping onto Google Earth (www.geog.qmul.ac.uk/research/trics/omegalocate/index.html) or Project Nightjar at the University of Exeter, which is using online games to investigate camouflage (nightjar.exeter.ac.uk). These types of public engagement projects model the ways in which we might rethink how we engage undergraduate and postgraduate students in our own or our department's active research.

Despite the potential benefits of aligning research and teaching, one of the fundamental reasons for a perceived disconnection is the variety of ways in which we might define these two activities and the contested nature of these terms within universities and across disciplines (Brew, 2012). Far from being stable or commonly agreed concepts, what we mean by both research and teaching are highly contextual and there can be considerable variation in different academics' understanding of the purposes and processes of research. These assumptions about what constitutes research can be influenced by personal beliefs about knowledge or what it means to be a researcher, disciplinary differences, the methodologies researchers use or even the types of research undertaken (Brew, 2001). These differences impact on how research and teaching are then seen to connect in practice and how research is, or is not, translated into the teaching context. Discipline differences, in particular, are seen to have a significant impact on when and how students become legitimate members of the research community. While undergraduate students studying in science-based subjects might not participate in original research, students in humanities subjects might engage in research and enquiry processes as a fundamental element of learning in the discipline (Robertson and Blackler, 2006).

The research–teaching nexus has been the focus of much attention over the last two decades and it is important to consider why such connections are seen as necessary in contemporary higher education. One of the main arguments for understanding and fostering connections between the research and teaching functions of universities is the recognition that research is not the exclusive preserve of universities but is undertaken by many people within and outside institutions. In particular, higher education is preparing students for future employment and professional lives in which accessing, assessing and using information will require them to have well-developed research skills in addition to sound content knowledge (Ozay, 2012). Many argue, therefore, that students' experiences of learning in university should better prepare them to undertake these types of enquiry. This means working with a broader and more inclusive definition of what we mean by 'research'. In Chapter 5 we explored how the different roles of teachers and learners can overlap or merge within a student-engaged approach to learning and teaching. This overlap suggests that, rather than attempting to connect the conventional higher education polarities of researching and teaching, we may do better to recognise and explore the mutual learning experience of researchers and their students at the centre of both activities. At its most fundamental, to integrate research and teaching in practice, 'rather than telling students what we know, we should show students how we learn' as experienced learners and researchers (DiCarlo, 2009: 260). From this perspective, when seeking to strengthen the research–teaching nexus we can focus on enhancing the teacher–student relationship around the shared engagement in the processes of research as continuous learners.

In this chapter we will begin by considering the different ways in which we might define research and how our definitions can diverge, depending on institutional context, discipline and our personal understanding and experience of the purposes and processes of research. We will then look at what linking research and teaching might be like in practice and how connecting research and teaching in different ways can both reflect and affect the teacher–student relationship. We will conclude by considering the benefits and limitations of connecting teaching and research for both teachers and their students using disciplinary examples of curriculum that provide authentic enquiry experiences for undergraduate and postgraduate students.

What do we mean by 'research'?

What we understand by the term 'research' and what we include or exclude as legitimate research activities can vary significantly depending on our context and our personal beliefs about what it means to 'do' research or 'be' a researcher (Brew, 2001). A number of studies have looked at how academics, doctoral supervisors and post-doctoral researchers understand what we mean by 'research'. They have identified differences in how individuals apprehend the aims of research as well as their expectations about the scope of impact (from individual advancement to the potential impact on wider society) and their emphasis on the products and outputs of research or the research process itself (Brew, 2001; Kiley and Mullins, 2005; Åkerlind, 2008). These differences are shaped by institutional setting, an educator's role and the academic or professional qualifications and experiences of researchers. Research can have empirical, conceptual, creative, commercial or societal drivers and outcomes with knowledge-transfer are an increasingly significant aspect of research. In the contemporary context, it is fundamental to recognise the breadth of researcher identities and activities that can be framed by the term 'research' within universities and wider society. Drawing on Pitcher and Åkerlind's (2009) survey of the literature on conceptions of research, four broad categories are proposed that reflect the diverse ways researchers might understand the idea of research. Research can be:

- a process with defined tasks, experiments, methodologies or specific steps aimed at successfully undertaking a recognised systematic enquiry in the subject;
- a route to achieving professional outcomes for the individual researcher in relation to gaining research grants, publications or other forms of academic prestige;
- a way to expand the knowledge of a field of study by creating new knowledge, surfacing new insights or developing the ways in which we might discover new knowledge in the subject;
- exploratory, with the aim of seeking new ways of seeing the world, illuminating new research problems or generating new lines of enquiry with outcomes that benefit wider society.

Although, in reality, an individual's understanding of research may not always fit within these categories, these definitions suggest that, for researchers, the principal goals, approaches and anticipated outcomes when undertaking research can vary. Research may be about fundamentally fulfilling an academic's professional role as a researcher or achieving particular indicators of success or status within their field or university. Alternatively, the primary motivation for undertaking research may be about extending or transforming knowledge in the discipline in ways that are relevant for the theoretical advancement of the subject or with significant professional applications in, for example, teaching, industry or business. The desired outcomes for those who primarily hold this conception of research can be directed towards changing the accepted paradigms of their subject or, if relevant, responding to social issues or real-world problems within the wider community.

In the current climate of evaluating research in terms of outputs and impact it is important to be reflective about what we mean by research, what counts as research (for example, in science disciplines as compared to professional or creative disciplines) and who primarily generates it (for example, academics, students, industry experts). In particular, our understanding of what counts as research can influence how we perceive both the opportunities for, and barriers against, integrating research content and processes into our undergraduate and taught postgraduate teaching (Brew, 2010). It shapes what role we think students are capable of playing as researchers within the scholarly community of a university or discipline. In examining student experiences of enquiry,

Levy and Petrulis (2012: 7) also identified differences in student conceptions of the role of research in their curriculum. Students understood that research can involve 'gathering information or exploring others' ideas' or as 'evidencing and developing [their] own ideas or making discoveries'. The former experience of research involves students engaging with an existing knowledge base that may be new to them though well known to their teachers, either through independent or teacher-led enquiry. Conversely, the latter student conception of research involves students having a greater role in knowledge-building in the field through discovery of knowledge that not only may be new to the student, but might also make an original contribution to their discipline. For many researchers, this latter form of knowledge generation is the definition of research. In thinking about how research and teaching are connected, however, we can work with a broader definition that includes both of these forms of research along a continuum from the production of knowledge that is new to the student to knowledge that is new to society. This continuum is summarised by Willison and O'Regan (2007) as the 'commonly known, to the commonly not known, to the totally unknown' (p. 394). This inclusive definition of research ultimately provides more scope for engaging all those involved in teaching, including teaching-only staff as well as students, in research.

Focus on practice

Thinking about a current research project you are involved in, consider the following questions to help you explore the most important factors of your experience of research and enquiry. Research can include synthesising the existing body of scholarship in your subject (for example, through textbooks) or preparing learning resources for teaching:

- What are your intentions when undertaking the enquiry? Who do you expect the research will affect or have an influence upon?
- What are the anticipated outcomes of the research? Are you chiefly focused on disseminating knowledge to others, extending knowledge in your discipline or providing solutions to problems that affect the wider community?
- In what ways is the enquiry undertaken? For example, is it focused on fact-finding and synthesising the work of others for a new audience or is it focused on developing new ideas or making discoveries?
- What do your answers to these questions suggest to you about how you understand the nature and purpose of enquiry? How likely is it that students could participate in the research and enquiry you describe?

Integrating research and teaching in practice

The integrating of research and teaching activities in universities has been informed by a growing demand from employers for problem-solvers with skills to undertake enquiry. In the face of rapid advances and innovation across many fields of knowledge, it is also increasingly important to prepare students to be lifelong learners able to continue to learn after graduation. Increasingly, the focus of work on the research–teaching nexus is not directed towards determining if there is a correlation between excellent research and teaching performance but how we can enhance the links between research and teaching activities in practice. Drawing on several surveys of contemporary higher education curricula, we can consider our curriculum approach in relation to six different categories of research–teaching linkages (Griffiths, 2004; Healey and Jenkins, 2009; Visser-Wijnveen *et al.*, 2010):

- teaching can be *research-led* so that the curriculum is informed by the outcomes of research and the emphasis is on developing students' understanding of existing research findings;
- teaching can be *research-oriented* where the focus is on the methodological processes of research in the discipline and students learn the practices of enquiry or how new knowledge is created and validated;
- teaching can be *research-tutored* where students are engaged in discussions about existing research findings and practices;
- teaching can be *research-based* where the curriculum is built almost entirely around students undertaking research activities;
- teaching can be *research-informed* where teachers (potentially in collaboration with their students) undertake enquiry into their teaching that, like all scholarly work, ensures teaching is evidence-informed, public and open to scrutiny by peers;
- research can be *teaching-influenced* where engagement of students in ongoing research can inform the direction, scope, methods and outcomes of a study. This can be particularly relevant when supervising research students where the experience of teaching and research is often blurred (Robertson and Bond, 2001), but is also possible in undergraduate teaching contexts (Trowler and Wareham, 2007).

Healey and Jenkins (2009) have mapped the first four dimensions of research–teaching links summarised above into a widely applied framework for thinking about the curriculum. They argue that research-led and research-oriented curricula respectively emphasise research content and research process but predominantly position students as an audience for disciplinary research.

Research-tutored and research-based curricula similarly focus on research content or process but locate students as participants in research. This framework, however, neglects the last two dimensions of research-informed teaching and teaching-informed research. The dimension of research-informed teaching is often excluded on the basis that it does not exclusively relate to disciplinary research outcomes or production but focuses on scholarly enquiry into the teaching of the discipline. Yet, as well as contributing to a teacher's understanding of their students' learning experience, involving students in asking questions about their learning in the context of the discipline can be a powerful way to develop their understanding of how they learn and improve their reflexivity (Barnes *et al.*, 2010). We will explore the ways in which we can make teaching research-informed in Chapter 12.

The dimension of teaching-influenced research is also often overlooked within institutional models for connecting research and teaching because even advocates of research–teaching links may still prioritise the research function over the teaching function. From this perspective the trajectory of the relationship between research and teaching is exclusively unidirectional: research can inform teaching but teaching does not inform research. Bringing research and teaching closer together, however, can be a reciprocal experience and many teachers recognise, in practice, that research projects benefit from new perspectives generated through student and teacher interactions or student involvement in live research projects. Bringing ongoing research into teaching helps researchers to collect or analyse data, refine conceptual ideas or evaluate methodologies and methods. In addition, skills such as being able to communicate complex ideas to non-specialists essential for teaching can also be re-purposed for disseminating research in ways that enhance its impact (Trowler and Wareham, 2007).

A rich and challenging curriculum located within the context of an active scholarly university community of both educators and their students ideally should include all these ways of connecting research and teaching (Healey and Jenkins, 2009). The different ways in which connections are made between research and teaching can be developed progressively over the length of a single module or cumulatively across different modules in a student's programme of study. In many cases, for example, curricula are planned to gradually introduce students to the existing knowledge base (research-led) and research methods (research-oriented) at the beginning of a module or programme to prepare them to undertake their own independent research projects or dissertations at the end of their programme (research-based). Introducing students to a teacher's or department's research outputs can lead students to report an increase in their depth of understanding of the subject and in their enthusiasm in response to a teacher's passion for their research, as well as prompting student interest in further study (Hajdarpasic *et al.*, 2013). While students also indicated some negative consequences as a result of academic staff prioritising their research over supporting students, this suggests that research-led approaches that draw on academics' engagement in research can be important for engaging students with the subject of their studies.

Such research-led curricula, however, also position students as relatively passive recipients of research conducted by experts. Students who experience research in their curricula predominantly in terms of information gathering from lectures and textbooks in this way have been found to align this to an approach to learning that is based on memorisation and the reproduction of facts (Levy and Petrulis, 2012). Therefore, in introducing research content into the curriculum it is important to frame this knowledge in terms of how such research is generated and understood contextually rather than as certainties dictated by the teacher as an authority. Including the research questions and problems that initiate the research and the processes of undertaking the enquiry alongside the outcomes emphasises research as a discovery process. If we want to support our students to develop their capacity to undertake independent enquiry and share our own experience of enquiry as learning, however, we also need to ensure that we create more opportunities within the curriculum to fulfil the types of engagement that are accounted for in research-tutored and research-based learning activities.

There are several aspects of the learning and teaching experience to consider in relation to the role research can play within undergraduate or taught postgraduate curricula (Visser-Wijnveen *et al.*, 2010; Healey, 2005). In reflecting on how to strengthen the links between research and teaching we need to examine several aspects of the curriculum:

- the orientation of the module or programme aims in relation to research;
- the role of the teacher in introducing research into teaching;
- the nature of the learning activities students undertake.

First, we need to consider if the curriculum focuses primarily on presenting research content or on developing student understanding of methodologies and processes. The curriculum may also be oriented towards developing the students' research dispositions and skills necessary to enable them to pose and investigate research problems themselves. Second, we need to consider the role that the teacher adopts in relation to integrating research into their teaching. A teacher may be positioned as an expert conveying the outcomes of their own research or the research of others in the discipline. If the aim of the module is to induct students into the discipline and support them to adopt appropriate research dispositions or disciplinary research skills, however, the teacher can be a role model and use their research experience to demonstrate to students how to be a researcher. Alternatively, if the curriculum is designed to enable students to undertake their own research independently or in collaboration with their teachers as research assistants, then the teacher will adopt a guiding or partnership role. Finally, the learning activities students are involved in can reflect the different stages of their engagement in research. For example, traditional learning activities such as attending lectures or reading allocated texts can be the basis for students learning about research. Creating opportunities for students to learn in research-like ways through enquiry tasks, small-scale research assignments or participation in live research projects will provide students with authentic research experiences. These different approaches to connecting research and teaching are summarised in Table 6.1.

Table 6.1 Connecting research and teaching in practice

Research-teaching nexus	Aims	Teacher role	Typical learning activities
Teaching is research-led	To teach current research, including the research of researcher-teachers	Researcher-teacher as expert	Listen to lectures and read texts that present the outcomes from current research
Teaching is research-oriented	To teach what it means to carry out research in the discipline	Researcher-teacher as role model	Engage in tasks that develop understanding and application of research methodologies, skills and techniques
Teaching is research-tutored	To share and discuss disciplinary research practices and outcomes	Researcher-teacher as mentor	Write, peer review and discuss essays or papers on research topics and processes
Teaching is research-based	To provide authentic research and enquiry experiences	Researcher-teacher as partner	Complete small-scale independent research assignments, collaborate with researchers as research assistants or participate in research placements
Teaching is research-informed	To employ systematic enquiry into learning and teaching to design, carry out and evaluate teaching	Teacher-researcher as developer	Undertake small-scale (collaborative) enquiry into specific learning and teaching activities
Research is teaching-influenced	To develop and enhance research processes and outcomes on the basis of engagement in teaching	Teacher-researcher as learner	Engage students in data collection, analysing raw data or peer reviewing conference papers or draft journal articles that are emerging out of ongoing or recently completed research

It is useful to critically reflect on how curricula map against the different dimensions of the research–teaching relationship summarised in Table 6.1. For example, how do we deliberately or tacitly position ourselves and our students in relation to the processes of disciplinary knowledge creation and dissemination? It can reveal gaps in our curricula and help focus our attention as educators on including a range of different ways to integrate research and teaching. In particular, it can reveal when we include research-based learning activities that give students opportunities to gain experience in enquiry in disciplinary and professional contexts. These experiences can often be lacking in the curriculum but can develop highly desirable intellectual capacities in students. Engaging students in learning tasks and assessments that are deliberately designed to replicate real-world enquiry experiences helps to foster enquiry skills that are relevant for critical thinking in the discipline as well as for future employment. In the next section we will specifically focus on ways to embed and evaluate enquiry processes when we design new modules. The following list provides suggestions, however, for strengthening the connection between research and teaching in existing curricula.

Include up-to-date research data and debates in the curriculum

Research-based elements of the curriculum can be developed by explicitly including the emerging outcomes of your own or colleagues' current research in the curriculum in lectures or seminars. Current research debates in the field can also be the focus for case studies or examples. Students can be directed to conference proceedings, abstracts or media reports on current research to engage with different positions and arguments at the cutting edge of the discipline. This helps to illustrate the contextual and contested nature of knowledge creation in the field.

Engage students with the progress of research projects and outcomes

Regularly updated reading lists or course packs that include recent outputs such as conference papers, presentations or journal articles can also provide ways to support student engagement with new research outcomes. Encouraging students to follow your own or colleagues' research blogs and other social media dissemination activities by linking these to module learning resources will also enable students to access and follow current information on live research projects.

Explore the process of departmental research in practice

Student understanding both of their teachers' research topics and the 'messiness' of the real research process, as part of a research-oriented element of curriculum, can also be developed by getting students to explore their teachers' experiences of research. Direct students to read some examples of the range of different written outputs from the research of departmental colleagues, such as journal articles, book chapters or grant reports, before conducting an interview about the research with the researcher. Dwyer (2001) used this as an assignment for first-year undergraduate students at the beginning of their programme as a way to familiarise them with their teachers' research work and begin the process of introducing students to the research culture of the department.

Initiate a student journal club

A journal club format, either integrated into teaching or as an optional complement to the curriculum, is one strategy for facilitating research-tutored elements. Journal clubs provide a space for students to read and evaluate research outputs, get exposed to different perspectives on the research of their teachers and peers and, in healthcare or other professional subjects, consider how they might use research as an evidence-base in practice. Roddam *et al.* (2009: 31) suggest that utilising prompt questions such as, for example, 'Was the study well-designed and is it the best way to answer the research question?', 'Can you identify whether the methodology is robust or are there any flaws?' and 'Were ethical issues considered?' will support student critical appraisal of published research.

Introduce assessments that are aligned to research and enquiry

Conducting research or enquiry as part of learning is seen as fundamental to facilitating a research-based approach to the curriculum. Completing the research process by being assessed in ways that replicate the dissemination practices of original research such as mini-conference papers, project reports or posters can support the communication aspects of research work in research-like ways. Embedding peer review of students' work develops their capacity to appraise research. Further to these curriculum-based strategies there are increasing opportunities for undergraduate students to disseminate their own research to a wider audience through conferences or publication in interdisciplinary undergraduate research journals. Research can include empirical research as well as literature reviews or conceptual papers. UK-based examples include *Diffusion: The UCLan Journal of Undergraduate Research*, published by the University of Central Lancashire, and *Reinvention: An International Journal of Undergraduate Research*, established by the University of Warwick and Oxford Brookes University and now published in collaboration with Monash University in Australia.

Developing student enquiry in the curriculum

Enquiry-based learning is sometimes used as a synonym for problem-based learning where the 'problem' comprises the entirety of the curriculum, but also includes standalone enquiry-based activities in a curriculum. For example, fieldwork, case studies, group work, student-led presentations and small- or larger-scale research projects and dissertations are all included within enquiry-based learning. In undertaking these activities, learners are not simply applying the disciplinary knowledge base to practice, but, by engaging in the processes of enquiry, they also actively engage in constructing their knowledge and understanding. An enquiry-based approach has the following characteristics (Kahn and O'Rourke, 2005; Justice *et al.*, 2007; Spronken-Smith and Walker, 2010; Levy and Petrulis, 2012):

- initiated by an open-ended task that is relevant to complex and contested real-world or professional problems;
- undertaken collaboratively by students with their peers and their teachers;
- requires careful input by teachers as facilitators to scaffold enquiry using questions as prompts or to challenge assumptions, to build trust and group dynamics, to direct students to relevant resources and to model appropriate expert enquiry processes;
- moves students towards a self-directed and situated approach to learning based on their own experiences of enquiry.

There are multiple examples of how enquiry-based learning can be embedded as elements within modules or can be used as the basis for full module design at undergraduate and postgraduate level across a range of disciplines and in different institutional contexts. The importance of dialogue and the open-ended nature of enquiry might suggest that enquiry-based approaches are more appropriate for humanities or social science subjects and for students in their final year or Masters level after they have learnt the foundational knowledge of a subject (for examples of humanities and social science enquiry-based modules see Hutchings and O'Rourke, 2002; Cox *et al.*, 2008; Kahn and O'Rourke, 2005). The following case studies, however, outline some of the ways in which the principle of enquiry can be introduced into science and engineering curricula where research engagement has been traditionally undertaken at postgraduate level. Though the examples vary in terms of the scope of the enquiry-based curriculum, the aim is to create not simply opportunities to apply knowledge previously introduced in lectures, but also strategies to develop student science understanding through the process of enquiry or opportunities for reciprocal benefits for researchers and students through introducing enquiry tasks into the curriculum.

Case study 6.1   Fieldwork in undergraduate geography (Nicholson, 2011)

A 20-credit enquiry-based physical geography module was developed for a group of 12 final-year undergraduates at Manchester Metropolitan University around a one-week residential fieldtrip. Students participated in two half-day workshops in advance of the fieldtrip to introduce the module and prepare them for fieldwork and research design. The learning outcomes for the module include demonstration of fieldwork skills, design and implementation of an investigation in the field and the analysis and synthesis of data from the field for a journal article. Two principles informed the implementation of the module: the provision of multiple opportunities for formative feedback as the students progressed through the module and the involvement of students in peer review. The module was assessed by a 1500-word portfolio of evidence and reflection on fieldwork skills and was open-ended to encourage student autonomy and innovation. The investigative design, analysis and synthesis outcomes were assessed by a 3000-word journal article supported by peer review to encourage reflection on learning and the development of student criticality as the basis for disciplinary understanding.

 Case study 6.2   An enquiry-based spectroscopy module for first-year undergraduates (Lucas and Rowley, 2011)

An enquiry-based module was introduced for 84 first-year chemistry students (divided into groups of six students) at the University of Birmingham. Students completed a pre-module questionnaire to determine their individual prior knowledge of spectroscopy and their levels of confidence in the topic. The results of the questionnaire were used to determine the group make-up. Student groups were allocated a discussion forum in the virtual learning environment and each group had to agree and post their ground rules for participation in their discussion forum after the first session. In the first meetings students were introduced to the module and the enquiry-based learning approach, practised an interpretation of the spectra of two simple molecules and received formative feedback on their interpretations. The module was then structured around four scenarios and students adopted the role of graduate chemists in a fictional chemistry laboratory to undertake progressively more complex enquiry-based tasks. After the five enquiry-based sessions students also attended five lectures on how theory relates to the interpretation of spectra. Assessment was by group and individual report on the scenarios and peer assessment.

Case study 6.3   The two-way relationship between research and teaching in undergraduate engineering (Casanovas-Rubio *et al.*, 2014)

The 'Constructionarium' was a six-day residential fieldtrip for undergraduate students on the Civil and Environmental Engineering degree. It was a partnership between Imperial College London and industry and involved the construction of student-run civil engineering projects. The 'Constructionarium' teaching event was identified as an opportunity to test the methodology of a proposed environmental impact model for construction works. At the beginning of the fieldtrip students were briefed on the study and volunteers were recruited to collect data during the lifecycle of the construction projects. The research aimed to evaluate the feasibility and validity of collecting the proposed environmental impact data on live construction projects. The four student groups were constructing scaled-down versions of Brewery Wharf Footbridge, Don Valley Stadium, Nuclear Island and the 'Gherkin'. The linking of research and teaching was found to have reciprocal benefits for the researchers and students. Conducting the research during the teaching fieldtrip enabled fast-track data collection at minimal cost with students as data-collectors. For students, participation in the research study enhanced their knowledge of up-to-date research on the environmental impact of construction projects as well as understanding of the process of conducting research.

In addition to showing how the characteristics of enquiry-based learning can be embedded, these examples also signal some of the considerations in introducing enquiry into the curriculum either as individual tasks in a more traditional curriculum or when using enquiry as a fundamental design principle in planning or revising a module. For example:

- all students need to be supported to develop as self-directed and autonomous learners by giving them greater control over what and how they learn (case study 6.1);
- different assessment methods, including formative feedback and peer review, enable students to demonstrate more open-ended and emergent learning outcomes (case study 6.1);
- technological interventions such as online discussion forums and blogs can be used to support collaborative learning outside timetabled sessions and validate independent student-constructed knowledge (case study 6.2);
- introducing research and enquiry into teaching can be a two-way relationship that develops students' understanding of current research issues and processes as well as enabling, for example, data collection or input into research outputs (case study 6.3).

These examples also signal the importance of the teacher's role in carefully guiding and organising student learning even within potentially less-controlled, open-ended enquiry. Enquiry-based learning has been criticised as ineffective and inefficient, resulting in inconsistent curriculum coverage as compared to more traditional curriculum approaches. While enquiry-based learning is advocated as a student-centred and transformative mode of learning, as we introduce enquiry into our curricula we also need to be cognisant of the diversity of our students and their prior experiences of, and expectations about, teaching and learning. Even at postgraduate level, the skills necessary for active learning and self-directed study may be new to those who have studied in more directed contexts. In particular, international students may not have confidence in their language fluency and the cultural knowledge required to participate fully in unfamiliar enquiry-based seminar discussion or group work without support (Bache and Hayton, 2012).

As the case studies illustrate, enquiry-based approaches require careful scaffolding to support and develop student understanding. Hmelo-Silver *et al.* (2007) suggest the following guidance strategies to ensure that an enquiry-based curriculum enables students to learn disciplinary ways of thinking. These approaches also provide models of disciplinary expertise for students:

- Make disciplinary expertise such as critical thinking skills visible by using questions that ask students to clarify their understanding or provide more evidence for their positions as the basis for supporting meaning-making. For example, 'What information is that claim based on?', 'How might you explain that interpretation to someone else?', 'Can you provide an example to demonstrate your point?' Teachers can also provide students with templates, models and tools for distinguishing between claims and evidence as ways to structure and make explicit the processes of argumentation and reasoning in the discipline.
- Plan expert inputs such as lectures, podcasts and other relevant resources at different points in the enquiry process to help support student meaning-making and ensure that disciplinary expertise is provided to scaffold learning.
- Recognise that the open-ended nature of enquiry can lead to students becoming overwhelmed; structure the enquiry through progressively more difficult problems or direct students to focus on some parts of a question. Simplifying the amount of data that might be generated out of an experiment or restricting options available for the enquiry to progress can also manage the process at a level appropriate to the students and their experience in the subject.

Focus on practice

Review a module you currently teach from the perspective of how it does or could better support student enquiry, drawing on the case studies described above. Think about how the different student and teacher 'knowledges' might be brought together and critically evaluated. In what ways are power relationships between you and your students framed? Also consider in what ways the process of enquiry is or could be scaffolded for the level and prior knowledge of the students. Spronken-Smith and Walker (2010: 729) suggest the following questions to help you evaluate the ways in which the module supports enquiry:

- 'Are there open-ended questions that lead to the formation of defensible answers?'
- 'Do students work [collaboratively] through the process of constructing knowledge?'
- Do teachers act as 'facilitators' and 'co-learners'?
- 'Do students reflect on the processes of constructing knowledge?'

Conclusion

In this chapter we have explored a range of strategies for strengthening the connections that we make between teaching and research as part of the 'dual economy' of higher education. For many staff and students in universities, teaching and research are conceived of as diametrically opposed activities, often working in tension. As with the previous chapter on student engagement, however, in this chapter we have explored ways in which we might reconceptualise the polarities of research and teaching around the shared experience of learning at the heart of both activities.

The borders of universities are becoming gradually more permeable in terms of their research function. Research outputs must now demonstrate an impact for wider society within a knowledge economy while graduates need to be able to demonstrate not only content mastery, but also flexible research and enquiry skills. High-status research is also being developed in partnership or wholly outside universities across a wide range of industries. It is timely, therefore, to explore and expand our definitions of 'research' and 'researcher' in ways that are more inclusive and embrace practice-based and applied research as well as more traditionally defined research. Similarly, by exploring more inclusive conceptions of who generates research we can see ourselves and our students in a range of different roles in relation to research and knowledge generation. The questions and case studies in this chapter should support you to evaluate your curricula and identify ways in which you can integrate research more fully within your teaching and assessment practices. Such approaches to connecting research to the curriculum will enable you to convey your enthusiasm for your discipline to your students. As with the discussion of a more student-engaged approach in the previous chapter, re-envisioning the relationship of teachers and students to research can and should be transformational for research. Engaging students creatively in live research problems or enquiry, or in understanding learning and teaching, can create new opportunities for a reciprocal nourishing of your own research by expanding the insights and perspectives that can be brought to the subject and how it is taught.

Further reading

Healey, Mick and Jenkins, Alan (2009) *Developing Undergraduate Research and Inquiry.* York: HEA.
This widely cited report provides an accessible summary of the different modes of research–teaching connection and includes a number of international disciplinary examples of undergraduate research in the curriculum.

'The Teaching-Research Nexus' (www.trnexus.edu.au).
An Australian-based site, this online guide brings together examples of teaching–research link activities organised by discipline and level, as well as examples of research into student learning to enhance teaching.

PART II

RETHINKING THE UNIVERSITY CONTEXT

CHAPTER 7

TEACHING FOR EMPLOYABILITY

Learning objectives

This chapter will support you to:

- Explore critically what employability and graduate identity means and how it can be integrated into the curriculum;
- Plan and implement opportunities for students to practice in work-related learning contexts within the curriculum;
- Support students to reflect on their university and employment experience as it relates to their graduate identity.

Introduction

Higher education has always been concerned with preparing graduates for future careers. Yet the recent expansion of highly qualified graduates seeking employment, the idea of the graduate job and the perceived central role of universities in the knowledge economy have demanded greater explicitness about how university prepares students for employment. Employability is a contentious issue for many stakeholders in this debate. Employers have repeatedly raised concerns about the quality of graduates and the shortcomings in the skills they bring to future employment. Likewise, the call to embed employability into traditionally non-vocational programmes has been resisted by some educators who consider this agenda to be focused primarily on providing students with a set of utilitarian skills driven by the short-term needs of employers. From this perspective the expectation that universities will develop student employability is seen as concerned with socialising students into existing workplaces and practices rather than equipping them with the capacity to analyse, critique and transform working environments (Laycock, 2011). Teaching for employability also raises other issues that question the conventional role of the academy in society. The complexity of modern post-graduation careers means that students are unlikely to progress within a single organisation or utilise a finite set of professional competencies. Employability, therefore, is not only about entry into graduate employment. Graduates will 'also require higher order, "meta" work skills – the abilities required to continuously recognise and capitalise on employment and training-related opportunities' (Bridgstock, 2009: 34). Mature entrants into higher education as well as part- or full-time employment or volunteering undertaken alongside studying also mean that many students are already bringing work experience into the university. This challenges the traditional framing of the relationship between university (theory) and employment (practice). Also, as we noted in Chapter 6, this challenges a view of the university as exclusively a place for knowledge creation and the workplace as a context for the application of that knowledge in practice. The workplace is also a valid setting for the generation of interdisciplinary knowledge that students might subsequently bring into, and test against, the traditional university disciplinary curriculum (Laycock, 2011).

These factors significantly impact on what employability means for higher education undergraduate and postgraduate curricula. Preparing students for future employment means developing their capacity to:

- demonstrate 'soft' skills and attributes such as communication, team-working, leadership, creativity, adaptability and critical reflection;
- analyse and evaluate critically the practices, values and priorities of the workplace;
- be self-directed and able to assess their current abilities and their future learning needs;
- negotiate and engage with complex, thematic and interdisciplinary problems in the workplace;
- be researcher-practitioners equipped to engage in reflective practice in the workplace.

While the context for exercising these skills is the workplace rather than the classroom, these desirable employability attributes are, in many cases, comparable to the higher-level critical thinking skills that have been traditionally developed within the disciplinary curriculum (Pegg *et al.*, 2012). This understanding of employability also emphasises the importance of preparing students to be 'critical agents' within the workplace rather than 'set up as objects to be transformed by employers' economic agendas' (Stibbe, 2013: 242).

In this chapter we will begin by looking at how the contested concept of employability is defined and how different approaches have been adopted to embed employability in university curricula. Lists of instrumental, and apparently transferable, graduate skills have been widely advocated as a way to enable students to demonstrate their employability as an outcome of university. More recent attempts to articulate what employability means for students as they leave university, however, have suggested a different understanding based on the development of graduate identity as an outcome of higher education study (Holmes, 2013). From this perspective, teaching for employability is concerned with helping students to analyse their learning experiences, identify their values and attitudes and articulate these to prospective employers in meaningful ways. We will reflect on the principles of employability pedagogies, audit existing curricula to explore how our modules or programmes develop employability and how we might teach and assess legitimately for employability. Employability accentuates experiential, student-directed and active learning that cannot wholly be taught within the university (Eden, 2014). We will therefore consider how work-based and non-work-based learning experiences can be combined to enhance students' understanding of employability. The capacity to problem-solve, reflect critically on experiences, reach well-informed decisions and act are fundamental for professional practice. Finally, we will consider how reflection on experience can be embedded into curricula to facilitate the development of future practitioners as critical enquirers in the workplace.

Employability: from graduate skills to graduate identity

Over the last two decades there has been a growing concern that the investment of individuals in higher education has inadequately prepared them for future employment. In Chapter 4 we considered the arguments for specifying the 'transferable' or 'generic' skills in subject benchmarks and learning outcomes with the intention to focus educators on developing graduate skills alongside disciplinary understanding. Nevertheless, there remain different views about how successfully graduates are being prepared for their subsequent working lives. In a cross-sector survey of employers, the UK Commission for Employment and Skills (UKCES) found that 83 per cent of employers in England, Northern Ireland and Wales and 85 per cent in Scotland considered graduates to be well-prepared for work (UKCES, 2014). The 2013 CBI/Pearson education and skills survey of employers from all sectors of the economy, however, identified perceived shortfalls in expected graduate skills in relation to self-management (32 per cent), problem-solving (27 per cent), literacy (20 per cent), team-working (19 per cent) and analytical skills (18 per cent). In addition, 41 per cent of surveyed employers identified a lack of relevant work experience as a significant factor in the employability of graduates (CBI, 2013). In 2014, the same survey flagged up a significant concern by 33 per cent of surveyed employers that, while science, technology, engineering and mathematics (STEM) graduates are viewed as highly employable in all sectors, the content of STEM-related qualifications were not relevant to business needs (CBI, 2014). Similarly, the Institution for Engineering and Technology (IET) survey revealed a perceived skills shortage by 54 per cent of employers of engineering, IT and technical recruits. In particular, employers in this sector identified lack of leadership skills (42 per cent), practical experience (24 per cent) and technical expertise (23 per cent) as contributory to this skills gap (IET, 2014).

Graduate employability and the challenges of aligning qualifications and graduate outcomes to the expectations of employers, therefore, remain a key issue for educators. The challenge for educators is how, through the curriculum or through support for extracurricular activity, we enable students to develop and demonstrate the skills and attitudinal attributes that we believe they will need to work and live. Employability is not about providing job-seeking skills or equipping students with the ability to secure employment. Employability is concerned with both potential and a longer-term view of a graduate's employment prospects, recognising their need to continue to learn in employment, manage their career and integrate work experience and university study or other professional development in meaningful ways. Even while agreeing that employability is not about getting a job, there are several ways to conceptualise employability in higher education. The surveys cited above signal a broad range of attributes that employers are seeking in their employees such as self-management, team-working, problem-solving, communication and literacy, business and customer awareness, positive attitude, creativity and entrepreneurship. Accepting that there is some equivalency with the higher-order learning outcomes that higher education traditionally aims to foster, these attributes pointedly differ from the types of skills and understandings that universities often emphasise in their graduates. These include research skills, managing complex information and critical thinking that reflect the academic and disciplinary orientation of university curricula (CBI/UUK, 2009).

For the CBI, employability is 'a set of attributes, skills and knowledge that all labour market participants should possess to ensure they have the capability of being effective in the workplace' (ibid., p. 8). While this definition includes soft skills such as communication or team-work, it also accentuates the idea of graduate skills as something that are acquired by a graduate and readily transferable to new settings.

While lists of graduate outcomes are appealing in helping institutions and students to be explicit about what graduates have learnt as an outcome of their studies, Yorke and Knight (2006) argue that employability is more multifaceted than the possession of a set of 'key' or 'transferable' skills. They propose that employability can be embedded into the curriculum as an outcome of four interrelated components:

- understanding of the subject matter;
- skilful practices in context;
- efficacy beliefs, personal qualities and self-theories;
- metacognition, including self-awareness and the ability to reflect on experience.

For Yorke (2006) this acknowledges the limitations of a skills approach and reflects the complex blend of disciplinary, social and personal factors that inform a graduate's employability. In particular, terms such as 'understanding' and 'skilful practices' 'signal the importance of a rich appreciation of the relevant field(s) and of the ability to operate in situations of complexity and ambiguity' (p. 13). The context-dependent and relational nature of 'skilful practices' and the capacity to analyse and reflect on experience constitute a more sophisticated model for embedding employability into our learning, teaching and assessment at university. Contemporary graduate careers are far more likely to be a 'patchwork of contract, part-time and self-employment' compared to a linear advancement within one company or even sector and, therefore, employability should also incorporate career management skills that engage students in reflection, evaluation and strategic decision-making processes (Bridgstock, 2009: 33).

These conceptions of employability emphasise the development of students' 'meta' knowledge to give them the capacity to self-appraise their academic and non-academic performance and understand their intellectual and technical skills as applied, situated and complex. While providing categories of attributes that 'work-ready' graduates should be able to demonstrate, these models also hint at possible alternatives to the conception of 'graduate employability as possession' (Holmes, 2013). As we explored in Chapter 3, while teachers might accept that, in the complex world our students will work and live in, the acquisition of disciplinary knowledge may no longer be an appropriate outcome of university, the performative language of skills can be equally problematic. As Barnett (2009) argues, our curricula and pedagogies should be concerned with the processes of being and 'the kinds of human being we want our students to become' (p. 440). Hence alternative, '"whole person" models of experiential learning [...] see employability as integrative, reflective and transitional' (Eden, 2014: 266). Taking Yorke's (2006) idea of 'skilful practices', more recent approaches to employability do not see being a graduate as concerned with having a set of desirable skills but instead emphasise graduate practices and identity (Hinchcliffe and Jolly, 2011). The transition from university to employment, therefore, is an 'identity project' for students in which they learn to 'become a graduate' by 'act[ing] in ways that lead others to ascribe to them the identity of being a person worthy of being employed' (Holmes, 2013: 549). From this perspective, we do not need to wholly reject the lists of graduate skills and attributes widely articulated by universities and employers. This terminology can instead provide students, educators and employers with a vocabulary for constructing narratives of graduate identity. Graduate attributes provide a 'discursive repertoire available to the various parties concerned, when warranting identity claims and ascriptions' (Holmes, 2013: 550). The Higher Education Academy (2006) collaborated with the Council for Industry in Higher Education to generate 53 disciplinary student employability profiles that state the skills that students develop in different subjects. Many UK universities now also specify the attributes that all graduates will be able to demonstrate in the context of their discipline at the end of their studies. Two examples are presented in Figures 7.1 and 7.2.

Drawing on these accounts of employability, supporting students to develop a graduate identity within the curriculum, therefore, involves several considerations: opportunities for practice, space for reflection and support to construct and explore their graduate identity narratives. First, recognising that practice is the site where graduate identity is constructed, modified and developed, the curriculum should provide opportunities for students to engage in practices through which they can form and test their personal values and ethics. These values include awareness of diversity, cultural difference and sustainability (Hinchcliffe and Jolly, 2011) and Barnett's (2009) qualities such as integrity, respect for others, openness and authenticity. Second, to be able to explore and integrate the learning from practice, students need to be able to reflect critically on their experiences and how they contribute to their graduate identity (Eden, 2014).

Finally, to be able to make claims about their employability students need to be able to access and use a shared vocabulary as a way to present their graduate identity to prospective employers. Being explicit about the graduate skilful practices that underpin learning outcomes will therefore help students

The University is committed to providing a culturally enriched and research-informed educational experience that will transform the lives of its students.

Our aspiration is for graduates who have developed the knowledge, skills and attributes to equip them for life in a complex and rapidly changing world.

In addition to their subject expertise and proficiency, the University's graduates will have the following attributes:

Professionalism, employability and enterprise

- The University promotes professional integrity and provides opportunities to develop the skills of communication, independent and team working, problem solving, creativity, digital literacy, numeracy and self-management.
- Our graduates will be confident, act with integrity, set themselves high standards and have skills that are essential to their future lives.

Learning and research skills

- The University fosters intellectual curiosity and provides opportunities to develop effective learning and research abilities.
- Our graduates will be equipped to seek knowledge and to continue learning throughout their lives.

Intellectual depth, breadth and adaptability

- The University encourages engagement in curricular, co-curricular and extracurricular activities that deepen and broaden knowledge and develop powers of analysis, application, synthesis, evaluation and criticality.
- Our graduates will be able to consider multiple perspectives as they apply intellectual rigour and innovative thinking to the practical and theoretical challenges they face.

Respect for others

- The University promotes self-awareness, empathy, cultural awareness and mutual respect.
- Our graduates will have respect for themselves and others and will be courteous, inclusive and able to work in a wide range of cultural settings.

Social responsibility

- The University promotes the values of ethical behaviour, sustainability and personal contribution.
- Our graduates will understand how their actions can enhance the well-being of others and will be equipped to make a valuable contribution to society.

Figure 7.1   University of Hertfordshire *Graduate Attributes* (Reproduced with permission from http://www.herts.ac.uk/about-us/student-charter/graduate-attributes)

to audit their own achievements through reflection. Creating time and space for students to articulate and receive feedback on their claim for graduate identity (through, for example, undertaking personal development planning or preparing professional portfolios) helps students to understand how to communicate their graduate identity to others (Holmes, 2013; Pegg *et al.*, 2012). In the next section we will explore further how these three principles of practice, reflection and identity narrative might inform learning and teaching practice when embedding work-related learning into students' university experience.

Discipline-based knowledge	Approaches to enquiry and learning
The Sheffield Graduate is ...	The Sheffield Graduate is ...
• knowledgeable in their subject area • competent in applying their knowledge and skills • information literate	• a skilled and ethical researcher • a critical, analytical and creative thinker • an entrepreneurial problem solver
Applying knowledge in the wider context	**Personal development and employability**
The Sheffield Graduate is ...	The Sheffield Graduate is ...
• someone who sees the big picture and understands the importance of context • experienced in working with clients, communities and partners outside the University • an active citizen who respects diversity and has the cultural agility to work in multinational settings	• a flexible team worker • an independent learner • an efficient planner and time manager • an accomplished communicator • skilled in the use of IT • professional and adaptable • a well-rounded individual, reflective, self-aware and self-motivated

Figure 7.2   University of Sheffield *The Sheffield Graduate Attributes* (Reproduced with permission from http://www.sheffield.ac.uk/sheffieldgraduate/studentattributes)

Focus on practice

Audit a module or programme to identify where graduate attributes or dispositions are integrated into the curriculum. You may want to look at the disciplinary graduate profiles (HEA, 2006), example lists in Figures 7.1 or 7.2 or use the graduate attributes published by your own institution as a starting point. Use the following questions to evaluate how employability is currently embedded:

• What kind of graduate identity is your module aiming to develop? What are the discipline-related employability skills, attributes or dispositions you want to cultivate?
• List the most important skills or attributes in the first column: for example, 'skills of independent and team-working' or 'have business awareness'. Identify where this is stated in the learning outcomes and consider what opportunities are available for practice, assessment and feedback on each attribute.
• How explicit are the ways students can develop and articulate their graduate identity in the module? Are there any gaps?

Developing learning, teaching and assessment for employability

University and employer graduate attributes can be wide-ranging from discipline-specific and technical skills to personal qualities and values. Increasingly, graduates will be working in complex and diverse global environments. Valuing diversity, cultural awareness and effective team-working skills are important attributes for graduates to be able to demonstrate to prospective employers. In the following chapters we will explore how students' capacity to work in inclusive and global contexts and as collaborative learners as part of their learning at university can be developed. Yet helping students to reflect on their learning experiences in diverse or international classrooms so that they can make wider claims about their graduateness and employability is also an important aspect of the curriculum. Student employability, therefore, does not mean always introducing work-related examples, activities or work-placements but does mean giving students the opportunity to reflect and abstract meaning from their learning and assessment experiences at university in ways that are meaningful for their future employment. The most important aspect of education for employability is that it is experiential: that is, that learning is derived from experience, whether that be experience of discussion in a diverse classroom or a group assessment or, alternatively, experience of authentic case studies, simulations, fieldwork or work-placements. Including more opportunities for students to experience authentic, work-related or workplace tasks – across all disciplines, not just traditionally vocational subjects – is a vital contributor to students' graduate identity. Learning from the workplace requires skills and attributes that are not always developed or tested in conventional, subject-based curricula: for example, 'how to analyse experiences, the ability to learn from others, the ability to act without all the facts being available, choosing among multiple courses of action, learning about organisational culture' (Tennant *et al.*, 2010: 119). Work-related learning provides the opportunity for students to practice these types of behaviours applicable to, or derived from, the complexity and uncertainty of real-world problems and authentic workplaces.

Work-related learning encapsulates work-based learning, such as part-time or full-time employment, volunteering, 'sandwich years', work experience and work-placements, as well as non-work-based learning in the classroom, such as case studies, simulations or role-plays. Working on live projects at university in collaboration with industry or business professionals or researchers and mentoring or work-shadowing interventions can encapsulate both work-based and non-work-based learning (Hills *et al.*, 2003). While work-related learning undertaken in the curriculum may involve learners applying theory to work contexts or developing theoretical principles from examples, work-based learning is 'active, purposeful learning which is derived from the workplace'

(Laycock, 2011: 7). This means that the workplace is a valid site for learning and knowledge creation, not just the location for the application of theory to practice; learning is more likely to be the result of the co-production of new knowledge through collaborative relationships in the workplace. While work-based learning is often built into curricula, if you want to introduce work-related experiences into modules that do not have formal work experience or placements there are a number of different learning and teaching methods that can be utilised to replicate the complexities of workplace problems or issues.

Case studies

Examples or case studies of relevant business or industry issues can be used to illustrate the application of theory in practice in lectures, seminars or problem classes. Alternatively, students can work through cases individually or in groups to identify key principles or comment on contextual factors that impact on workplace decisions.

Simulations or scenarios

Students participate in simulated work situations in groups to solve problems or work through typical scenarios. New data or resources can be released periodically to students as they reach points in the simulation to imitate decision-making in situations based on incomplete data. In situations where there are multiple alternative outcomes students can subsequently reflect on and justify their decisions.

Problem-based learning (PBL)

A real or typical workplace problem can be used as a stimulus for student research, analysis, synthesis of information and decision-making. Students identify the information they need, action plan to solve the problem and make decisions about individual roles in the group and how the group will work together and communicate.

Business or industry briefing or research project

Students work individually, in pairs or in groups to undertake work-related research and prepare a report or briefing for senior management or business clients on a specified workplace or sector topic. This requires students to investigate sector trends and organisational or workplace culture and draw conclusions or make recommendations for action that take into account business realities, commercial risk factors or resources. Alternatively, they prepare a learning resource: for example, a short guide or website on a topic for a specified audience such as adult learners, patients or children. Students will develop their research and information-management skills as well as communication and presentation skills.

Case study 7.1   Three initiatives for embedding employability into the classics curriculum (Barrow et al., 2010)

Although classics graduates enter a range of professions including law, education, business, journalism and the civil service, three initiatives were used to embed employability into the Classical Civilisation degree at Roehampton University. In two modules students completed a group presentation on a chosen object at the British Museum or National Gallery in London. This provided an opportunity for students to practise team-work as well as experience communication in a workplace environment to a potentially diverse audience, particularly when visitors to the galleries also listened to the presentations. The second initiative for second-year students required students to undertake an independent research project to design and construct a website on a mythological topic such as a mythical character, a theme, or a narrative event, such as the Trojan War. They were also expected to complete an oral presentation to explain their content and design decisions in relation to the intended audience for their resource. Students were supported with workshops, led by academic and e-learning staff, to support the research and website design. The small-scale research project provided preparation for the longer dissertation assessment in the final year while also developing skills such as time management, problem-solving, research organisation and communicating through new media. The third strategy was an optional work-placement module in the second or third year. Students were responsible for identifying and gaining a relevant short-term placement: for example, on an archaeological excavation, in a school, at a museum or gallery. Students engaged in a range of activities including teaching Latin, cataloguing collections or preparing exhibitions. The module included workshops on making applications, writing CVs and presenting at interviews and an e-journal tool supported recording and reflection on the learning experience.

Live project

Students collaborate on authentic, time-specific ongoing projects in collaboration with professionals. Examples include an advertising campaign, a grant submission, a research project or a gallery exhibition. Participation in live projects gives students opportunities to reflect on roles in group tasks, working to deadlines, professional responsibility and autonomy and communicating ideas or proposals to different professional audiences.

Presentation or pitch

Students work collaboratively to put together a short presentation or make a pitch to a business or funding body. Students need to research the topic and synthesise data to respond to a specific brief. The task means they have to think about how to communicate information to a particular audience, practice oral and written skills and plan how the task will be undertaken by the group. If groups need to produce several outputs – for example, poster, PowerPoint presentation, a short video or written brochure – the students will also need to consider the impact of genre they are using to communicate and the skills to use these tools effectively.

Case study 7.2   A 'project pitch' assessment to embed employability in geography (Smith, 2012)

Smith introduced a new project assessment into the second-year Environmental Management module in the Environmental Science and Geography, Physical Geography and Environmental Earth Science programmes at Aberystwyth University. The aim was to enhance students' understanding of employability and have the opportunity to practise relevant work-relevant skills. The 150 students on the module were divided into small groups and given the task to make a 'pitch' for one of five grants at a professional conference at the end of the module. The pitch included a five-minute video and oral presentation, a poster and five sides of the conference programme to present a written outline of the pitch. Each pitch was based on a real-life grant or contract: for example, 'Pitch for a wind farm option to develop'. Each pitch should take account of the budget and scope of work for the planning process, design and construction. Students were encouraged to approach the pitch professionally and 5 per cent of the assessment criteria included teacher assessment of team coherence and professionalism. The assessment not only developed students' disciplinary skills but also helped to develop evidence of employability behaviours such as team-work, time management, budgeting, project management, oral defence of a proposal and poster design skills.

Guest lecture or master class

Inviting industry or commercial experts or professional practitioners to contribute to the design and content of a module, deliver lectures or facilitate master classes creates opportunities for students to gain insight into the typical challenges, solutions and professional practices of work. Ensuring students also have access to relevant trade or professional journals alongside textbooks and academic publications emphasises that the relationship between theory and practice and between the academy and the workplace is not one way.

Mentoring

Mentoring by experienced professionals or alumni working with current students can develop their skills and attributes by helping them to audit their existing skills and to action plan and reflect; this arrangement can facilitate workplace visits, job shadowing or other short-term work experiences. Mentors can also be drawn, however, from more experienced students in the same cohort or from other stages in the programme. As more students are returning to study after a period of employment or are working full- or part-time while at university, they bring valuable and up-to-date workplace experience into the classroom to support students with no work experience.

Case study 7.3   Drawing on students' industry experience as a resource in civil engineering (Davies and Rutherford, 2012)

One-third of students on the BEng in Civil Engineering at Coventry University are part-time students working in industry alongside study. A number of strategies are used to embed the development of employability and industry awareness into the curriculum such as authentic project work, industrial simulations, practitioner input and work experience. Yet the experiences of students with current professional roles in industry are also a resource for the full-time students on the programme. Two methods were used to draw on this experience in the classroom. First, part-time students were invited to act as mentors of first-year full-time students as part of their own learning and leadership development. Mentors met with four to five students who did not have professional experience and were encouraged to discuss their experiences in civil engineering practice as it related to the course. Second, teachers managed group formation for project work to ensure each group included at least one part-time student to give all students access to their professional knowledge and authentic workplace skills. These interventions supported students to discuss and reflect on team roles and professional skills as well as draw on the organisational and time management skills of the mentor in project work. A major benefit of these strategies was the opportunity to integrate into the programme real workplace examples and, in particular, authentic physical artefacts such as drawings, photographs, sample documents and templates.

Many of these activities also create group or individual outputs that are assessable. For example, individual or group reports, professional portfolios, industry-facing presentations, posters, case studies or briefings can all be assessed tasks within modules as a way to foster employability at undergraduate and taught postgraduate level. Peer feedback and peer assessment is also widely used in assessment for employability (Brown, 2012). Not only are students assessed in relation to their disciplinary knowledge and skills, but also their understanding of workplace issues and business awareness, as well as graduate attributes such as effective communication, problem-solving, research skills and team-working. Developing students' employability, however, means not only creating opportunities for practice, but also supporting critical reflection on the application of theory to, or development of knowledge in, the workplace, reflection on practice and reflection on individual learning.

Enhancing student reflection on practice

Being able to translate workplace and university-based work-related experience into meaningful learning is not only important for integrating theory and practice knowledge in the curriculum, but also develops students' capacity to structure self-directed, lifelong learning in their future careers. The relationship between experience and reflection is often depicted using a cyclical model that is based on Kolb's (1984) experiential learning cycle. Students use experience of work-related learning opportunities to inform reflection individually and collaboratively. They use evidence from their reflection and relevant literature or data to evaluate their experience before planning for future action based on their analysis. It is a model that can be used to frame learning from a single activity such as preparing and delivering a presentation or from longer-term work-placement activities. Reflecting on work-related experiences helps students to draw out the skills and challenges of an experience and identify meaningful resolutions for future practice, as well as capture their learning and articulate this to others. In particular, while communication skills or research skills may be evidenced in more traditional presentation or written assessments, reflection can be particularly valuable for drawing out more complex graduate attributes such as professional values and cultural awareness. There is a range of methods that encourage students to capture and reflect on their practice experiences during classroom activities or placements; these are summarised in Table 7.1.

Table 7.1 Strategies for encouraging reflection on work-related learning

Activity	Strategies for supporting and reflecting on experience
Learning journals or blogs	Posting short personal accounts of work-related experiences captures the emotional experience as well as recording action plans and setting goals for practice before an activity. It enables reflection on incidents in practice, evaluation of progress and recording of achievement of goals (Jackson, 2015)
Reflective interview with peers	Students develop and use pre-agreed questions to conduct a reflective interview with each other about practice experiences and work through implications for future practice. The interview helps students to draw out learning points from multidimensional experiences (Ryan and Ryan, 2013)
Reflective portfolio	Portfolios allow students to collect together artefacts that record their achievements and experiences in practice. The process of creating the portfolio, however, not only records experiences, but also facilitates deeper levels of making meaning through personal reflection and, if involving peer review or group tasks, collaboration. Portfolio learning involves 'processes of planning, synthesising, sharing, discussing, reflecting, giving, receiving and responding to feedback' (Jisc, 2008: 6)
Critical incident analysis	Students identify an incident that stood out for them in practice and work through a series of questions that prompt them to describe, analyse and evaluate the experience and draw conclusions. Question prompts should ask students to describe the incident, explore their initial responses including emotions, consider issues raised by the incident, relate the incident to theoretical and policy contexts in the module and identify outcomes (Green Lister and Crisp, 2007)
Group-memory work	In this collaborative activity students initially write reflective personal narratives on a mutual experience of a work-related activity. These are shared with others and, through individual and collaborative analysis of these accounts, students draw out the individual values and assumptions their accounts reveal as well as implications for future professional practice (Ryan and Ryan, 2013)

Strategies for enhancing collaborative learning such as small group discussion and self- and peer feedback (explored further in Chapter 11) also create occasions for students to explore experience, test ideas and interpretations as they connect theory and practice. Through reflection students engage with their full experience of learning in practice, validating subjective, emotional, ethical and bodily responses to events alongside theoretical and cognitive outcomes. Reflecting on and articulating their practice experiences, however, is challenging and, without scaffolding or careful facilitation, it is possible for it to be purely descriptive and be unproductive. Research into reflection has identified different hierarchical levels of reflection that structure progressively more complex engagement with experiences (Ryan and Ryan, 2013). When initiating reflective activities, therefore, it is valuable to provide students with prompts to help them develop their reflective accounts and access richer understandings of their work-related experience. For example, Smith (2011) identifies four domains of reflection: self-critical, interpersonal, contextual and critical. The self-critical domain of reflection focuses on a students' own thoughts and actions whereas the interpersonal domain seeks to concentrate reflection on interaction with others. Contextual reflection engages students in reflecting on theory or methods and critical reflection focuses on the political, social and ethical context for action. Similarly, Jay and Johnson's (2002) typology of reflection distinguishes between three dimensions: descriptive, comparative and critical. Descriptive reflection is the first step in describing what will be reflected on, defining the parameters of the action and capturing the emotional and subjective response to the situation. Comparative reflection seeks to reframe that experience taking into account other perspectives or theoretical positions. Critical reflection takes these alternative perspectives and asks students to consider the implications for personal values and political and ethical position. As students seek to record and interrogate their work-related experiences, guiding questions will support them to develop their reflection. The following questions can be used within the methods described above and are applicable to analysis of a single incident or longer-term experiences (Green Lister and Crisp, 2007; Jay and Johnson, 2002; Smith, 2011).

Questions to initiate description and analysis of a work-related experience

- What happened? What is the context of the work-related experience? Who is involved? What was my role?
- What do I understand and what do I not understand about this experience? What are my questions about what happened and why are those questions important?
- How am I feeling about what happened? Why am I interested in this experience?
- Can I draw on my subject knowledge or prior experiences to better understand this experience?

Questions to contextualise and reframe a work-related experience

- What other views might there be about what happened? Whose perspectives are missing from my account of this experience so far?
- What practice dilemmas does the experience prompt? What values and ethical issues does it highlight for me?

- Are there relevant disciplinary theories, frameworks or models that might help me develop my understanding of this experience?
- How might my analysis of this experience contribute to my, or others', knowledge or understanding of professional practices, workplaces, professional relationships or disciplinary-based theory?
- If I had analysed this experience from a different perspective would I have reached the same conclusions? How have my assumptions influenced my reflection?

Questions to develop a critical perspective on a work-related experience

- How might legislative, organisational or policy contexts explain the experience or determine ways to respond to it?
- Taking into account different perspectives on this experience and my personal and professional values, what are the alternative ways to respond?
- What are the implications of my response? Do my conclusions, recommendations or actions serve the agenda of some people and not others?
- Has my reflection informed or changed my perspective on this experience? What work-related skills or capacities has this experience drawn on or developed?

Encouraging students to explore work-related incidents and experiences in this way supports them to find ways to evidence in more complex, situated and critical ways how they have developed their graduate identity. The third principle of teaching for employability is to create opportunities for students to practice and get feedback on their narratives about their graduate identity. Written reflection engages students in the process of making claims about learning as an outcome of experience that are available to others and mentors, teachers or peers can then give feedback on the quality of the account.

Focus on practice

Drawing on any gaps you identified in the audit of a module or programme in the previous 'Focus on practice' activity, consider how you might introduce a work-related element into the curriculum. Design a work-related activity or assessment task relevant to your discipline. Use the principles necessary for effective work-related learning (practice, reflection and graduate identity claims) to structure the activity or assessment. Write a proposal for colleagues outlining the rationale for the new work-related intervention or prepare a briefing for students to introduce the activity or assessment.

Conclusion

Integrating employability into the curriculum is a contentious issue for educators, particularly given some instrumental and uncritical approaches to defining generic or transferable skills relevant for employment. More sophisticated understandings of employability, however, suggest the importance of preparing students to make claims about their graduate identity as an outcome of university. Developing students' capacity to learn in work-related and workplace settings, reflect critically on that learning and plan for future action are important ways in which we can ensure students have greater agency in undertaking and shaping their future careers and lives. This understanding of employability, emphasising the process of students 'becoming' critical members of society, mirrors the types of self-directed and critical thinking that many disciplines seek to develop. Being able to live and work in a diverse, global, networked and collaborative world are essential features of students' contemporary experiences in university as well as their future employment and citizenship. Universities provide unique spaces for students to practice, reflect and articulate how these experiences have informed their perspectives, beliefs, ethics and values central to their graduate identity. Over the next four chapters we will explore further how paying attention as teachers to diversity, internationalisation, technology and engagement with peers will not only enhance all students' learning at university, but also support them to critically evaluate these experiences.

Further reading

Pegg, Ann, Waldock, Jeff, Hendy-Isaac, Sonia and Lawton, Ruth (2012) *Pedagogy for Employability*. York: HEA (https://www.heacademy.ac.uk/sites/default/files/pedagogy_for_employability_update_2012.pdf).
Employability is a key work stream of the HEA and there are a range of resources to support practitioners to integrate work-related learning into the curriculum. This resource summarises some of the key issues for implementing employability in teaching and learning. Other resources and outcomes of disciplinary projects to embed employability, including student employability profiles, are available from their website (www.heacademy.ac.uk/workstreams-research/themes/employability).

Vitae (2013) *The Career-Wise Researcher* (www.vitae.ac.uk)
The focus on employability often targets undergraduate and taught postgraduate students, but this practical guide supports postgraduate research students to evaluate their own areas of expertise, career aspirations and career management and to reframe their experiences to demonstrate their employability.

CHAPTER 8

DEVELOPING INCLUSIVE LEARNING AND TEACHING

Learning objectives

This chapter will support you to:

- Develop a critical understanding of student diversity as the basis for inclusive learning and teaching and assessment;
- Critically reflect on personal approaches to student diversity and inclusive teaching in practice;
- Plan and facilitate inclusive teaching environments that engage with student diversity and inclusive practice to enhance the learning experience for all students.

Introduction

Over the last two decades there has been a major imperative to expand access to higher education globally, driven by both economic demands for a skilled labour force in the post-industrial age and an increasing social justice argument for equity of educational opportunity for all. In the UK, from the 1990s, there has been a significant commitment to both expanding numbers and widening access to what was regarded as an exclusive higher education system available only to some members of society. 'Traditional' students were likely to be white, from higher socio-economic groups and entering university directly after A-levels. The New Labour pledge, in their 2001 election manifesto, to increase participation in tertiary education to 50 per cent of 18- to 30-year-olds by 2010 committed the UK higher education sector to transform itself from an elite to a mass and meritocratic system. Alongside these commitments, current legislation, including the Disability Discrimination Act (2005) and the Equality Act (2010), have meant university-level education provision must be inclusive and equitable for all in terms of both access and practice.

While admission trends have evidenced increased levels of participation of students aged 18 to 21 and participation rates for black and ethnic minority students are higher than for white students (Sanders and Rose Adams, 2014), the participation gap between those from high and low socio-economic backgrounds remains profound. There also continue to be significant variations in participation in terms of the ethnicity, disability, age and nationality of prospective students between disciplines and between institutions. Despite policies to facilitate access to tertiary education, it has been acknowledged that increasing participation does not always equal widening participation (Cunningham, 2013). The entrance of 'new' or 'non-traditional' students into higher education has not been equal across the sector. While universities have become more diverse than they were two decades ago, there is significant differentiation across the sector and a continued hierarchy of institutions, often reflecting the original two-tier organisation of universities (Brennan and Osborne, 2008). The specific mission of some universities – for example, to respond to regional or local populations or employment needs – as well as institutional size or range of subjects can also impact on the diverse nature and student make-up of individual universities. On that basis, different institutions have different levels of diversity in their student body and dominant groups in one institution may be actually marginalised in another. For example, participation by social class can vary considerably between different post-1992 universities and older Russell Group universities (Reay et al., 2010).

Fairer access to higher education, however, is not the only consideration. Perhaps even more fundamentally, once students have entered university there can also be a significant gap in the attainment between 'traditional' and 'non-traditional' students. For example, in 2012–13, the Equality Challenge Unit reports that in science and engineering subjects 70.2 per cent of students aged 21 or under received a first or upper second degree compared to 59.9 per cent for mature students, a 13.1 per cent attainment gap. More profoundly, while 73.2 per cent of white UK-domiciled students received a first or upper second degree, 57.1 per cent of black and minority ethnic UK-domiciled students achieved a comparable qualification. Though this has reduced from a peak of nearly 19 per cent a decade ago, this still constitutes a 16.1 per cent attainment gap between UK white and ethnic minority students. If gender is also taken into account, the attainment gap between UK-domiciled white male and black male students is 27.1 per cent (ECU, 2014). Drawing on 15 years of data, Richardson (2015) argues that the 'odds of a non-White student obtaining a good degree are about half of a White student' (p. 280). The retention of students after they enter their programmes of study, as well as the variances in attainment between students from different demographic groups, is multidimensional, but it has been widely argued it reflects the ongoing tensions between the cultural and structural values and practices of universities. This includes the pedagogic approach of educators and the learning experiences they foster, as well as mis-alignment with the needs, experiences and talents of a more diverse student body. Engaging with diversity in higher education, therefore, requires teachers to reflect critically on differences between, and also within, institutions as well as the individual differences between students in their classes.

Brennan and Osborne (2008) suggest there are several aspects of diversity to take into account when reflecting on the student experience. There can be diversity that is 'imported' into higher education and relates to student social identities, including gender, age, socio-economic status, ethnicity, sexuality, religion, nationality, migrant or refugee status and disability, as well as student prior educational experiences. There are also differences that are contextual and 'externally generated' such as student financial circumstances, their need for term-time employment, part-time or full-time registration status and domestic commitments such as caring responsibilities or living arrangements. Finally, there are differences that relate to the student's learning experience that are 'internally generated' by the structures of the institution and different student responses to the pedagogic environment. These can reflect curriculum organisation and flexibility, the relationship between curriculum and co-curriculum activities and variation in student levels of engagement and learning approaches. Inevitably, in reality, these diversity factors are not mutually exclusive. Students from low-income families may be more likely to have to work to support their studies, for example, and may have prior educational experiences that do not provide them with the academic skills expected to succeed within existing higher education structures implicitly designed for students from a different social and educational background.

In this chapter we will begin by looking critically at the assumptions and expectations about the academic capacity and learning needs of a more diverse student group in the context of the institution and discipline. Changing 'imported' and 'externally generated' factors, that frequently reflect the social inequalities of wider society, are for the most part outside the scope of individual teachers.

Crozier *et al.* (2008) argue, however, that the 'interplay of the structural with the personal, the familial, social and academic experience' (p. 175) means that the existing structures of higher education, such as the teaching and learning methods or the assessment tools we use, are not neutral choices for all students but are ideological and potentially discriminatory. This can mean that our practices may inherently reward the skills, values and dispositions of 'traditional' students over those of students from different socio-economic or ethnic backgrounds. Rather than enabling the social mobility or social justice outcomes of education which many educators would subscribe to, our teaching, learning, assessment and other curriculum choices might, in reality, serve traditionally privileged social groups by ensuring some students are implicitly or explicitly advantaged over others. We will, therefore, look at how 'internally generated' factors in the university, including curriculum content, academic support, learning and teaching strategies and assessment, can all be addressed to fulfil more inclusive aims.

We will explore how developing inclusive pedagogies that adjust to the wider needs of a diverse student cohort can not only challenge the reproduction of traditional privilege within universities, but also, in doing so, transform learning for all students and prepare them to engage in society and employment in more progressive ways. Recognising that the internationalisation of higher education and the development of intercultural learning experiences are a significant aspect of a contemporary globalised higher education, this specific dimension of institutional and student diversity is considered in more detail in the following chapter. Taken together the approaches examined in both this chapter and Chapter 9, however, are relevant for rethinking the culture of institutions as a whole and how that culture can be experienced by those unfamiliar with the expectations and assumptions of university education in the UK.

Focus on practice

Think about a student group you are teaching and reflect on your answers to the following questions:

- What are the differences between students in your group in terms of 'imported' and 'externally generated' factors?
- Are there differences in the expectations, participation and attainment of students from different social groups? What student characteristics or external commitments might be possible reasons for student poor performance, different levels of participation or even withdrawal?
- What are the respective roles and responsibilities for individual students, you and your institution in responding to these differences?

Different conceptions of student diversity in context

Alongside international student recruitment, the expansion of higher education through improved access for previously excluded groups in the UK has resulted in greater student diversity. This can be found across cohorts or institutions or be located in silos within particularly disciplines or programmes. Teachers will perceive this in different ways and how we respond to student diversity has implications for the teaching and learning strategies we utilise. Research by Gordon *et al.* (2010) and Leach (2011), in Australia and New Zealand respectively, has defined several different responses to diversity. This research has suggested that teachers' recognition of student difference can be categorised along a continuum from what they describe as a homogeneous perspective to a group perspective, a comprehensive perspective and an individual perspective.

Homogeneous perspective of diversity

From this position, teachers may not acknowledge any diversity within a class nor anticipate any effects of student differences on learning and teaching. It can be based on the assumption that in teaching and assessment all students have an equal opportunity to succeed. From this perspective it is believed that if 'non-traditional' students have comparable ability, perseverance or confidence then they will achieve equally with their more 'traditional' peers (Devlin, 2013). This approach also reflects educators' concerns about the risks of cultural pluralism and a commitment to being 'blind' to differences. From this perspective, questions of unity and similarity between individuals are the focus; equality (the same for all) rather than equity (tailored to need to achieve a level playing field for all) is the objective in teaching. Indeed, it may be perceived to be unethical to provide additional support for one group or student over another. As Leach (2011) warns, however, what might be seen as a culturally neutral position, one of gender- or colour-blindness, can actually reflect the tacit but specific position of an individual teacher. Existing structures and pedagogies within universities may be perceived to be politically and socially neutral. Yet the identities, experiences and attitudes of 'traditional' students (white, male, middle-class, non-disabled) may, in reality, define those apparently culturally neutral or 'colour-blind' norms and it is therefore those students who participate more successfully within them.

Group perspective of diversity

An alternative perspective is one in which the diversity of students as members of different demographic groups is both recognised and valued by teachers. This means seeing 'imported' differences such as gender, ethnicity, disability or social status and how these differences impact on learning. Recognising these differences may also involve acknowledging student intersubjective identities and understanding that individuals are not exclusively members of one cultural or social group. Teachers with this perspective might try to relate to the different cultures within the class or implement specific support for students from different demographic groups. They might also, however, share the concerns of those with a more homogenising perspective in recognising student diversity but still believing that it is necessary to provide equal learning experiences for all students.

Comprehensive perspective of diversity

The comprehensive position on diversity is categorised by Leach (2011) as an individual-group perspective in which the identity of a demographic group is recognised but so too are the individual differences between students within these cultural or social groups. It reflects an appreciation that, while group identities may convey certain values, beliefs and experiences, it is important to acknowledge that students are not defined by their membership of one or more groups. Intersectionality recognises that, for example, race, gender, class, disability or sexuality are not separate experiences of identity. Nor do we necessarily represent, as individuals, the groups we may be seen to belong to. It is an important, nuanced position that counters the dangers of stereotyping or bracketing individual students because of their perceived group affiliations and identities. This position can lead teachers to attempt to relate to individual student cultures and implement focused strategies to support learning within their practice. Gordon *et al.* (2010) define this as a comprehensive position because it reflects the broadest level of engagement with student diversity and recognises both differences between groups and differences between individuals.

Individual perspective of diversity

The reverse position to the homogeneous view that conflates or ignores difference is described as the individual perspective in which multiple differences between all students are recognised regardless of any demographic group affiliation. Each student is understood to have different motivations, interests, experiences, learning needs and preferred learning approaches to which the teacher should tailor their teaching and resources as far as possible. It is a position that avoids generalising the learning experience across a cohort of students and resists an all-purpose curriculum that, in reality, might serve only some individuals. The danger of this position, however, is that supporting the wide variety of needs becomes quickly unfeasible within large groups. As Leach (2011) argues, by focusing on individuals, teachers with this perspective may ultimately also neglect the real benefits of group affiliations or peer collaboration because they do not provide the opportunity to build connections between students or explore the shared beliefs or similarities between individuals. It is a position in which 'Each student then becomes a self-contained, independent island, isolated from other students, reliant on the teacher to foster their learning' (p. 260).

Within this continuum of perspectives of diversity, the 'group' and the 'comprehensive' perspective allow the most scope for responding to student diversity. While noticing student differences generates greater sensitivity to variations in student learning experiences, it can also reveal teachers' personal beliefs about typical student characteristics that lead to success or failure. Research has suggested that teachers can hold strong preconceptions about the impact of 'imported' and 'externally generated' factors on student success. Popovic and Green (2012) interviewed teachers in the UK and the USA about the key characteristics of undergraduate students whom they perceived as doing either well or not well at university. The teachers they interviewed identified a number of characteristics of students they expected to perform well at university including:

- attend university full-time;
- belong to particular ethnic groups (usually white);
- do not have dyslexia;
- have a particular gender (differing depending on the subject studied);
- perform some paid or voluntary work but not excessive hours;
- enjoy doing activities outside their curriculum that relate to their programme;
- talk with their teacher and ask questions;
- actively form their own study groups.

When scrutinised against empirical evidence of assessment performance, the researchers found that these often deep-seated assumptions had no validity in determining student success. While some expected behavioural characteristics such as lecture attendance, a proactive approach to developing study habits for university study and keeping up with assigned readings were found to be significant, assumptions related to 'imported' and 'externally generated' differences were not upheld. Nevertheless, such assumptions influence the way we consciously or unconsciously articulate expectations and appropriate behaviours in academic contexts. Yet, while our preconceptions may be widely off the mark, there are still attainment gaps between students from different groups. As educators, we need to understand why, although student ethnicity, social status, gender or other factors are not deterministic, students from some groups are performing less well than others in university.

The recognition of the potential different needs, experiences and motivations of 'new' students in higher education flags up difficulties and barriers to achievement, both within the organisational structure of the system or particular university and within traditional pedagogies and assessment regimes. The presence of 'non-traditional' students may compel institutions and teachers to conjure up a 'normal' student against which the 'new' entrant is measured and potentially seen as lacking the necessary academic understanding or skills to succeed. The danger is that mature students entering universities through different qualification routes, students from working-class backgrounds, ethnic minority or disabled students can all 'represent "the masses": homogenized, pathologized and marked as "Other" compared with existing students' (Leathwood and O'Connell, 2003: 599). If 'new' students struggle to meet the academic achievements of their 'traditional' peers, one response is to consider the fault to lie with the student. Failure to fulfil potential and take advantage of the opportunities of the university can be seen as a result of a student's lack of appropriate motivation, attitude or aptitude. Their difficulties can also quickly confirm assumptions about the capacity of individual students to be at university in the first place. This is a deficit model of 'non-traditional' students that fundamentally problematises them as legitimate participants in higher education (Devlin, 2013).

Much of the research into the experiences of 'non-traditional' students from working-class backgrounds entering university, however, draws on the work of two sociologists, Bourdieu and Bernstein. Their work helps us to understand the nature of the difficulties students from a wider social range might face (Crozier *et al.*, 2010; Zepke and Leach, 2007). Bourdieu's (1973) theory of social reproduction can be used to understand the university as a space whose norms, in terms of appropriate values, attitudes and practices, have been defined and continue to be regulated by the dominant class in society, which previously had exclusive access to higher education within an elite system. These norms create an institutional 'habitus', with rules and codes of practice that are not equally understood by all students, particularly those who come from outside the dominant social groups. Academic values and practices, therefore, are not politically or socially neutral but are 'classed, raced and gendered' (Crozier *et al.*, 2010: 73) in ways that can become barriers to some students. From this perspective 'traditional' students from the middle and upper socio-economic backgrounds are better prepared for university because they may be already familiar with these rules or have knowledge, skills or attitudes (or 'cultural capital') that will help them succeed. Conversely, students who lack this specific 'capital' will experience incongruence between their own culture and the middle-class academic values they encounter in universities (Devlin, 2013). The 'habitus' of university comprises what Bernstein (2000) describes as an 'invisible pedagogy' where expectations of academic study are coded or unclear to some students in ways that reflect and reinforce existing social inequalities and sense of belonging at university. As we explored in Chapter 4 when we considered the 'hidden' curriculum, the 'curriculum is a cultural artefact' that 'represents a set of choices about what knowledge and values should ultimately be transmitted to preserve the community that holds such values' (Nunan *et al.*, 2000: 71). For students who sit outside these values or the community that created them, the curriculum and learning and teaching can be experienced not as neutral or straightforward but as challenging, disorienting or exclusionary. Some of the principles of a purportedly student-centred curriculum, such as independent study, active learning and the emphasis on student-led academic support and information-seeking behaviours, may be unclear to those with different prior learning experiences, levels of academic confidence or expectations of university. For example, research into the impact of gender and ethnicity suggest that differences in attainment may in part be the outcome of black and male students misunderstanding the demands and expectations of higher education study (Cotton *et al.*, 2015).

The barriers to achievement that have been identified for working-class students have also been investigated in relation to students with disabilities and, in some cases, can provide a far more literal manifestation of the impediments experienced in other ways by many 'non-traditional' students in university. A social model of disability suggests that, while identifying different learner needs and interventions can ensure that appropriate resources are directed to support some students (for example, wheelchair users, blind, partially sighted, or deaf students, students with dyslexia or mental health issues), it is important to avoid this deficit focus. Instead, we might want to look at the experience of the university and consider in what ways the physical and educational environment itself discriminates or disables some students but not others (Matthews, 2009). At the physical level, this can mean identifying when a student will need a note-taker or the modifications required in a laboratory to ensure the workspace is at the correct height for wheelchair users. But this can also prompt us to reflect on the wider disabling factors (physical, educational and social) of the learning environment rather than the perceived disability of the individual and how these might be addressed. Although some solutions might involve specific adjustments for individual students, making visible the possible inequities within the university curriculum and classroom can ultimately help us to improve the learning experience for all students.

When student diversity and any related inequalities between the experiences and outcomes of 'traditional' and 'non-traditional' students are not considered, Gordon *et al.* (2010) suggest the primary response of teachers is to ignore the specific needs of some students and attempt to treat all students the same. When inequalities are acknowledged, however, educators can identify what is responsible for the disjunctive experiences of 'non-traditional' students that might result in poor outcomes or retention. There are several ways in which we can approach learning and teaching in an attempt to generate more equal opportunities for all students.

Study skills approach

One response is to adopt teaching strategies that attempt to enable all students to succeed within the existing values, attitudes and practices of university by rectifying the perceived deficits that 'non-traditional' students might have. This is achieved by providing remedial 'bolt-on' study skills for those entering university with different prior knowledge and experience. It might also mean giving compensatory help to enable some students to undertake the same tasks as 'traditional' students. For example, allowing 'special arrangements' for disabled students to give them extra time in exams or a scribe so that they can complete the same tasks as other students on an equal basis.

Alternative approach

A second way to support 'non-traditional' students is by acknowledging that it is not that individual students lack essential skills but that the rules of the game of university might not always be clear. We can respond to this by making the academic requirements of tasks more transparent and by expanding the range of existing content, teaching, learning and assessment methods we use for some students if we see them as excluding or disadvantaging some students. For example, for students with dyslexia, sight problems or those working in English as a second language, large volumes of reading or essay-based assessment may be more demanding than for other students without enabling their assessors legitimately to determine differences in understanding or academic potential. Introducing alternatives such as video or podcast resources alongside set reading or offering an oral viva or presentation task, as well as a written essay or report, can ensure such students are not disadvantaged by traditional pedagogic tasks. For some teachers, this response raises fears of lowering standards to accommodate the needs of students who lack the perceived skills and understanding to participate in higher education to the detriment of other students. It is important to consider, however, whether traditional, text-based tasks are the only way to differentiate between, for example, levels of conceptual understanding or critical thinking.

Inclusive approach

We might, however, draw on the possibilities of student diversity to question the existing traditional learning and teaching values, expectations and practices of the discipline or the university. This can be the basis for transforming higher education teaching and learning for all students. This might involve expanding the range of ways in which all students, not just those who have been identified as needing additional support through study skills or compensatory measures, might learn or demonstrate that learning in assessment. In adopting this teaching approach, teachers acknowledge and 'utilise' the diversity of students as a teaching resource, not a problem to solve (Gordon *et al.*, 2010). This is described as an 'inclusive' approach to teaching and assessment in which alternative methods are embedded in the curriculum and available to all students regardless of their status as 'traditional' or 'non-traditional' students. It recognises that common signifiers such as 'traditional' and 'non-traditional' over-simplify the complexities of all student identities in higher education and the conservatism in some of the ways we teach and assess. In particular, an inclusive approach provides a productive critique of the overemployment of traditional methods and assessment tools such as the written essay or examination (Waterfield and West, 2006). For example, engaging all students in showing their learning in alternative formats such as artworks, video, collage, drama and performance can inspire and challenge students in ways that writing may not (James and Brookfield, 2014).

Focus on practice

Revisit your answers to the previous 'Focus on practice' activity in the light of debates outlined above and consider what your approach to student diversity is:

- How valid are some of your assumptions about the factors for student success or failure in your context? What evidence could you provide to uphold your position?
- How would you categorise your approach to diversity and what are the implications for your practice? Are there disadvantages to your approach?
- In what ways might the existing attitudes, assumptions, values, content or teaching, learning and assessment methods of your curriculum be 'disabling' to students?

Responding to diversity in practice: the example of teaching academic writing

The ways in which students are asked to demonstrate their learning using the specific rules of academic writing in their discipline provides an example of how the different responses to diversity outlined about are manifested in practice. Lea and Street (1998) have defined three ways in which student academic writing is developed in higher education. They suggest that the teaching of academic writing may be addressed by:

- teaching students a set of technical writing skills;
- socialising students into the best ways to communicate in the discipline;
- recognising and engaging students in making individual meaning as a social practice.

The first approach emphasises teaching students a set of skills to create a text that meets the demands of academic writing in the discipline. These skills focus on the surface elements of academic writing: for example, the use of appropriate academic rather than everyday language, the way an essay or report is structured and correct approaches to citing sources to avoid plagiarism. These can be taught as atomised and de-contextualised practices that are distinct from the subject matter or learning environment and readily transferable from one context to another. As such, writing skills can be efficiently taught through study skills classes outside the curriculum. Alternatively, the socialisation approach requires an appreciation of the specific demands of the disciplinary academic culture and the implicit, or explicit, ways that the different genre and discourse conventions of a discipline are learnt. Writing is taught by making transparent the expected ways we communicate in the discipline and then socialising students into these conventions by providing examples, offering opportunities for students to practice their writing and giving them feedback. Yet this approach also assumes that once students have understood and mastered the academic ground rules they will be able to replicate these conventions straightforwardly. Both the study skills and socialisation approach to academic writing reflect what is described as a normative position in terms of reinforcing the existing values, attitudes, practices and communication patterns of the university as correct (Lillis and Scott, 2007).

While these approaches seek to address any discrepancies between students' prior knowledge or experiences and the requirements of the new university and disciplinary learning environment, they do not challenge these requirements or the issues of identity, power and authority that these practices can instate. These remedial and compensatory responses to student writing development, perhaps unsurprisingly, continue to dominate curriculum design and instruction (Lea and Street, 2006). An inclusive approach to writing, however, reflects a more transformative recognition and valuing of differences in the way we communicate. Instead of enforcing one permissible way of writing in university, what Lea and Street describe as a multiple, academic literacies approach supports students' critical exploration of writing and communication and how it relates to their identity. From this perspective, supporting students to write within the dominant modes of higher education such as the academic essay can be balanced with other opportunities to reflect on and challenge these conventions. Lillis (2006) argues that discussion about writing practices is central to this more inclusive pedagogy. She suggests a number of stages of dialogue about writing that create space for teachers and students to reflect on and test these academic conventions:

- teachers clearly explain the rules of different texts to explain how and why texts are written in the ways they are;
- teachers help students to identify these rules in practice so that the specifics of the language (for example, vocabulary, sentence or paragraph structure) and the genre (how the type of written task is organised and how it differs from other written formats, how reference is made to other texts) are made visible to students;
- students are given the opportunity to 'talk back' (Lillis, 2006: 42) to the texts they have written within: for example, the conventions of the academic essay. This means giving students space to 'say what she likes and doesn't like about the conventions she is expected to make meaning within' and explore other ways of expressing themselves outside these conventions. This could include exploring the potential of, for example, blogs, hypertext-enabled writing, visual and multimodal formats or collaboratively written wikis to disrupt the traditional essay or report as the sole mode for communicating academic knowledge.

This approach focuses on the texts 'in process' and creates opportunities for teachers and learners to examine, evaluate and generate new ways of communicating that are inclusive of a wider range of identities and meaning-making.

 Case study 8.1   An online approach to developing academic literacy in pharmacy (Wingate and Dreiss, 2009)

A discipline-embedded resource, the Scientific Writing Online Tool (SWOT), was piloted as part of the module 'Communicating Science' in the Pharmacy Department, King's College London. The aim of the tool was

(Continued)

(Continued)

to support students' understanding of a range of literacy tasks in their degree such as writing laboratory reports, essays and journal critiques and reading a range of academic and professional texts. The difficulties students experienced included how to synthesise information from scientific texts and use scientific terminology appropriately for different audiences. Students completed activities such as identifying the typical features and writing conventions of scientific writing in different texts such as an academic journal article, a pharmacy practice magazine article and material from newspapers. Other activities included identifying the criteria for 'good' and 'bad' laboratory reports using teacher feedback and applying these criteria to a previous student's assignment. Additional practical activities were designed to enable students to organise paragraphs in an unstructured text and divide long sentences into shorter sentences.

 Case study 8.2 Scaffolding students' understanding of genre in history (Wrigglesworth and McKeever, 2010)

Colleagues at the University of Portsmouth investigated the literacy challenges of students studying history by looking in detail at the structure and language of a document commentary which is a specific writing task for first-year undergraduate students in the department. They recognised that, far from there being an agreed single genre of history writing, students have to work with different source texts, different historical interpretations and expectations about how history is written. Building on their research into the nature of the genre, they developed learning activities, embedded into the curriculum, to help students understand and deconstruct the way the texts worked to make meaning. They created annotated exemplars of student document commentaries, including audio recordings with teachers talking about how the texts were constructed and demonstrate how experienced writers and assessors thought the text should be organised, what it should contain and the language it should use and why.

Drawing on the examples above, the following recommendations provide strategies to support all students to engage critically with the conventions of academic writing, as well as providing creative space for students to find alternative ways to express meaning:

- Give students an example of several different types of writing in the discipline: for example, a journal article, book review, newspaper or magazine article, textbook chapter or researcher's blog. Ask students to discuss the main purpose of each type of writing. Who is the intended audience? What is the intended use of the writing? How is this reflected in the language used, the formality of the voice or the structure of the writing? What are the advantages and disadvantages of the different genre for communicating meaning? Who might be included and who might be excluded by a particular mode of writing?
- Ask students to prepare a style guide for a specific literacy task that is used in the subject such as an essay, laboratory report, a business report, a reflective portfolio or an oral presentation. Give students prompts to help them structure their style guide. For example, should the writer/speaker be objective or subjective? What are the key structural features that are expected? How should you make reference to other sources? How formal is the language? Post up the best guides in the programme learning environment as a resource.
- Include a formative feedback opportunity for students to submit draft written work or a draft outline and get peer or teacher feedback on the format as well as the content of the written work. Use the student-developed style guide above as a self-assessment cover sheet or develop with students an assessment criteria matrix to evaluate the written work in relation to the disciplinary genre and language they have identified. Alternatively, set the students the task of annotating their written texts to elucidate the ways in which the text creates meaning and how the writer anticipates their reader's needs. Such activities provide opportunities to recognise the process of an assessment task as well as the product.
- Introduce alternative assessment formats that give students opportunities to explore and attempt to make meaning in different ways. Consider offering a range of assessment modes for all students using different genres. For example, offer students the choice of a written, narrated slideshare or oral presentation assessment to demonstrate how they fulfil learning outcomes. Introduce e-portfolio, blogging or patchwork text assessments which are made up of smaller written or visual pieces created during a module. These are then 'stitched' together in a final assessment often with an overarching narrative that ties the 'patches' together (Winter, 2003). The patchwork text assignment can be used specifically to provide space for students to collect different genres together and explore critically how differences in format or voice affect meaning-making (Trevelyan and Wilson, 2012). Concept maps, group presentations, podcasts, observed simulations or recorded presentations can also offer other ways to vary assessment tasks and emphasise different strengths across the curriculum as a whole (see case study 10.4).

Implementing inclusive learning and teaching in practice

Hockings (2010) defines inclusive learning and teaching in higher education as 'the ways in which pedagogy, curricula and assessment are designed and delivered to engage students in learning that is [...] accessible to all'. It is an educational approach that sees 'difference as the source of diversity that can enrich the lives and learning of others' (p. 1). This recognition of diversity where, for example, cultural differences between students from different countries can provide a rich resource for teachers, is explored in more detail in the following chapter on internationalising learning and teaching. Diversity of student perspectives can also inform a more critical understanding of the curriculum and the key texts, concepts, practices and traditions of the discipline. Inclusivity is also about ensuring equity, fairness and social justice in the classroom through careful reflection on the ways teaching, learning and assessment are accessible for some students while excluding others. Teaching inclusively is about:

- finding ways to diversify the teaching environment and challenging intentional and unintentional discrimination through inclusive learning and teaching;
- opening up the curriculum to contestation and different perspectives aligned to the needs, interests and experiences of all students;
- evaluating how we enable all students to demonstrate achievement without advantaging or disadvantaging some students over others.

Inclusive learning and teaching

For some teachers, meeting the needs of all students, particularly in terms of disabilities and 'hidden' disabilities (for example, dyslexia, dyspraxia, Asperger syndrome, epilepsy or mental health issues) or bringing unfamiliar inclusive content into the curriculum, is an alarming and overwhelming demand outside their expertise (Matthews, 2009). While in specific cases alternative equipment and support will need to be implemented, such as a scribe, additional time or alternative formats, in many cases putting in place inclusive learning and teaching practices is simply about putting effective learning and teaching into practice for all. The further readings at the end of the chapter have suggestions for ways to develop your inclusive practice but the following list suggests some initial ways to create an inclusive learning environment:

- Ensure all hand-outs, presentations and online materials meet accessibility requirements and use a sans serif font (Arial, Calibri) of at least 12pt for documents and 24pt for slides so they are easier to read for students with visual impairments or dyslexia.

- Insert alternative text (or 'alt text') or captions for images, tables or figures in presentations, videos and web resources for those using screen readers.
- Vary teaching methods such as lectures with more interactive methods of teaching and learning. Use visual and oral strategies as well as text to present new content. For instance, think about how you might present concepts or examples using mind maps, diagrams, images, graphs, videos and podcasts.
- Be sensitive to and, when necessary, challenge language, assumptions and stereotypes in terms of gender, sexuality, religion and race. Consider addressing questions of language and self-naming for different groups as part of the ground rules for discussion at the beginning of a module or seminar.
- Include a breadth of relevant topic examples that include ethnic minority, disability or gender diversity and manage group dynamics to ensure all students can be heard. Encourage students to relate topics and issues to their own experience but avoid asking students to 'speak' for any particular group.
- Counteract segregation in group work using formal mechanisms such as the allocation of random numbers or letters as the basis for organising students to work with peers both within and outside their usual social group. Create space to talk about the process of group work in diverse groups as well as the outputs (Singh, 2011).
- When introducing contentious topics use what Brookfield and Preskill (1999) describe as the 'five-minute rule' which is a strategy that enables the airing and testing of perspectives. It allows anyone to identify a neglected viewpoint or position and open it up to serious scrutiny for five minutes without criticism. This means believing that position and brainstorming the following questions: 1) What is interesting about this view? 2) If you believed this position, what would be different? 3) Under what conditions would this position be true?
- Peer assessment and peer-assisted learning can be useful for clarifying expectations about participation in specific teaching and learning activities and for calibrating students' understanding of assessment standards (Stevenson, 2012).

Inclusive curricula

Bhagat and O'Neill (2011) have suggested that when thinking about inclusion it is fundamental to consider the curriculum as an artefact and, in particular, the canonical texts, ideas, people and works of a discipline that are drawn upon to make the curriculum that are historically, contextually and socially situated. Auditing our curriculum for inclusivity means we need to ask critically:

- Whose perspectives and values does the curriculum put forward?
- Is the curriculum relevant and meaningful to a broader range of learners?
- Who does the curriculum include and who does it exclude?

For creative arts, humanities and social sciences disciplines, where the fundamental ethos of a curriculum can be predominantly interpretative, the possibility of opening up curricula to other points of view is entirely supportable, if not always enacted in practice. For those working in scientific disciplines, particularly the physical sciences, where scientific knowledge may be perceived as universal and acultural, such questions might seem initially irrelevant. It has been argued, however, that science education must similarly acknowledge the potential to have both an ethnocentric and androcentric bias. The university science curriculum can be seen to be dominated by Western and male interests and perspectives and may not acknowledge or value alternative perspectives or the contributions of the traditions of other cultures or women to scientific enterprise. The traditional Western male perspective, Bianchini *et al.* (2002) argue, has influenced research questions, methodological and interpretative practices and theoretical constructs as well as the way in which the results of scientific research are used in society. For example, how we classify race and ethnicity remain important concerns for understanding and using genetic research in biomedical science. Curricula in all disciplines, therefore, will benefit from a critical audit of the content and consideration of how it might reflect more pluralistic views. Including theories and examples from 'non-white' and 'non-Western' contexts in teaching and in reading lists helps to validate a wider range of perspectives (Stevenson, 2012).

Importantly, however, making the curriculum more inclusive needs to go further than introducing additional, potentially tokenistic, topics or perspectives outside the Western or white canon. An inclusive curriculum not only recognises a wider range of views but puts the traditional values of the disciplinary curriculum under critical scrutiny and engages students in debating potentially contentious and challenging topics. Diversifying the curriculum is about revisiting the content and structure in ways that recognise the contestability of knowledge, wider perspectives and accommodation of students' different experiences. One way to do this is by introducing contentious topics such as social justice, racism, misogyny or other discriminatory perspectives as productive issues within a curriculum across disciplines, not as marginal concerns but as central to the debates in the discipline. For example, the Race Relations (Amendments) Act can be examined in law, in medicine and nursing (the impact of religious and social differences such as these impact on healthcare decisions) or post-colonialism and feminist perspectives in relation to historical sources.

Inclusive assessment

Assessment is inevitably a key context for questions of parity and unequal attainment across a diverse student cohort. Some assessment choices might advantage some students while disadvantaging others in ways that are not relevant to differences between students' capacity to engage critically with subject material or master complex concepts. An inclusive approach to assessment means revisiting existing assessment methods and ensuring that the language and format used for the assessment is accessible and explicable to all students. An important next stage in developing inclusive assessment is recognising that module and programme learning outcomes can be assessed equally using different formats of assessment. Rather than just introducing these alternative formats exclusively for students with declared disabilities, using different modes of assessment for a single assessment task or using a range of assessment tools over a module or a programme for all students seeks to make assessment inclusive for all students. Clear criteria and scrutiny of assessment tasks and criteria for bias helps to ensure fairness in assessment (Stevenson, 2012; Singh, 2011). As an educator looking to develop a more flexible and inclusive assessment strategy, it is important to consider:

- What are the learning outcomes you want to assess? For example, is accurate spelling and grammar always essential when assessing quality of understanding or can assessment criteria be more flexible?
- What are the barriers for different students in relation to successfully demonstrating achievement of the learning outcomes in each mode of assessment?
- How might these learning outcomes be assessed using different modes of assessment open to all students? For example, how might you utilise a range of different tasks emphasising visual, oral, written and performance skills across the curriculum?
- How can feedback be given to students using different formats – for example, written narrative feedback, podcasts, oral one-to-one or group feedback, annotated exemplars or in tabulated formats – to enable students to receive feedback at different times in ways that align to their preferences as well as clarifying expectations and assessment criteria?

Focus on practice

Select a module you currently teach and audit it in relation to the learning and teaching strategies you use, the curriculum content and processes or assessment. The further reading suggestions can help with this audit. How are you responsive to the diversity of your group and how do use this diversity to inform learning and teaching?

Conclusion

In this chapter, we have considered the ways in which educators conceptualise and respond to the differences in experience, prior knowledge, perspective and approach that widening participation in higher education should bring to the debates, questions and practices of universities. An inclusive curriculum is multi-dimensional, needs to take into account a range of issues and is context-specific: minority participants in one context might constitute the majority identity of students in other contexts. Critically auditing current practice in terms of ensuring equal participation for all students is an important aspect of responding to student diversity. Ultimately, however, inclusive practice that recognises the needs of all students and engages critically with contentious and multiple perspectives underpins a curriculum that is good for all students, not just those who might be identified as 'non-traditional'. Recognising and incorporating diversity of experiences, values and views into learning and teaching is enriching for all students. Inclusive approaches can create transformative opportunities for teachers and challenge the reproduction of existing structures of power and privilege through curricula that have historically excluded individuals on the basis of differences of ethnicity, gender, sexuality, religion and disability.

Further reading

Grace, Sue and Gravestock, Phil (2009) *Inclusion and Diversity: Meeting the Needs of All Students*. New York: Routledge.
A comprehensive text providing a detailed account of the implications of inclusivity and practical strategies in relation to small and large group teaching, online learning and the wider student experience outside the classroom.

Griffiths, Sandra (2010) *Teaching for Inclusion in Higher Education: A Guide to Practice* (http://www.qub.ac.uk/directorates/AcademicStudentAffairs/Centrefor EducationalDevelopment/CurriculumDevelopment/Inclusion/).
A detailed guide to auditing and enhancing practice based on research on student experience. Designed as a workbook, it offers suggestions for inclusive practice in relation to learning and teaching, curriculum, assessment and teaching spaces.

Jisc TechDis (http://www.jisctechdis.ac.uk/techdis/resources).
A set of resources to support educators to prepare and evaluate presentations, documents and webpages to ensure they are accessible for all students.

'Universities Scotland Race Equality Toolkit' (http://www.universities-scotland.ac.uk/raceequalitytoolkit/)
A resource providing guidance on how to integrate race and equality debates into the curriculum across a full range of disciplinary curricula and embedding inclusivity into learning, teaching and assessment practice.

CHAPTER 9

INTERNATIONALISING TEACHING IN PRACTICE

Learning objectives

This chapter will support you to:

- Develop your understanding of international undergraduate and postgraduate students' learning experiences and how you can internationalise the curriculum;
- Plan and facilitate inclusive approaches to content, teaching, learning and assessment that create effective intercultural experiences for all students;
- Explore the skills and knowledge that educators need to contribute to effective international collaboration and participate in transnational education.

Introduction

As the social and professional spheres of individual experience have become increasingly globalised, universities are adapting to the opportunities for economic, technological and cultural mobility and integration. Many universities and employers are now emphasising the need for graduates to be competent world citizens capable of acting effectively across cultural and national borders. For many prospective students, the opportunity to travel and study in countries away from their home is seen as an important contributor to their personal growth and future employability. In the UK in 2012–13, international students made up 18 per cent of the UK student population. There is, however, significant variation in international student numbers between regions and between disciplines. For example, data for 2011–12 shows that over a third of all students enrolled in business studies, engineering or technology subjects are international compared to a tenth of students studying subjects related to education, history, philosophy or biological sciences (UKCISA, 2015). In the context of this rapidly changing international student market, there are three related strands to the internationalisation agenda for UK higher education (Knight, 2004):

- international student recruitment and the enhancement of the international student experience;
- the inclusion of an international, intercultural or global dimension into the curriculum as the basis for enabling the development of intercultural skills and a global world-view for all students. This is often called 'internationalisation at home';
- internationalisation activities that are focused on working with students in countries outside the UK through distance learning, collaborative agreements with other universities or governments, branch campuses or franchises. This is cross-border or transnational education with students studying in a different country to the awarding institution.

The university you work in, the subject and level you teach and the institutional mission can, therefore, determine the nature and extent of internationalisation you will encounter. It is also important to recognise the complexities involved in developing an internationalised curriculum and effective intercultural pedagogies. National cultures are not static or homogeneous entities but dynamic and constantly evolving. Categories such as Western, Asian, Middle Eastern or Confucian do not encapsulate the diversity of the individual cultural experiences and affiliations of students within these identities. In addition, as we explored in the previous chapter, a student's national or cultural background intersects with other identities such as gender, economic background, class, sexuality and race that will also inform a student's beliefs, perspectives and world-views. This has led some to critique the term 'internationalisation' because it overlooks how these other identities intersect with nationality. Welikala (2011) suggests that the alternative term 'multi-perspective curriculum' encapsulates the diversity of perspectives beyond what is traditionally represented by nationality. This includes interdisciplinarity, alternative world-views and comparative approaches to teaching and learning. In this chapter we will begin from the position that engaging with the internationalisation agenda can be about identifying ways to work with and integrate international students into the UK context. A 'multi-perspective' approach, however, enables us also to use international experiences to question the pedagogic norms and conventions of our discipline or institution in creative ways.

The lucrative recruitment of higher fee-paying international students to UK institutions can be seen as a primary motivation for the promotion of an international agenda. The internationalisation and marketisation of higher education are often connected in describing the changing nature and purpose of higher education in the UK (Kandiko, 2013a). Ensuring that international students are effectively integrated into the classroom and supported in their studies is often seen as the first challenge for many teachers. Yet approaches to internationalisation have progressively emphasised other, more critical goals.

In a global employment market, many graduates will need to be able to communicate and collaborate across cultures even if they do not live or work abroad. A diverse university community represents a microcosm of that future globalised world of work. International students bring with them a cultural and intellectual diversity that can contribute to an international learning environment. Their experiences and knowledge create the opportunity for a diversified student cohort to interact and collaborate in ways that foster mutual intercultural understanding as the basis for developing student world-mindedness. The aim is not to assimilate international students into a UK academic culture but to benefit from their different perspectives. Such objectives can be underpinned by a commitment to cultural tolerance, pluralism, global ethics and sustainability (Haigh, 2002; Otter, 2007). This form of internationalisation can enrich academic knowledge and pedagogies by extending the range of perspectives from different intellectual traditions that are applied to complex issues. As we explored in Chapter 3, global challenges such as environmental sustainability, international development, food and water security, health, geopolitics, poverty and globalisation can only be addressed through the interdisciplinary and international collaboration of experts from a range of fields (Knight, 2004).

A further dimension of internationalisation is the growing international mobility of academic staff. You or your colleagues may be teaching and researching in English as a second language and have studied and worked in different cultural and educational systems. These differences can usefully bring an international perspective to the curriculum content and teaching and learning approaches. Yet the assumptions, expectations and practices of both local and international teachers may also add to the complexity of managing the intercultural learning environment of contemporary UK campuses (Slade *et al.*, 2012; Luxon and Peelo, 2009). Conversely, where institutions are expanding their provision beyond the borders of the UK, educators may find that they are working online or face-to-face with students who all share the same linguistic or cultural background and are studying in their 'home' country. In these contexts, it may be the teacher who is the 'outsider' and expected to conform to the host nation's culture and conventions (Leask, 2007; Smith, 2009).

Despite the opportunities that internationalisation can offer for enhancing student learning, the proximity of local and international students and teachers in a university does not automatically garner positive outcomes or achieve the types of intercultural learning that might be projected (Leask and Carroll, 2011). The challenges that many teachers and students perceive include:

- lack of integration between students from different nationalities and cultural backgrounds;
- variable language proficiency and cross-cultural communication problems;
- Anglo-centric or non-inclusive curricula that do not encourage contributions from different perspectives or value alternative ways of making or validating knowledge;
- learning and teaching approaches that clash with prior educational experiences and cultural norms: for example, in relation to participation in class or academic skills such as critical thinking;
- lack of clarity about assessor expectations, including difficulties in decoding assessment rubric and unfamiliar forms of assessment such as group tasks, portfolios or presentations;
- mismatches between different conceptions of authorship, originality and plagiarism and alternative, culturally determined understandings of argumentation and academic referencing;
- generalising or stereotyping of international student behaviours and attitudes (De Vita, 2007).

The potential consequences of not responding to these challenges are reinforcing cultural misunderstandings and stereotypes as well as the loss of transformative learning opportunities for all students (Haigh, 2002).

Importantly, however, although these challenges impact on the experiences, retention and outcomes of non-UK students studying in UK institutions, in many cases, they are not exclusive to international students. Homogenising the perceived behaviours of students from different national and cultural backgrounds and polarising international and local students oversimplifies the complex issues of diversity that exist across a student cohort (Tian and Lowe, 2013).

National and cultural identities have been used to better engage diverse student groups. In understanding the international classroom it is fundamental to remember, however, that 'the culture is not the person' (Cortazzi and Jin, 1997: 89). As well as recognising that nationality is only part of any student's identity, in the context of the discipline, department and the university, 'All students are to a large degree "cultural others" seeking acceptance in the academic cultural community' (Leask, 2006: 187). To become acculturated into the academic community of the department and university, both local and international students have to understand and learn to work appropriately within the often unfamiliar conventions of the university. Teaching and assessment strategies that seek to explicate these rules for international students, therefore, are likely to benefit all students, not just international students (Ryan and Carroll, 2005).

Building on the debates we began to explore in the previous chapter, we will examine how the international student experience is enhanced through more inclusive teaching, learning and assessment strategies. Moving on from addressing the initial challenges that internationalisation might pose, however, we will then consider how the diversity of local and international students is an asset that enriches the learning experience of all students and teachers. Fundamental to this enhancement is awareness of differences between diverse perspectives and identities, the introduction of multiple and comparative perspectives into the curriculum that profitably challenge a Western-centric view of knowledge and deliberately building the capacity of students and their teachers to understand the relationships and resource-rich context of multicultural modules (Tange and Kastberg, 2013). Finally, we will examine the demands of undertaking international academic roles in transnational education and how professional practice is developed through critical reflection on intercultural collaborations.

Working with international students

Many responses to the international student experience adopt, either deliberately or unintentionally, a deficit perspective (Ryan and Carroll, 2005). This is sustained by the dominance of a European or Western world-view across academic, cultural, political and economic spheres. Post-colonial analysis has exposed how this position is constructed through political, intellectual, cultural and moral discourses. This includes prioritising the values, interests and language of Western intellectual traditions and their educational systems (Said, 1978). For international students, the educational and academic work (scholarship, publications, conferences) of UK, US and Australian higher education are often perceived as a 'centre' in unequal relation to the 'periphery' of other intellectual and educational traditions (Canagarajah, cited in Robinson-Pant, 2009: 419). These are regarded as education 'systems with status, power and valuable knowledge, especially English language competence'. Within these systems, international students can experience their own positions as deficient in terms of the academic skills and knowledge required for study at the higher level (Koehne, 2006: 244–5). The presence of these dominant cultural beliefs may 'imply that students need to free themselves from previous learning identities in order to be successful in a "Western" educational system' (Montgomery, 2010: 124). From this perspective, working with international students primarily involves acculturating them into the practices of UK institutions as rapidly as possible.

The association between a student's cultural background and their perceived approaches to learning is widely reported. Montgomery (2010) notes, for example, the claim that Chinese students are more likely to adopt memorisation or rote learning practices aligned to poorer learning outcomes. She also identifies individualist and collectivist societies as another conventional way of distinguishing between cultural backgrounds to understand student behaviours. Individualist societies include those found in western and northern European, Australasian and north American countries. Collectivist societies include those found in Asian, African and eastern European countries. Further research, however, has suggested that the easy binaries of 'deep' and 'surface' approaches to learning, 'Western' and 'Eastern' cultures or individualist and collectivist societies are reductive and inappropriate ways to understand the complexities of the international student lived experience. A fundamental consideration when seeking to understand the international student experience as an alternative to this deficit view is that all students bring with them an individual, personal history. They will have experiences of different, sometimes multiple, intellectual traditions that they need to adapt to the specific demands of their new institutional context (Koehne, 2006).

The main conclusions of this research identify three principles that can frame our practice when working with international students:

- the academic practices of the 'Western' university are not culture-free but embedded in the values and discourses of the dominant intellectual and educational tradition of their context;
- international students are 'bearers of alternative knowledge, perspectives and life experiences' and their presence in the classroom and in the curriculum is a 'source of dialogical strength, not a liability' (Ryan and Carroll, 2005: 9; Brookfield and Preskill, 1999: 99);
- many students, not exclusively international students, entering university can feel 'estranged from the language, culture and practices' of the university.

This has 'the potential to provoke the sense of [...] disorientation, of invisibility, voicelessness, and ineffectualness' (Mann, 2001: 10–11). Hence, enhancing practice to engage rather than alienate international students is likely to be of some benefit to all students (Ryan and Carroll, 2005).

The implication of these principles is the need to scrutinise the assumptions about learning, teaching and knowledge creation that both teachers and students bring to the classroom. As we explored in Chapter 2, as an experienced member of the academic and subject community, through doctoral study or professional experience, you may be so familiar with the specific ways of understanding and communicating your subject that these are essentially invisible to you (McLean and Ransom, 2005). Identifying the implicit culture of teaching, learning, knowledge creation and assessment regimes in the disciplinary and institutional context is central to supporting all students. The high population of international students doing doctoral research in the UK also requires a specific focus on how the supervisor–supervisee relationship can be managed in intercultural contexts.

Focus on practice

Identify and reflect on an occasion in your teaching or research practice where there was a misunderstanding on the basis of the different national, institutional, cultural or educational background of those involved.

- What assumptions or values did this misunderstanding reveal about the way you and others engage in academic practice regarding, for example, beliefs about student participation, collaboration or responsibilities?
- How did you make your expectations explicit to everyone involved?
- How did other perspectives on knowledge creation and communication impact on your own assumptions? In what ways could the experience enable you to critique the norms and conventions of your own cultural, educational or intellectual position?

Teaching and supervision in the international classroom

Ryan and Viete (2009) identify three principles for successful learning in the international classroom: 'feelings of belonging; being valued as a person with knowledge; and being able to communicate effectively, creatively and confidently' (p. 309). These reiterate the principles of a student-engaged classroom. Creating a safe space that acknowledges and works with diversity is the basis for the future interactions of a multinational group and building a sense of belonging in the group (De Vita, 2000). This is particularly important where students may feel isolated because of the cultural, social and emotional aspects of living and studying in a new country. Including icebreaker activities that help to surface diversity of background and experience in non-threatening ways can also serve to clarify academic expectations in a new context and set ground rules for participation. Some examples of introductory activities that could be adapted for use at the beginning of a module are summarised in Table 9.1.

Table 9.1 Icebreaker activities for international groups

Activity	Description
Stereotypes	Students individually begin by giving examples of the stereotypes of their own country of origin and then evaluate the validity of these different stereotypes. Use this as the basis for challenging stereotyping behaviour and encouraging learning more about the different cultures, including those of UK students, represented in the group (De Vita, 2000)
Naming ourselves	Students individually reflect on the ethnic, cultural or class group or groups they most identify with. Then everyone takes it in turn to introduce themselves, the group or groups they belong to and how they would like that group to be referred to in future discussion (Brookfield and Preskill, 1999). It encourages students to think about identity, intersectionality and the negative and positive power of language
Line up	If students are only working with a few members of a group, one way to encourage working with new people is to manage groups. Ask the whole group to line up in order based according to a specified category. For example, alphabetically in relation to first or family name, birth month order, journey time to the session. Use this to organise seating positions or groups as a way to integrate the group and get students to sit and work with different colleagues (UKCISA, 2009)
Comfort zones	Students are encouraged to discuss reasons for choosing their seat. Ask students to then talk to someone they do not normally work with and explore the barriers or discomforts of talking to someone new. Consider what the benefits might be in speaking to different people on a topic and how to maximise their learning through collaborative working (UKCISA, 2009)
Ground rules	Students collaboratively develop ground rules for small group learning processes, including, for example, the different roles of teachers and students in discussion, expectations about turn-taking, silence and participation or respectful listening (Ryan, 2005). This clarifies expectations and assumptions for all students about their role in potentially unfamiliar learning contexts
Commonalities	Small groups of students create a list of the things they all have in common. These might relate to prior study or areas of interest in module topics or might be related to hobbies or other personal experiences or skills. Then each group identifies something that is unique to each member of the group. These common and unique interests, characteristics, traits or skills provide the opportunity to encourage discussion, to explore shared beliefs or values and identify potentially valuable skills and knowledge that different students bring to the group

Some of these activities emphasise difference in the group (for example, naming ourselves, comfort zones) and others promote unity by emphasising what different students have in common (commonalities). There are risks in opening differences up to scrutiny in such explicit ways and we need to judge carefully whether a group is ready to manage the outcomes of these activities (Brookfield and Preskill, 1999). If the purpose is made clear, however, they can be powerful tools to engage critically with the different values, perspectives and expectations represented in the class as the basis for learning.

 Case study 9.1   Valuing student cultural knowledge and skills in engineering (Rodriguez-Falcon *et al.*, 2011)

Colleagues in the Department of Mechanical Engineering at the University of Sheffield wanted to embed multicultural awareness into the engineering curriculum by building on the knowledge, skills and experiences students bring to their learning. The aim was to develop students' understanding of working in international engineering projects. A third-year module on Engineering Management includes the learning outcome related to successful project management through cross-cultural working. After a lecture on managing international projects, students and teachers share personal cultural anecdotes and students are asked to identify the behaviours that someone must and must not demonstrate to participate socially or professionally in their country of origin. These examples can relate to personal habits, greetings, relationships to colleagues and typical business, governmental or administrative practices. For example, students suggest that a project leader in Kuwait must socialise and get to know project colleagues but must not leave a meeting without drinking tea or coffee. These suggestions are discussed, critiqued and collated into a peer-learning guide and distributed to all students on the module as a tool for raising awareness of cultural differences in professional contexts.

In the case of postgraduate supervision, different cultural and educational backgrounds can influence supervisor and student expectations about the supervisory relationship and the aims and practices of research. For example:

- language proficiency, disciplinary literacy and the anticipated role of the supervisor in editing text, particularly if students are writing in English as a second language;
- the role of the supervisor and student during supervision, such as autonomy and equal engagement with the supervisor as a colleague in the academic community (Wang and Li, 2011);

- uncertainty about the aims of a thesis and the need for the student to develop an original argument and express their position in relation to the field (Knight, 1999);
- in social science and related disciplines, challenges in undertaking fieldwork in new cultural settings or using new, potentially contentious, research methodologies in their home context (Robinson-Pant, 2009; Robinson-Pant, 2010);
- in sciences, socio-cultural challenges such as student discomfort in seeking guidance when experiments are failing or seeking support in laboratories (Frost, 1999).

Again, many of the challenges that international postgraduate students may experience reflect those of UK students who may be equally uncertain about their relationship with their supervisor or demands of thesis writing. As with working with undergraduate students, however, it is important to recognise the value that international research students bring both to their own and other's research. Deficit views of research students that focus on assimilating them into UK doctoral practices overlook the ways in which research students bring new perspectives that can enrich research questions and outcomes. The initial tensions between supervisor and student views about knowledge creation can provoke powerful insights that problematise some of the assumptions and norms of the discipline. This can generate theses that will draw productively on more than one academic tradition (Cadman, 2000).

Strategies for supporting international students

There are a number of ways in which you can ensure that your teaching reflects the principles of inclusivity for international students:

- Consider how you can make it possible for students to 'see themselves in the curriculum' (Leask, 2007: 88) by including not only UK examples, but also case studies and other relevant teaching materials from cross-cultural contexts.
- The conventions of university small group or discussion-based teaching may be unfamiliar, so be explicit about your expectations at the beginning of the programme and model respectful interactions yourself (De Vita, 2007). For example, what is the purpose of discussion? Is it acceptable to interrupt someone? Do you have to wait until you are asked a direct question to contribute? Is silence appropriate?
- International students will have context-specific and authentic knowledge and perspectives that can enhance your learning and that of their peers: for example, in-depth knowledge of a relevant issue such as immigration,

technology use, environmental sustainability or healthcare in their home country. Alternatively, they have experiences of working in a second language or of culture shock and transition. This gives you scope to give different students the role of expert at different points and value their specific knowledge and experience (Cruickshank *et al.*, 2012).

- Bilingual students may have slower reading and listening speeds than their English-speaking counterparts even though they have achieved the language requirements for the programme. In both lectures and small groups pay attention to the pace of delivery, use repetition to ensure that key points are clear and use a range of oral and visual prompts to convey key terms or concepts in presentations (De Vita, 2000).

- Large volumes of reading can be difficult for bilingual students and they may not be clear about the relationship between independent reading and taught sessions. Consider uploading presentations in advance of a lecture as well as providing a glossary and annotated reading lists if appropriate. Instead of long reading lists, indicate key texts and chapters to help focus reading (Ryan, 2005).

- Critical reading, sourcing information and evaluation of arguments may also be unfamiliar academic skills, especially if prior educational experiences have adopted more didactic models of teaching. Scaffolding reading by providing students with prompt questions to support critical approaches can make these academic demands more explicit (McLean and Ransom, 2005). Examples of these prompts are suggested in Figure 2.2.

- Be aware of your communication practices and avoid colloquial speech and idioms. Humour, popular culture references, analogies and brand names are often culturally specific and hence potentially meaningless to those from other contexts.

- Bilingual students may find it helpful to practice or test out ideas before contributing them to the rest of the group in English. Cruickshank *et al.* (2012) recommend encouraging students to work on a task alone, then exchange their ideas in pairs before contributing to the class as a whole. This works towards improving international student confidence to participate equally in discussions.

- In the case of doctoral candidates, being explicit about expectations at the beginning of the supervision process in relation to supervision roles and thesis writing is fundamental, especially if students are new to the UK context. Early on in the relationship discuss expectations about supervisor and student responsibilities, how feedback is given and received, how meetings are scheduled, who sets the agenda and how records will be kept in line with institutional requirements (Wang and Li, 2011).

International students and assessment

If participation in unfamiliar teaching and learning methods can pose problems for students when the purpose and rules are not explicit, assessment is where cultural difference can be converted into disadvantaging some students. There are a number of issues that may arise in relation to the assessment of international students. First, assessment mechanisms may equate proficiency of language use, accuracy of spelling, grammar and confidence in communication with academic ability and high-level outcomes such as critical thinking (Ryan, 2005). Also assessments that are based wholly on recognising and rewarding work that reflects a 'Western-template of knowledge' may disadvantage international students (Mackinnon and Manathunga, 2003). In UK higher education the written essay or report dominate assessment, though this is not the case internationally (Duhs, 2013). No single assessment tool is culturally inclusive. Using a range of different assessment methods over the course of a programme can enable you to reward different ways of knowing and address the potential cross-cultural gap in relation to essay writing practices (De Vita, 2007; Robson *et al.*, 2013). The process of giving and receiving effective written feedback on assessment is more powerful if it is understood as a dialogue, as we explored in Chapter 5. Written comments convey a number of messages about the purpose of academic writing. This can include the nature of knowledge in the discipline and the conventions of academic practice (Ivanič *et al.*, 2000). As with other forms of cross-cultural communication, however, the feedback conversation between teachers and students can be fraught with miscommunication. When written feedback is given, it is important to remember that 'both the intended and the received meanings pass through cultural filters' that can impact on the academic and emotional experience of feedback (Tian and Lowe, 2013: 585). There is limited empirical evidence to suggest international students are more likely to plagiarise than UK students, yet it is recognised that what is defined as plagiarism is culturally dependent. It has been suggested that international students, and specifically those working in English as a second language, may be at increased risk of using literacy practices such as 'patchwriting', a form of paraphrasing where novice writers link multiple source texts together (Pecorari, 2003). This approach can lead to an allegation of plagiarism without the student necessarily intending to cheat (Maxwell *et al.*, 2008; Abasi and Graves, 2008).

Unless accuracy of English-language use is a specific learning outcome, assessment judgements about the quality of argument and demonstration of critical thinking should be made on the basis of how well a student has achieved these outcomes. This is without diminishing the robustness of the assessment process itself, which is sometimes a fear of teachers in response to the specific issues international students pose for traditional assessment regimes (Duhs, 2013). The form and function of academic writing and the meanings of critical analysis or evaluation are not neutral or universal concepts. They are reflective of particular cultural values and ways of making and communicating meaning. Students working in English as a second language may not be familiar with assumptions about the hierarchical organisation of argument, authorial voice or critical evaluation that is expected as a matter of course in the UK context. English rhetorical style has linear ways of organising an argument using connecting words or phrases to link ideas, sentences and paragraphs. Connecting phrases such as 'also', 'in contrast', 'so that' or 'for example' enable a native English writer to extend an argument, compare and contrast, provide examples and order ideas. Different discourse styles, however, reflect culturally different ways of making meaning and may not utilise these ways of building an argument. For example, other languages may adopt more circular, digressive or repetitive rhetorical patterns (De Vita, 2000; Mackinnon and Manathunga, 2003). In addition, the notion of adopting a position by critically evaluating and drawing conclusions from a range of alternatives is central to English-language conceptions of argumentation. This may not be an obvious or, indeed, comfortable expectation for students if their prior academic experience has been shaped by educational values such as respect for expert authority or demonstration of content mastery (Cortazzi and Jin, 1997).

A dialogue-based approach to assessment feedback is a fundamental opportunity to clarify the expectations of assessment and make explicit some of the tacit assumptions about the type of student engagement with module content that is desirable. As well as conveying important messages about the values of the discipline and institution, feedback on assessment also has a significant emotional dimension and impact on self-esteem (Mutch, 2003). If strategies that led to assessment success in prior education result in poor outcomes in the UK environment this can significantly impact on students' feelings of self-efficacy and confidence in the new setting (Tian and Lowe, 2013).

Strategies for assessment and feedback for international students

There are a number of ways to enhance the experience of assessment and feedback for international students that will, inevitably, also improve the assessment process for local students. These strategies do not aim to lower standards but to ensure that the expectations and assumptions of assessment are made more explicit. This ensures that the assessment is not testing the capacity of students to decode the assessment process itself but rather their engagement with the content and the quality of that engagement. The following strategies will help to clarify assessment and enhance feedback for all students:

- Demystify assessment tasks and criteria by getting students to adopt a more active role in assessment. Engage students in discussion about the nature of the assessment task, including what it is that an assessor is looking for by analysing the assessment criteria. For example, scaffold peer assessment activities using feedback grids mapped to assessment criteria or use interactive cover sheets that increase student responsibility for self-evaluating their learning. 'Interactive cover sheets' are submitted with an assessment and have space for students to self-evaluate their work against the criteria or to identify what specific aspects of the assessment they would like to receive feedback on. When giving feedback, the marker responds to these student-generated questions about the work (Bloxham and Campbell, 2010).
- Include marks to recognise the process as well as the product of assessment tasks (for example, information handling and organisation of the argument rather than reproduction of the lecture or textbook). The academic essay is 'a coded artefact which is judged by what are inherently language based criteria (quality of original expression, accordance with convention etc.)' (Walden and Peacock, 2006: 203). Including evidence of the process of researching a topic, such as notes, keywords, data sources or mind maps, that help to explicate the process of developing ideas and managing information as part of the assessment ensures students are recording their sources and thinking about how they use them in the final essay or report.
- Use text-match software such as Turnitin as the basis for developing a critical engagement with source-use rather than only for detection of plagiarism. Introduce a short formative assessment early in a module as part of the introduction to academic practice in the discipline: for instance, alongside information on referencing conventions in the module handbook. Teachers or peers then focus specifically on giving feedback on examples of poor paraphrasing, plagiarism and poor citation as well as other aspects of the writing process (Ireland and English, 2011).
- In the case of doctoral candidates, Kamler and Thomson (2006) suggest that writing a thesis should be understood as identity work and that students are writing themselves into being scholars. The process of writing shapes their identity and, vice versa, their emerging identity as researchers shapes their writing. Scaffolding critical reading of example theses, conference papers and research articles can explain the different institutional expectations and academic conventions. This supports international students to critically evaluate issues such as voice, audience and how arguments are built (Li and Vandermensbrugghe, 2011).

Developing intercultural learning for all students

Building on the benefits of the international experience for students travelling to study in other countries, the 'internationalisation at home' agenda focuses on how to draw intercultural encounters and international content into the curriculum. Internationalising the curriculum aims to achieve outcomes for all students such as greater openness, respect and understanding of 'otherness', a breadth of international perspectives on fundamental debates and professional work environments and also a greater capacity to be self-aware and critique their own cultural position (Haigh, 2002). One rationale for designing global curricula is to create programmes that will appeal to international students in the competitive global marketplace. Internationalising the curriculum at home can take a number of forms (van de Wende, cited in Dunne, 2011):

- curricula with a unifying international theme such as Global Health, International Management or Global Environmental Change;
- curricula with an interdisciplinary and area studies focus such as European, Asian or African Studies;
- approaches to internationalisation that focus on including beginner or advanced language modules as core elements of the curriculum;
- curricula where the traditional subject content has been infused with international and comparative approaches and content so that there are case studies, examples and references from 'non-Western' and 'non-white' perspectives.

Programmes designed specifically to engage with international and interdisciplinary subjects often build on the international research and professional experiences of teachers and researchers. Internationalising more traditional curriculum experiences, however, can be challenging. Research has also suggested that attitudes to internationalisation are discipline-dependent. Social sciences, applied and humanities subjects may be more likely to engage with international perspectives as part of the content. In science subjects, however, it has been suggested that there is more resistance to the idea of internationalising the curriculum (Clifford, 2009; Sawir, 2011). In these subjects the content might be considered to be already international on the basis that factual content is ostensibly objective or value-free and hence universal. In already-packed curricula, there are also inevitable concerns that introducing additional international elements into the curriculum dilutes disciplinary learning (Kandiko, 2013b). As Clifford (2009) argues, however, many science students will be applying science knowledge within international careers and hence will also 'need some understanding of global issues and have ways of making ethical judgements about their work' in different cultural contexts with different moral or ethical parameters (p. 142).

Embedding intercultural learning into existing curricula develops cross-cultural communication skills, promotes inclusive and tolerant approaches to diversity and develops critical awareness of different ways of creating knowledge that are essential for living and working globally (Summers and Volet, 2008). It is only through deliberate strategies such as intercultural group work that such outcomes are translated into the lived experience of students rather than an abstract topic in the curriculum (De Vita, 2000). Despite the increase in international students in the classroom, however, there still may be limited interaction between international students and UK students. UK and international students can also express negative attitudes towards working with their peers or view intercultural group work as a diversion from achieving disciplinary outcomes (Leask and Carroll, 2011; Cruickshank *et al.*, 2012).

Designing and implementing intercultural learning in multicultural groups

There is general agreement about the factors that will facilitate effective intercultural activities in the curriculum:

- Activities should be designed to draw explicitly on the diversity of perspectives and experiences of group members to complete the task (Arkoudis *et al.*, 2012). For example, in medical-related disciplines a task could draw on students' experiences of community pharmacies or healthcare provision in different countries to compare legal, ethical or professional practices (Edmead, 2013).
- Anticipated intercultural objectives should be discussed at the beginning of tasks and included explicitly in learning outcomes. Assessment should also be structured in ways that ensure students understand what and how intercultural skills are being assessed (Leask, 2009).
- Interaction is, in itself, insufficient for achieving intercultural learning unless opportunities for reflection are built into the task and assessment (De Vita, 2005). It is important for teachers and students to experience and reflect on intercultural differences in ways that enable them to 'make strange' and appraise critically their own cultural position as part of their developing personal awareness (Leask, 2013). Reflection might include, for example, examination of multicultural behaviours and communication patterns. Prompts to support this include: 'What is the most important thing you have

learnt from working in a multicultural group?'; 'What is the most important thing to remember when working in a multicultural team?'; 'What information about other people's culture or country have you been able to learn?' (Woods *et al.*, 2011: 64).

Case study 9.2   Internationalising the undergraduate chemistry curriculum (Overton and Bradley, 2010)

Overton and Bradley developed a case study as part of a first-year undergraduate chemistry programme at the University of Hull to include an international context. This reflected the increasing globalisation of chemistry and particularly the expansion of the manufacturing and pharmaceutical industry in Asia. The 'Titan Project' case study provided opportunities to explore applied chemistry related to cultural internationalisation in an industrial scenario. The case study was based on the industrial production of titanium dioxide; students needed to reach conclusions about continuing, expanding or replacing the current production processes at a location in India. Drawing on trade press reports, students had to evaluate the available options at the fictional site in relation to local industry customers, raw materials, ports and the power and transport networks. The case study was assessed by oral presentation of their recommendations, review of analytical methods and peer assessment of group work.

Focus on practice

Choose a module in which you would like to develop students' international and intercultural understanding. How can you revise the module learning outcomes to include a global dimension relevant to the subject? For example, in medicine, the learning outcome 'Select and justify an appropriate diabetes patient treatment plan' could be revised to include awareness of cultural differences: 'Select and justify a culturally sensitive diabetes patient treatment plan'. In computer sciences, the learning outcome 'Design and build a software application fit for a specific business use' could be revised to take into account the global business market: 'Design a software application for international business use that takes into account cross-cultural users'. What learning and teaching strategies will support students to develop these revised learning outcomes?

Teaching across borders: internationalisation abroad

With the expansion of international collaborative agreements between institutions and new international campuses, more teachers are engaging in short-term transnational education activities. The intensive face-to-face teaching experiences of 'flying faculty' have distinctive demands that can be under-supported by institutions. In addition to the intercultural issues comparable to those faced by teachers working with international students at home, the challenges of teaching for short periods of time in other countries include:

- physical and emotional stress as a result of jet-lag, intensive teaching work-loads in the transnational context, ongoing teaching workloads for domestic students during absence and culture shock;
- working collaboratively with local teachers in transnational teaching teams;
- tensions between a perceived need to deliver UK-equivalent curriculum experiences for international students and the adaptation of curricula to fit local needs;
- tensions between respect for cultural values in the transnational context while also creating a bridge between the international campus and UK-based institution;
- different goals, motivations and experience of students undertaking trans-national programmes.

Although there is still limited formal support for staff undertaking these types of activities and equally limited research into the experiences of transnational staff and students, there are a number of recommendations for preparing for this type of teaching (Gribble and Zirguras, 2003; Dunn and Wallace, 2006; Smith, 2014).

Building on the suggestions above for working with international students or managing intercultural groups as a transnational educator you can:

- Familiarise yourself with country-specific information concerning the local education system, cultural, political and legal context, as well the regional labour market, to develop your understanding of student prior experience and motivation.
- Explore opportunities to collaborate with local teachers to understand the teaching environment and share understanding of how to develop key student intellectual skills such as critical thinking and reflective practice in context.
- Review curriculum content, learning, teaching and assessment to explore how it might be infused with appropriate international perspectives such as

country-relevant case studies, examples and opportunities to consider application of concepts to host country.
- Review the availability of country- and language-specific scholarly journals, books and other resources to augment existing resources.

As when working with international students in the UK context, valuing student prior knowledge and experiences is central to developing intercultural teaching in international contexts and can also enrich the transnational curriculum. Transnational teaching experiences, however, also provide valuable mutual learning opportunities for travelling educators. The experience of working in new contexts with culturally different students and colleagues can lead you to see teaching in your home institution through a new lens. The experience of being 'other' in transnational contexts raises critical questions about the assumptions we bring to our role and relationships in our teaching, learning and assessment. Using the experiences of working in contexts that defamiliarise 'normal' teaching practices can be transformational (Smith, 2009). Reviewing your curricula and your practices in the light of these experiences will foster valuable insights into the experiences of both local and international students.

Conclusion

Internationalisation of higher education is a real and present issue in the transformation of academic practice in the UK. In this chapter, we have explored how the changing demographics of students as more international students enrol in UK universities, as well as the global nature of post-graduation employment, have impacted on teaching and the curriculum. Working with international students can raise a number of challenges to the traditional practices of the UK classroom. Rather than adopting a deficit view of international students needing to be acculturated into the UK system, we have explored how intercultural encounters can enrich the modules we teach. Internationalisation can broaden curriculum content and pedagogy by introducing new perspectives, examples and ways of addressing real-world problems. Supporting intercultural integration in class not only benefits international students new to the UK, but also helps all students become familiar with the demands and expectations for global careers. International experiences at home or in transnational contexts help us to critique the conventions and assumptions of our disciplinary and institutional practices. This capacity to 'make strange' what we might take as the norm is a powerful prompt for the ongoing intellectual renewal that is fundamental to our learning as educators and researchers advancing our fields.

Further reading

Ryan, Janette (2005) 'Improving teaching and learning practices for international students: implications for curriculum, pedagogy and assessment', in Jude Carroll and Janette Ryan (eds), *Teaching International Students: Improving Learning for All*. London: Routledge. pp. 92–100.

Scudamore, Rachel (2013) *Engaging Home and International Students: A Guide for New Lecturers*. York: HEA. (https://www.heacademy.ac.uk/sites/default/files/RachelScudamoreReportFeb2013.pdf).

UKCISA (UK Council for Student International Affairs) (2009) *Discussing Difference, Discovering Similarities: A Toolkit of Learning Activities to Improve Cross-Cultural Exchange between Students of Different Cultural Backgrounds for Academic and Support Staff/Students*. London: UKCISA. (www.ukcisa.org.uk/resources_download.aspx?resourceid=35&documentid=33).

All three of these texts provide practical tools, ideas and techniques for supporting international students to engage with the demands and unfamiliar practices of studying in a UK context. They also suggest ways to support intercultural group work and communication as an outcome of international students working with UK students.

CHAPTER 10

ENHANCING LEARNING IN THE DIGITAL UNIVERSITY

Learning objectives

This chapter will support you to:

- Consider the potential ways in which technology can be utilised to enhance existing learning and teaching practices;
- Plan interventions in practice that use technology to achieve learning and teaching outcomes;
- Explore critically the issues of social presence and digital literacies in the context of the digital university.

Introduction

Technologies have always been used to support and to change the ways we learn and teach. From printing and photocopying to the introduction of presentational tools such as overhead projectors or PowerPoint or the availability of electronic databases, repositories and the internet, new technologies have always shaped pedagogic processes. Yet, for many university teachers, the exponential growth of technologies over the last decade can be overwhelming and profoundly test both their technical competence and confidence. The wider access to, and suggested opportunities offered by, the internet have raised questions about how traditional, face-to-face pedagogies might be translated into, or altered by, virtual encounters in online environments. The emergence of Massive Open Online Courses (MOOCs) has also posed the tantalising proposition that wholly online, tuition-free, collaborative courses will not only ease the pressures on an overstretched system but profoundly transform the way that 'staid' universities currently work (*The Economist*, 2014).

While MOOCs still remain for the moment a fringe route for individuals to access the academy (Walker *et al.*, 2014), the collaborative Web 2.0 technologies upon which MOOCs build have offered new ways to participate and engage with learning and with learners. These tools allow users not only to access materials (as was possible in first-generation Web technology), but also to interact with, create, re-purpose and re-create resources themselves. Social media tools are now used extensively by students and teachers formally and informally to support learning within higher education contexts. Diverse applications such as blogs, wikis, document sharing, discussion forums, virtual laboratories, podcasts, lecture capture, screencasts and e-portfolios have the potential not only to transform learning online, but also how we teach in face-to-face environments (Garrison and Kanuka, 2004). Many universities have invested heavily in the infrastructure necessary to support these digital technologies. Key drivers for this outlay include the potential that technology might increase teaching capacity in the context of rising student numbers as well as the need to fulfil student expectations about the availability of Wi-Fi and support mobile learning using smartphones, tablets and laptops (Kirkwood and Price, 2013).

These drivers for investment are often reflected in how technologies are perceived and employed in universities. The plethora of frequently interchangeable terminology used to describe the relationship between technology and learning (for example, e-learning, virtual learning, blended learning) also reveals different assumptions about the purpose of technology in educational contexts. While the term 'e-learning' had currency a decade ago, the implication of using web-based and other technologies exclusively to support learners and learning at a geographical distance from the university has been replaced by the more expansive idea of 'technology-enhanced learning' for all students. Technology-enhanced learning encompasses the use of technology for distance learners as well as blended models for full- or part-time students studying on and off campus, both inside and outside lectures, laboratories, studios, seminars and libraries. From this perspective, technology 'adds value to learning' for all learners (Jisc, 2009: 8).

In 2009, the Higher Education Funding Council for England identified three levels of technological intervention for learning in higher education. Technology can be implemented for the purposes of:

- 'efficiency (existing processes carried out in a more cost-effective, time-effective, sustainable or scalable manner)';
- 'enhancement (improving existing processes and outcomes)';
- 'transformation (radical, positive change in existing processes or introducing new processes)' (HEFCE, 2009: 2).

As Kirkwood and Price (2013) note, however, many claims for the added value of learning with technology can be understood as 'operational' and related to efficiency gains such as better access to resources, management of learning for large student numbers, e-submission, e-marking and the freedom for students to choose when and where to study (p. 332).

There are also assumptions that the 'affordances' of technology – that is, the potential properties and effects of different technologies or applications – are sufficient to justify their use in learning contexts. The anticipated ways that a tool might engage learners can therefore override consideration of the type and value of learning experiences we want to create for our students. This 'technological determinism' means that 'technology is unquestioned because questions about efficiency and productivity replace political and ethical questions about use' (Oliver, 2011: 374). At the same time commentators suggest we are now moving from a 'digital' to a 'post-digital' age where technology is so embedded in our practice and lives that we no longer need to pay particular attention to the 'digital as a mode of production' and can instead begin 'attending to agendas other than technology in education' (Beetham, 2014). As educators we need to be attentive to the pedagogic purpose of integrating technology into learning and teaching. Yet we have to do that in a context where technology use is becoming, in many ways, unremarkable and often indistinguishable from the other means we use to communicate and collaborate in academic and everyday life.

In this chapter we will first look at the types of learning activities that we can engage students with and how technology can be used to stimulate, support or make this possible. As such we will initially focus on technological interventions that seek to *enhance* the learning experience. Technology is also influencing the content of disciplinary curricula. For many disciplines, technologies are inevitably transforming our knowledge: for instance, by changing what we can 'see' micro- or macroscopically, what we can create through computer-aided design or three-dimensional printing and the skills students will need, in terms of programming, to use and manipulate software. These changes to what we teach intersect with how we teach it. As learners engage with technology, it has been argued that existing theories of learning are insufficient to account for new ways of knowing in a networked world. Though the need for new theories to accommodate digital technologies is questioned (Mayes and de Freitas, 2013), advocates for a distinct theory of technology-enhanced learning suggest that connectivism or rhizomatic models can be productive in helping to understand the ways we create, interact with and share knowledge in a digital age through connectivity and interaction (Siemens, 2005; Cormier, 2008).

A recent survey of technology-enhanced learning, however, suggests some disciplines see digital technology as less relevant to their modes of teaching than others. While science and medical disciplines might be early-adopters of technology for teaching, art, design and the humanities are potentially less likely to integrate technologies into existing pedagogies (Walker *et al.*, 2014). As the examples and case studies in this and other chapters demonstrate, however, digital technologies have been utilised in all disciplines in valid ways to replicate, augment and alter disciplinary pedagogy. We will therefore consider how our interactions with technology might challenge our ways of knowing and understanding in our disciplines and *transform* the ways we teach in both real and virtual contexts.

As we consider the transformative potential of technology-enhanced learning we will return to two interrelated issues that we have explored in other contexts in previous chapters. These issues have particular resonance for teachers and learners as they move, often seamlessly, between real and digital environments. First, the relationship between technology and learning raises important questions about 'social presence' in digital spaces where the physical and temporal connections of face-to-face learning environments are altered (Kehrwald, 2010). Our identity as we venture into virtual spaces is an important consideration for learning. Prensky (2001) configured this in generational terms by suggesting students are 'digital natives' who are '"native speakers" of the digital language of computers, video games and the Internet'. Unlike them, many teachers who have, enthusiastically or otherwise, adopted and adapted to digital technologies are only ever 'digital immigrants' (pp. 2–3). While Prensky's categorisation of learners and their teachers has now come under considerable critique, the intersection between identity, language and multimodal texts in the digital environment remains an important consideration for educators. Second, we therefore also need to consider students' textual practices, or 'digital literacies', as they negotiate the new technology-mediated environments of the digital university and the nature of the 'texts' these practices create (Lea and Jones, 2011). Although digital literacies have been narrowly defined as a set of technical capabilities or attributes, we will explore the learning and teaching implications of a richer account of the literacy practices and the 'texts' and non-written forms of making meaning and representing knowledge that are possible in digital spaces.

Enhancing learning with technology

For many teachers in higher education, teaching practice now adopts a 'blended' model where face-to-face teaching and technologies within a virtual learning environment are integrated into student learning experiences. This can include how students search or access the library, engage with content and teaching and learning experiences, complete and submit assessments and receive feedback. The fluid slippage between participating in face-to-face and technological spaces is also evident in ways that refute binary distinctions between 'real' and 'virtual' encounters. Using laptops, tablets or smartphones, students can not only take notes or record and share audio or visual images, but also search and follow-up references during as well as after a lecture or seminar. Close-up live footage of a teacher carrying out an experiment or performing a technique that is simultaneously projected onto video screens in a laboratory, clinic or studio also blur the line between 'real' and technologically-enhanced learning experiences. Students may also review a recorded lecture that they previously attended in person for revision and collaborate or share work with their peers using email or social media to prepare for a face-to-face group presentation.

While technology is inevitably fast-moving and such lists are quickly outdated, widely used and comparatively durable technologies employed for learning include:

- virtual learning environments, such as Blackboard Learn or Moodle, including a content management system that assembles together module information, calendars and multimodal content, as well as interactive technologies such as discussion forums, wikis and e-assessment tools;
- conferencing or webinar tools such as Adobe Connect and Blackboard Collaborate;
- text-matching, e-submission and e-assessment software such as Turnitin;
- e-portfolio software such as Mahara or PebblePad;
- blogging software such as Wordpress, Blogger or microblogging applications such as Twitter;
- document-sharing software such as SharePoint, Google Docs and Dropbox;
- podcasting, screencasting or lecture capture using software such as Camtasia or Panopto;
- electronic voting systems (also called audience response systems) using handset 'clickers' such as TurningPoint that plug into PowerPoint or web-based applications using students' own mobile devices such as Poll Everywhere;
- social bookmarking or annotation tools such as Diigo, Delicious and Pinterest;
- social or professional networking applications such as Facebook and LinkedIn (Walker *et al.*, 2014).

Yet despite the pervasiveness of these technologies within higher education, Kirkwood and Price (2014) query what is actually 'enhanced' in technology-enhanced learning. They suggest that enhancement with technology can take different forms: to replicate current face-to-face teaching methods, to complement existing teaching and learning practices or to transform learning and teaching processes. As such they warn that the use of technology does not guarantee innovative or transformative teaching and learning. For example, 'if a teacher uses PowerPoint or a video-enhanced podcast to deliver a lecture it does not make it anything other than a lecture' (Kirkwood and Price, 2013: 333). As such 'when a new technology arrives we tend to use it in old ways' (Weller, 2009: 181). Kirkwood and Price suggest that often technologies are utilised because of what a tool can do rather than because of a specific educational objective. This can mean that there are ultimately 'deterministic expectations that introducing technology would, *of itself*, bring about changes in teaching/learning practices' (Kirkwood and Price, 2014: 26, emphasis original). They suggest that the transformative impact of technology is only enabled when teachers focus on achieving a qualitative change in the learning they are trying to foster. This means attending to the types of learning activities and outcomes we are seeking for our students and using technologies as part our learning design to support the reflection, knowledge-building, student engagement, collaboration or sharing that contribute to an enriched learning experience in real as well as virtual contexts (Kirkwood and Price, 2013, 2014).

Nevertheless, we need to be cautious about claiming that a 'captured' lecture that has been recorded from a single viewpoint, possibly edited or transcribed and certainly available to pause, skip or replay, is 'anything other than a lecture' that was experienced in live form by the students present. The texts mediated through, and made possible by, certain applications also mean that writing and meaning-making in online environments will be fluid, hybrid, multimodal and intertextual in ways that print-based texts are not. McKenna and Hughes (2013) argue that the increasingly legitimate academic texts that are created by scholars and students through wikis, blogging or microblogging are dialogic, co-created and dependent on audience engagement in ways that challenge traditional notions of authorship. Drawing on actor-network theory, Lea argues, therefore, that we should not privilege people over technologies but 'see technologies as actants in different contexts and scenarios. Students work with and not through technologies' (Lea, 2004, cited in Lea and Jones, 2011: 384). As we integrate technologies into our teaching we need to be cautious about claims that the introduction of technology will unquestionably enhance learning while recognising that our students' interaction with technology has already changed traditional learning practices.

In previous chapters we have explored the types of activities that we might want students to engage in during their learning in face-to-face as well as virtual contexts. In the networked environment enabled through web-based technologies, Beetham (2013) defines these activities as: 'discovering; developing and sharing ideas; collecting, gathering, recording and remixing/editing; solving problems and developing techniques; and working with others' (p. 41). While Beetham does not specifically sequence these five technology-enhanced types of active learning, Nerantzi and Beckingham (2014) suggest that we can design students' learning pathways with technology using the 5C model (communicating, connecting, collaborating, creating and curating) 'that enables learners to progressively engage in more complex learning and teaching activities' online (p. 6). Their 5C model mirrors, to some extent, Salmon's (2013) staged model for engaging students with learning technologies. Salmon depicts this progression as a process of initially socialising students into online learning environments and developing their online identity and technical skills to manage the tools, encouraging students to participate in exchange and collaboration with their peers and their teachers and moving them towards the active creation as well as consumption of knowledge in the online environment.

As we integrate technologies into our pedagogic practices, it is useful to think critically about how we prepare and scaffold these activities, both technically and socially, in ways that ensure students are participating in constructive, challenging and productive learning experiences. Drawing on these learning-oriented objectives for integrating technology into learning we can explore how we plan and use technologies to support particular interventions in practice through discovery, developing and sharing, collaborating, connecting and solving problems. Importantly, what the case studies below illustrate is how online learning activities can be designed to directly feed into face-to-face learning contexts and vice versa in ways that helpfully blur the binary between online and offline learning. Some of the interventions with technology presented here do require that teachers have high levels of technical competence or collaborate with technology-enhanced learning experts, but others are possible to implement with open-source software (freely downloadable and modifiable by users) or the tools within existing institutional virtual learning environments.

Discovering

The volume of information available via the internet constitutes a rich resource for enquiry-based learning. Siemens (2005) argues that 'when knowledge is abundant, the rapid evaluation of knowledge is important'. Even five years ago teachers were concerned about the quality of the online sources students were drawing on, but, increasingly, websites, blogs and Twitter microblogging are seen as legitimate references in academic contexts. A discovery learning process, however, should include opportunities for students to evaluate the sources of information they access or locate. Case study 10.1 gives an example where resources are brought together by teachers in one location, requiring students to navigate and make decisions about multiple perspectives, potential source-use and value. More experienced students can be asked not just to access or accumulate information but, for example in 'WebQuests', to develop search terms or questions to drive their enquiry and locate as well as make judgements about the quality and validity of the information they find. Through discovery-based activities students also learn how to collate and manage digital as well as non-digital artefacts in ways that are personally and collectively meaningful. It is also possible to use virtual resources to explore simulated environments and real locations before or during site visits by bringing together resources that facilitate discovery.

'WebQuests' were developed at San Diego State University in the 1990s (http://webquest.org/) and are widely used in compulsory, museum and English-language education in the UK, but are adaptable to the higher education context as a way for students to become familiar with using search engines and databases for research (Hassanien, 2006). A 'WebQuest' is a student-centred enquiry-based activity in which the teacher identifies a topic relevant to the module and a task that involves students in working towards a goal. This could be to compile resources into a particular useable form such as a field guide or a short encyclopaedia entry for a specified audience. Alternatively, students collate resources into a campaign site or a policy briefing or analyse different arguments relevant to a topical issue for an online news posting. Students can work individually or in groups and can keep a journal of their experience of enquiry to record and reflect on their selection of search terms and search tools for their quest or inclusion and exclusion criteria for evaluating the quality of resources (Barkley, 2010). Students' use of Wikipedia and other collaborative information sources are often a source of anxiety for educators. Engaging students in critically reviewing, for example, Wikipedia entries for key topics relevant to the module comparing website information with lecture and seminar materials, finding errors, misattributions or supplying missing references is a valid way to support enquiry and engage students in learning to critically evaluate all sources they access.

Virtual field guides are another strategy to bring together materials and resources that help students engage in fieldwork before and after field visits, as well as connect results from laboratory work to observations in the field. For example, Liverpool John Moores University has developed a virtual field excursion of Ingleton Waterfalls Trail in Yorkshire for students on the Foundation-level module 'Introduction to Geosciences' and second-year undergraduate module 'Caving and Karst Landscapes' (Stott *et al.*, 2014). The interactive field guide includes text, videos, maps, photographs, cross-sections, a glossary of terms and references as well as questions and prompts to support fieldwork (https://ljmu.ac.uk/NSP/ingleton/index.htm).

Students access these resources to prepare for the visit, use the questions in the site virtually to scaffold observation and recording and revisit the site after the fieldwork to supplement their field notes.

 Case study 10.1   Collecting and curating resources online in Foundation-year Anthropology (Pearce and Learmonth, 2013)

Colleagues at the University of Durham saw the potential for digital resources and artefacts to supplement readings and lectures and support revision as part of a ten-week introductory, Foundation-level Anthropology module. Pinterest (https://uk.pinterest.com) is a social media application that enables users to 'pin' multimedia resources from multiple sources onto a virtual 'pin board'. These can be grouped around a theme or topic and can be visible to others online. The application was used by the module team to group relevant online resources around each of the topics of the weekly lecture, such as rites of passage or biological anthropology. The collecting and connecting of the resources together in this way reflected the anthropological concept of bricolage by bringing together existing objects or resources and reusing them to create something new. A student project assistant, who was a previous graduate of the module, collated resources from academic blogs, online museum archives, online newspapers and social media sites to build thematic 'pin boards' for each topic. Students could subsequently access, share and re-pin the resources to their personal 'pin boards'. The collating of these resources required students to explore multiple perspectives on a topic rather than a definitive answer or definition. The non-linear organisation of the pinned objects also meant they had to evaluate the resources individually and, because each pinned item retained information of its original source, further explore beyond the pinned link and module. The openness to public view and the capacity to share and discuss resources with each other through other social media also encouraged peer learning and collaboration. Although, in this example, the 'pin boards' were collated for the students as they were new to studying at university, the module team recognised that as students became more experienced they could be encouraged to collect, collate, evaluate and share their own resources.

Developing and sharing ideas

Collating resources, annotating them or communicating them with others in ways that sit outside the traditional format and voice of 'academic' writing can contribute to deepening student understanding of new concepts. As well as generating new ways to make content available, digital technologies have reinvigorated how we communicate visually and orally within academic and professional contexts. Free or subscription tools such as CMap Software (http://cmap.ihmc.us/) or WebspirationPRO (http://www.mywebspiration.com/) support visual modes of communication such as collaborative concept mapping (Ching and Hsu, 2011). Social bookmarking (case study 10.2) or a jigsaw wiki (case study 5.1) are other strategies that help students to explore and share their ideas by experimenting with voice and playing with traditional notions of authorship through the co-creation of text. Alternatively, podcasting is a communicative form that has been utilised to develop student understanding of important topics by providing short introductions or overviews of concepts. Podcasts are digital audio recordings that are made using mobile technologies such as digital recorders, smartphones or laptops and, if necessary, edited using open-source recording and editing software such as Audacity (www.audacity.sourceforge.net). Alternatively, relevant TED talks (http://www.ted.com), videos on YouTube (http://youtube.com) or television and radio broadcasts archived through services such as Box of Broadcasts National (http://bobnational.net/) can be used as stimulus for discussion. While full or edited lecture podcasts or audio-visual materials may be included in module resources, student-created, rather than more widely utilised teacher-generated, podcasts also offer student groups the opportunity to create and share their work in modes other than text (Guertin, 2010).

Case study 10.2   Supporting students to develop disciplinary research practice using social bookmarking in undergraduate history (Wood, 2011)

Developing students' capacity to search, analyse and evaluate sources is an essential disciplinary practice in history. Locating and sorting valid sources is only part of this research process. Students also need to be able to pose questions as part of enquiry-based learning as well as develop their information literacy skills such as using internet databases and search engines effectively and critically. To support the development of their research skills first-year history undergraduates at the University of Sheffield were introduced to social bookmarking as a tool to collate and share resources. Although there was a detailed module reading list, as part of their independent study each week students had to locate primary and secondary sources relevant to the topic for the next week. They had to bookmark the resource using a 50-word description of the webpage, article, podcast or image and tag it using appropriate keywords to aid searching and categorisation of the resources. Students could also use the tools within the social bookmarking software to highlight and annotate a resource in more detail. Finally, each student had to post a question in the module discussion forum that the resource raised for them;

these were available to other students. The independent bookmarking and question-posing activities were supported by in-class opportunities to practise navigating and using the software and aligned to questioning, evaluating and interpreting sources and developing arguments in line with the assessment for the module. The collated resources and the questions that students posted enabled the teacher to monitor student preparation for the seminar and adapt the seminar discussion to the interests and direction of the students' own enquiries or introduce alternative arguments. The questions and resources therefore fed directly into the discussion and activities of the seminar.

Collaborating

Discussion forums, wikis and other group tasks can all be used to engage students in working collaboratively with their peers. Digital technologies enable that to happen outside timetabled teaching to support independent study with students at a geographical distance and, distinctively, asynchronously as well as in real-time. We will explore effective peer interaction in virtual collaborative spaces in Chapter 11, but digital technologies can also be used to enhance face-to-face collaboration in powerful ways. Although the 'flipped lecture' format potentially reinforces a transmission approach to knowledge acquisition, if well planned it can be used to ensure independent and face-to-face time is interactive and collaborative rather than didactic. Case study 10.3 illustrates how introducing technologies both outside and inside the face-to-face environment facilitates active self-regulated learning approaches outside the lecture and interactive peer-assisted learning during timetabled contact hours.

Case study 10.3   A flipped lecture approach to support peer instruction in undergraduate electrical engineering (Imran and Arshad, 2013)

A flipped lecture approach was developed for 70 students on a module in electrical engineering at the University of Surrey using short videos to explain fundamental concepts. The videos were in the form of pencasts (http://www. livescribe.com) that combined audio explanation with an interactive digital version of the teacher's handwritten notes. Students could watch the whole video or jump to specific explanations by clicking on a location on the digitised page. To encourage engagement with the material in advance of the face-to-face session, students completed a pre-lecture assessment which tested their understanding

(Continued)

(Continued)

of the concepts rather than necessarily the correct answer. The pre-lecture assessments were conducted every fortnight to make the marking and feedback manageable, and contributed 10 per cent to the final module grade. The videos enabled the teacher to use contact hours for questions and answers or enquiry-based learning rather than exposition. At the beginning of the lecture good examples and typical errors or misconceptions in students' work were explained and key concepts briefly revised. An electronic voting system was used to test understanding of the concepts and the group results were shared with students immediately. Students then discussed the concepts collectively in small groups using peer instruction to help correct errors and share understanding before a re-poll checked all students had understood the concept. The provision of short lectures in advance of timetabled teaching allowed students to learn independently and at their own pace outside of the lecture and increased collaboration with each other and the teacher during face-to-face timetabled sessions.

Connecting

Proposed theories of learning that explicitly seek to take account of the affordances of technology suggest that in a complex and networked world 'knowledge is distributed across a network of connections' and hence 'the capacity to form connections between sources of information, and thereby create useful information patterns' is a core skill for learners (Downes, 2007; Siemens, 2005). The complexities of pattern recognition as meaning-making can be explored through reflective activities that help students to examine the connections they create both between different digital artefacts and between individuals within a community of learners. Mapping activities and 'patchwork' portfolios (see Chapter 8 for a description of this as an alternative assessment format) capture these processes and allow students to reflect on how they identify, explore and test these connections.

 Case study 10.4   Media-rich patchwork portfolios to facilitate personalised learning and reflection (Arnold *et al.*, 2009)

Building a media-rich portfolio is a valid and inclusive assessment strategy in the context of work-based learning. Students in professions such as nursing, banking, teaching and charity administration were required to enquire into practice issues as part of their studies on a fully online undergraduate programme at Anglia Ruskin University. An adapted online version of the 'patchwork text' provided the opportunity for the personalisation of learning through the creation of multimedia 'patches' that made up the assessment and e-submission of the final portfolio. Students were encouraged to use low-cost and accessible technologies such as mobile phone-recorded videos and open-source blogging tools to create objects.

Central to the process of developing the portfolio was discussion and collaboration online. The online environment created a 'community space' within which students could negotiate their understanding of the assessment requirements and subsequently make available to other students completed 'patches' for peer review before submission. The process of peer review initially provoked student anxiety, but ensuring students sought and received teacher feedback within the shared learning environment rather than through private communication methods such as email meant that the constructive process of giving feedback was modelled for students. Grouping students into smaller sub-groups for giving feedback also helped to build trust in the group and make the number of comments manageable. Students submitted 'patches' in a wide range of genre and media: essays and reports, audio-visual presentations, posters, animation and comic strips and play scripts or storyboards. Some students also made their 'patches' available to wider public review through YouTube or online blogs.

Solving problems

Digital technologies can be used when teachers want to develop student problem-solving skills or create opportunities for them to master disciplinary techniques. This is especially valuable in contexts where access to laboratories or expensive chemicals is limited or if there are health and safety or ethical considerations that reduce the practicality of repeated practice. In medical and veterinary education, where hands-on experience is essential, patient welfare must be prioritised over educational outcomes. In veterinary medicine, internal examinations to locate and diagnose, for example, pregnancy or fertility are a situation where teaching is also done 'blind' because the expert must trust the student's account of their competency to identify anatomical features internally that cannot be observed in practice. A collaboration between the Royal Veterinary College, University of London and the University of Glasgow led to the development of a three-dimensional Haptic Cow simulator. This simulator enables students to examine and palpate simulated organs repeatedly but also, importantly, allows the teacher to observe the technique on a computer and provide detailed feedback on the student's clinical skills (Baillie *et al.*, 2010). Other problem-solving interventions can utilise the standard discussion tools within a virtual learning environment to support collaboration, problem analysis, research and visualisation as part of the creative process. For example, Sykes (2012) created an e-studio for undergraduate creative advertising students at Leeds College of Art using the discussion forum as a collaborative space within which students participated in a competitive live brief to simulate a 'pitch' to a client.

Case study 10.5   Using virtual experimental scenarios in biology (Levin *et al.*, 2014)

Laboratory-based experimental work is an important opportunity to explore the practical application of the theory introduced in lectures. Financial resource constraints and safety considerations in relation to some types of experiments mean physical laboratory experiences are not always possible. A virtual laboratory was introduced at the University of Manchester as one solution that gives student access to experimental scenarios in a second-year undergraduate module 'Principles in Developmental Biology'. Teachers storyboarded five interactive scenarios and created them using scenario-building software; these were hosted in the institutional virtual learning environment. A scenario was made available every two weeks during the term in parallel with the lectures, as well as at the end of the module to support revision. In each scenario, students take on the role of a postgraduate research student in the laboratory. A hypothetical rather than pre-existing model organism was designed for the virtual laboratory so that students had to test concepts in a novel context. In working through the scenarios students could make a limited number of experimental decisions and if, for example, they chose the wrong experiment they had to return and select an alternative. The scenarios also included quiz questions with immediate feedback which they could attempt multiple times. While the simulated laboratory experiences could not completely replicate the real-life experience of the experimental laboratory, students have positively evaluated the opportunity to consolidate learning from the lectures and get immediate feedback on their understanding.

Focus on practice

Identify a learning objective or activity, including assessment, in a module you teach where integrating technology might enhance the learning experience or overcome a particular teaching challenge.

- What type of technology intervention could you use to support the activity?
- Do you and your students have the skills to engage in the activity successfully and, if not, how will you develop these skills?

- What different roles do students, teachers and technologies play in the activity?
- What is the benefit for learning for all students?
- What evidence can you draw on to demonstrate that this has enhanced learning?

Supporting student learning with technology: social presence and digital literacies

Many claims are made that digital technology is changing not only the way we work, communicate or socialise, but also the fundamental way we learn and create knowledge. For instance, Cormier's (2008) rhizomatic theories of learning suggest that the 'fluid, transitory conception of knowledge' exemplified in the fast-changing, adaptive and 'ephemeral nature of the Web' challenges traditional, measured practices of knowledge creation and validation by experts. For Cormier the 'curriculum is not driven by predefined inputs from experts; it is constructed and negotiated in real-time by the contributions of those engaged in the learning process. This community acts as the curriculum.' Yet, if we accept the formulation of 'community as curriculum' where we 'learn from each other, through each other, from each other's learning' rather than from expert-approved resources (Cormier, 2010), then technology-enhanced learning must focus less on content management and more on facilitating interaction between learners. But the way individuals engage with technology and participate in online learning spaces can vary significantly.

Prensky's (2001) distinction between younger 'digital natives' and older 'digital immigrants' obscures many students' lack of skills and confidence in using the tools and platforms we introduce for learning. While students may easily use social media to share and communicate in their personal lives this may not translate straightforwardly to competent usage of the virtual learning environment, library e-resources or internet as a research tool. White and Le Cornu (2011) have suggested an alternative typology of 'visitors' and 'residents' that characterises users not on the basis of age but in relation to their motivation for participating in online social spaces. Visitors 'see the Web as primarily a set of tools which deliver or manipulate content'. They 'are users, not members, of the Web and place little value in belonging online'. Conversely, residents 'see the Web primarily as a network of individuals or clusters of individuals who in turn generate content'. While visitors reject 'non-expert opinion and notions such as the wisdom of the crowd', residents 'do not make a clear distinction between concepts of content and of persona'.

Individual students may sit at some point along a continuum between visitor and resident types and may well adopt a visitor or resident approach to engaging with technology depending on context. As White and Le Cornu (2011) suggest, conventional assessment in higher education, for example, may still reward visitor approaches that seek 'expert' over community knowledge as an outcome of online learning. Yet as more collective forms of knowledge develop, our online identities and sense of belonging, or 'social presence', are therefore significant factors in our participation and interaction in online environments.

Social presence constitutes 'the degree to which a person is perceived as "real"' in a virtual space and the connections they establish within a group. It contributes to achievement, motivation, satisfaction and interaction in online learning and, hence, a fundamental condition for an effective learning experience (Sung and Mayer, 2012: 1738; Kehrwald, 2010). In the absence of the social cues typical of face-to-face interactions, Sung and Mayer (2012) suggest there are five factors involved in creating social presence online:

- social respect: contributions to discussion forums are valued and timely responses are received from others in ways that make interaction worthwhile;
- social sharing: personal information such as beliefs, values and motivations are shared between members as the basis for building social relationships;
- open-mindedness: the collaborative space is open and welcomes the expression of opinions and feedback;
- social identity: learners and teachers address each other by name;
- intimacy: personal stories and individual experiences are shared with others.

In planning online learning experiences we need to take account of these factors and find ways to foster our own and our students' social presence in digital environments. The following suggestions are ways to do begin to do this in practice:

- Use icebreaker activities to initiate participation online as well as establish students' and teachers' social identities. For example, at the beginning of the module each student creates an autobiographical webpage using images, video, hyperlinks and text to introduce themselves to other members of the group, focusing on their previous learning experiences or attitudes to the module or discipline. Alternatively, put students in pairs and ask them to interview each other about their interests or past experience, using one of the communication tools that you will use in the module such as email, discussion forums or Twitter; then introduce them to the rest of the group (Barkley, 2010).

- Acknowledge contributions or postings in discussion forums or wikis and use student names to refer or respond to comments. In an active online discussion it might be difficult to respond to all contributions, so track the overarching debate, highlighting different positions and drawing connections between comments either online or, as in case study 10.2, to inform face-to-face sessions.
- Set up a knowledge and skills exchange where students share experiences and tips for successfully working online or identify their strengths, weaknesses or views in using specific digital tools that will be employed in the module (Salmon, 2013).
- Create space to talk about and reflect critically on the different roles that online environments and communicative practices require of teachers and students. Haythornthwaite (2013) summarises the range of ways students can take an 'active role as shapers of conversations, contributors of knowledge, and creators of new knowledge' in online contexts such as e-facilitators, 'braiders' or 'patchworkers' (p. 63) as they take a lead in mediating and managing online conversations or the creation of artefacts. Assigning specific roles to individuals, as with face-to-face groups, can help to make these actions visible and open to scrutiny.

In virtual environments identity is demonstrative and dynamic. To be 'present' you 'post' into discussions, edit, re-purpose, tag, rate, 'like' or interact with objects or contributions (Kerhwald, 2010). As such, virtual social presence inevitably intersects with students' digital literacies as they explore and make meaning through hybrid, multimodal and technology-mediated texts. These new ways of creating, co-creating and interacting with digital texts have the 'potential to disrupt some of the more conventional literacy practices of the academy' (Lea and Jones, 2011: 377). In particular, online literacy practices often challenge the traditional notion of authorship. Many of the tools used in digital environments such as wikis, blogging, microblogging and document sharing make collaboration and co-authorship central to the process of text production. Similarly, open educational resources or resources with a licence that permits open access and variable levels of usage are challenging a static and proprietorial concept of creator or author. This has foregrounded what Hilton *et al.* (2010) describe as the four 'R's of reuse, redistribution, revision and remixing as individuals engage with online objects. Unsurprisingly, this has also prompted anxieties about plagiarism and inappropriate referencing in student work as we move between new and traditional academic writing tasks.

While detection and punitive policies for plagiarism are one strategy for responding to these concerns, an alternative approach is to embed in teaching a deliberate and critical engagement with the new genres that online environments make possible. The suggestions for supporting students to evaluate academic writing conventions in Chapter 8 can be integrated into a discussion about the hybrid nature of online writing conventions. The disruptive potential of online literacy practices, however, can be explored with your students in the following ways:

- Unlike printed texts, online texts are mutable, ephemeral and, in many ways, never final (Lea and Jones, 2011). This is especially the case if teachers are assessing work such as wikis, blogs or e-portfolios where it may be difficult to lock down a final version of the work after a submission deadline. The non-definitive status of the work, however, is a powerful stimulus for focusing not on the text as a product but on the practices of creating the text (Lea, 2013). One strategy is to encourage students to evidence and reflect on their processes of creation and collaboration in formative and summative assessment. Students can include in assessment submissions, for example, editing histories on wikis, samples of discussion forum threads, argument maps, reflective journals recording the experience of writing, annotated resources or annotated essays to demonstrate how they have engaged with ideas from resources and peers.
- Consider including a range of different modes for assessment that extend the choices for exploring and representing learning beyond the traditional essay or report. Wikis, blogs, websites, podcasts, e-portfolios and social bookmarking all provide opportunities for students to experiment and reflect on tone, intertextuality, hypertextuality and audience – central to new digital literacy practices. Gray *et al.* (2010) suggest that while teachers have integrated these tools into their assessment practices very few, in reality, exploit the distinctive features these technologies offer. Although using online applications, often such assessments could just as easily be fulfilled by traditional essay-based assessments or oral presentations. To encourage more critical use of the different technologies, they argue that assessment criteria should include, for example, marks for editing practices in wikis, user experience of websites, student social presence in online environments through posting, the quality of the presentation in podcasts or innovative use of the specific features of a chosen format.
- The capacity to engage with non-written forms of communication in digital environments creates opportunities to challenge the privileging of the written word in traditional assessment regimes. While the impermanency of the Web interrupts our received ideas about texts, conversely the availability and flexibility of technologies such as smartphones that record relatively high-quality video and audio material means emergent, temporary

or improvisational practices can be captured. Barton and Ryan (2014) argue that in many creative disciplines reflective practice is often expressed using forms other than writing. Multimodal forms of reflection such as oral, performative, visual and embodied reflection can all be enabled and shared through digital technologies such as podcasts or videoed performances in ways that challenge the dominance of textual reflection for assessment and give more scope for experimentation with other ways to represent understanding.

Conclusion

In this chapter we have explored some of the ways in which digital technology is impacting on higher education learning and teaching practices. Learning technologies give us and our students the freedom to work when and where we choose; open up, almost instantly, a breadth of knowledge and global experience that was not possible even a decade ago; and create opportunities for students to be creators, not just consumers of knowledge. Yet the propensity in some contexts to reify technology means that we do not always pause to ask critical questions about why we might use a digital tool in our teaching. Working with technology can subtly and powerfully alter our ways of communicating, of working with others and how we understand creative or authoritative acts of knowledge-making. Yet many technological interventions focus on 'operational' efficiency or cost-effectiveness rather than pedagogic 'enhancement' outcomes. Undeniably, operational and enhancement outcomes are not always distinguishable. Increased efficiency in the submission of assessments or accessing of resources can allow teachers time to improve the quality or frequency of the feedback provided to students or broaden the range of texts students read. Yet, as we introduce technology into our practice, Kirkwood and Price (2014) remind us to ask the important questions: what is 'enhanced' through technology-enhanced learning and what evidence can we draw on to demonstrate that enhancement? In particular, digital technologies increase opportunities for active engagement, collaboration and peer learning and the case studies in this and previous chapters have demonstrated how this can be meaningfully put into practice. This is a dynamic dialogue between understanding what new technologies can do or enable and critical engagement with what we are trying to achieve or could achieve as educators. Therefore, while it is important to avoid technological determinism (what can a tool do and how it can be used), technologies create distinctive or new conditions and opportunities for learning. As we work creatively and thoughtfully to exploit these technologies, we can begin to explore the possibility that existing and future technologies might radically transform our existing pedagogies and allow us to think differently about how we learn, teach and create knowledge.

Further reading

Jisc (2015) 'Jisc Digital Student' (http://digitalstudent.jiscinvolve.org/wp/exemplars/).
This collection of exemplars from UK universities provides strategies for responding to the typical challenges teachers face when integrating technologies into their practice, including preparing students to study with digital technologies, inclusive use of technologies and involving students as digital change agents.

Salmon, Gilly (2013) *E-tivities: The Key to Active Online Learning*. 2nd edn. New York: Routledge.
This practical guide includes practitioner resources for supporting teachers to design and implement 'e-tivities' to scaffold student access, collaboration and knowledge creation.

CHAPTER 11

SUPPORTING COLLABORATIVE LEARNING

Learning objectives

This chapter will support you to:

- Explore critically how students learn individually and collaboratively in relation to the aims and practices of higher education;
- Enhance your understanding of the approaches and implications of collaborative learning for undergraduate and postgraduate students;
- Develop teaching, learning and assessment strategies to support student collaborative learning.

Introduction

As we have explored in the preceding chapters, the context for learning in higher education has undergone dramatic changes over the last two decades. The expectation that higher education will prepare students for employment, a revolution in the demographics of the student population and technological innovation have all transformed the aims and practices of universities. This is never more evident than in the ways we configure the contexts within which learning happens. Increased student numbers mean that the staff–student ratio has significantly altered. Across a range of disciplines and institutions, students must increasingly learn in larger classes with sometimes limited individual contact time with their teachers. As we explored in Chapter 10, new interactive technologies enable learning to happen in spaces and times unrestricted by traditional, face-to-face timetabled classes or the exclusive learning relationship between expert teacher and individual student.

Over the last four chapters we have examined these changes as they impact on the curriculum content and practices. In this chapter we will consider in more detail the implications, challenges and opportunities that learning alone and learning in groups presents in these new contexts. This particular focus on the role of groups and collaboration for learning is necessary because it underpins many of the fundamental debates about university teaching. Gibbs (2009) has asserted that class size is a more important indicator of quality than the total contact time a student experiences in their studies. At the same time, the joint Higher Education Policy Institute (HEPI) and Higher Education Academy survey of student academic experience also reveals students' belief that learning that takes place one-to-one with a teacher or in small groups of under 15 students is of greater educational benefit than learning in large group contexts. While 88 per cent of students surveyed rated learning in small groups (groups of six to 15 students) positively, this compared to a positive rating of only 51 per cent when learning in groups of over 100 students. In the same survey 28 per cent of students also explained why their higher education experience did not meet their pre-enrolment expectations by pointing to a perceived lack of support for private study (Soilemetzidis *et al.*, 2014). While teaching all students in small classes may not be possible in practice, how we plan and support the relationship between self-directed learning and learning in groups is an important determining factor in the perceived quality of students' experience.

Learning collaboratively, however, is also an important opportunity in and of itself. As we explored in Chapter 7, as well as influencing the inclusion of work-based experiences within the curriculum, preparing students for employment has meant a demand for graduates who have developed leadership skills and the capacity to work effectively in teams (Caple and Bogle, 2013). The affordances of Web 2.0 social media technologies have made possible new forms of social and professional collaboration that inevitably shape how we work in both higher education and subsequent employment. Preparing students to operate in a networked world, therefore, is increasingly an important further outcome of their higher education experience. The new ways of describing learning in a digital age, such as rhizomatic learning or connectivism explored in Chapter 10, inform our understanding of the potentialities of peer, collective and connected learning. These factors will impact on how we conceptualise, plan and manage group work and how we develop student capacities to fulfil independent learning outside of contact hours. In addition, the political, social and moral demands for greater environmental accountability, which recognise an individual's relationship to their wider community as well as their intergenerational responsibility, not only impacts on what we teach but also how we teach. In Chapter 3, when we explored interdisciplinarity in higher education, we looked at how education for sustainable development calls for interdisciplinary and systems-thinking approaches (Cotton and Sterling, 2012). Sustainability pedagogies, however, also require us to reconsider our learning and teaching approaches to include participatory, collaborative and collective learning based around learning communities, group work and discussion (Cotton and Winter, 2010).

The aim in this chapter is to consider how collaborative learning can underpin the purpose and processes of teaching at university. This means considering how we support students to learn independently as self-regulated learners while also understanding their responsibilities for, and the benefits of, learning with others in collaborative group contexts through peer learning. While the opportunities of peer learning are widely advocated, as Boud and Lee (2005) warn, 'peers do not necessarily learn as a natural outcome of their being peers' (p. 515). We will look, therefore, specifically at three opportunities for collaborative learning in higher education and how we structure them for learning. We will begin by building on the debates in the previous chapter about learning in digital contexts to focus specifically on how social media applications are creating spaces and forms of collaboration that support collective knowledge creation. We will then consider how peer-assisted learning and peer feedback can be utilised to develop collaborative learning in which undergraduate and postgraduate students draw on collective knowledge and experiences to reach relevant and meaningful outcomes. Finally, we will consider how education for sustainable development raises questions about self-regulation, collectivist knowledge and co-responsibility as an important set of principles for responding to the challenges of environmental, social and economic sustainability.

Working in groups to foster collaborative learning

Focusing on how to enhance and embed opportunities for collaborative learning is not a disingenuous response to alleviating the realities of teaching larger groups in a mass higher education system. Nor is it a failsafe answer to the pressures on teachers' time to provide individual support and feedback in the context of high student numbers. For many teachers and researchers, collaborative learning is a vital paradigm for reconceptualising learning, knowledge and experience that is relevant to the challenges of responding to complex world problems. The benefits of collaborative learning are inevitably contested, but research suggests that working in groups:

- fosters problem-solving in the context of multidisciplinary and multi-professional teams;
- raises student awareness and the capacity to negotiate diverse perspectives;
- increases student understanding of the interdependence and mutuality of their individual knowledge and outcomes and the collective knowledge and outcomes of the group (Ackermann *et al.*, 2007).

Yet, despite these strengths, Johnson and Johnson (1999) argue that, at all levels of education, individualistic and competitive approaches to learning and assessment are dominant. In individualistic approaches, students work alone to achieve specific outcomes unrelated to the outcomes of others. In competitive learning, individual students work towards outcomes that are beneficial exclusively to themselves and simultaneously may be detrimental to others. Selective admissions and inappropriate norm-referenced assessment approaches are examples of how the competitive principle of learning still operates at significant moments in higher education. In this chapter, however, we will explore in more detail how collaborative learning offers a productive alternative to individualistic and competitive learning approaches when it is embedded into the curriculum to support other kinds of learning outcomes for students.

Collaborative learning can be enabled through, for instance, group writing, problem-solving and group projects in virtual and face-to-face contexts, but learning in group settings is not synonymous with collaboration. Learning in groups can instead involve cooperative learning in which students distribute elements of a group task between members and work individually. Alternatively, groups could work collaboratively whereby they have a shared understanding of the task and realise that the outcomes are only achievable if they coordinate their activities together (Witney and Smallbone, 2011). While cooperation is a form of group working, it is only within collaborative learning that students recognise the value of collective knowledge and the interrelationship between their own learning and that of their peers. In implementing group learning in ways that deliberately seek to encourage students to adopt collaborative learning approaches, we therefore need to find ways to make the process of working together more transparent as well as capture the collectivist knowledge outputs of group working. Social media technologies can fulfil these two requirements by both facilitating and making visible the process of student collaboration while also providing the space for user-generated content that is, when supported and used effectively, more than the sum of the individual contributions.

Using social media technologies to support collaborative learning

There are a range of applications that we can use specifically to support student collaboration and presentation of co-created work for assessment. Document collaboration software at its simplest can include the widely used peer review, commenting and track changes features in Microsoft Office Word or co-authorship of Google Docs. These tools allow both simultaneous and sequential writing and editing that can be shared with peers via email or cloud-based file-sharing services. While enabling collaborative working, one of the disadvantages of these applications, however, is that it can be difficult to track the final contribution individual students have made to the group activity. A wiki is a social media application that enables students collaboratively to write, edit and hyperlink documents or learning resources while also making more transparent the role individual students have played in completing the task. It takes the form of series of hyperlinked text and multimedia web pages that can be open or restricted to specific users. Wikis have a number of features that support group working and collaborative writing (de Wever *et al.*, 2011):

- they allow students to author content, integrate multimedia resources and links and to share this with their peers and teachers;
- they support editing and updating of other students' contributions and in-text feedback from teachers;
- the history functionality makes it possible to go back to previous versions of pages after editing and analytics can track individual student contributions to group tasks (Caple and Bogle, 2013).

If well designed, a wiki-based activity encourages students to collaboratively co-construct subject knowledge, develop and record their team-working skills and enhance their ability to give peer feedback. Collaborative learning through the collective knowledge-building and co-authoring facilitated by social media applications creates opportunities for students to reflect on content from multiple perspectives, understand their own writing from the perspective of different readers and appreciate how their individual knowledge and experiences can 'serve as a learning resource for the learning of others' (Laru *et al.*, 2012: 30).

There are a number of tasks which use wiki or bookmarking and annotation tools to facilitate collaborative writing, to create a repository for student-generated learning resources or to support opportunities for individual reflection on experiences using peer review and feedback. For example, students can use wikis to:

- build a glossary of key terms and concepts (Meishar-Tal and Gorsky, 2010);
- compile a collaborative annotated bibliography or literature review for a specific topic or question;
- create and share a reflective journal of learning experiences in professional or disciplinary contexts (Kear *et al.*, 2010);
- write a lab report to record notes and results with the added value of annotation or amendment by peers;
- capture group brainstorming, problem-solving or compile a report to track the progress of a research project;
- prepare learning resources for peers such as a reading pack, textbook, instruction manual, user documentation for a tool or a protocol for conducting an experiment (Parker and Chao, 2007).

Social bookmarking and annotation applications also make it possible for students to work together to collate, comment on and annotate documents, multimedia and webpages. Social bookmarking tools such as Delicious (https://delicious.com/) and social annotations tools such as Diigo (https://www.diigo.com/) have also been used and researched in educational contexts. Social bookmarking enables teachers and students to assemble web resources and share them with their peers while the tagging option allows teachers to link resources specifically to the curriculum and learning outcomes using keywords 'tagged' to the pages. Rating and tagging options also allow students to organise and share these resources in ways that are meaningful to them (Farwell and Waters, 2010). Social annotation applications are designed to allow users not only to organise material but also to highlight, annotate, link and share documents, webpages and multimedia resources with their peers. Social annotation can be used by students to read and discuss online material and uploaded documents through a process of 'remixing' content; teachers can also embed questions and notes into the text of pre-set readings to direct students to key arguments or ideas (Gao, 2013: 76). Case study 10.2 is an example of using social bookmarking not only to support collaboration, but also to introduce students to enquiry-based learning and develop their research skills.

The affordances of wiki, social annotation and bookmarking software for facilitating group work, co-authorship, peer review and the publishing of student-generated and student-owned module content for sharing with peers make these highly desirable tools for educators. Yet, ultimately, wikis and other social media technologies cannot achieve these outcomes without careful thought given to the pedagogical as well as the technical aspects of the task (Witney and Smallbone, 2011). Specifically, rather than engaging students collaboratively, wiki tasks can result in students simply breaking up a larger assignment into smaller activities which are then delegated to individuals. Students might also work collaboratively in other spaces (when working in person or using email or track changes in documents) but cooperatively in the wiki itself (Naismith *et al.*, 2011). In using wikis and other social tools to support students to work collaboratively and exploit the opportunities for peer-to-peer interaction, it is important to recognise some of the challenges of social media and the process that needs to be in place to scaffold student learning to foster more collaborative approaches.

New technologies do not make equal student participation in, and contribution to, group work any more likely. Even the possibilities of tracking more explicitly the extent and quality of contributions of individuals might not assuage student concerns about 'free-riding' within group tasks. For many students, as indeed for more experienced academic writers, the act of editing, amending or even deleting the work of others in a wiki is a highly complex and sensitive issue requiring high levels of trust between co-authors. Nor does the opportunity for collaboration necessarily mean students will automatically know how or want to work together. Ultimately, how a collaborative task contributes to assessment will drive how students will work together (de Wever *et al.*, 2011). For example, if we use a wiki either to support group learning or explicitly as an assessment task we need to decide if the process as well as the product of collaboration is recognised and if, and how, group and individual grades will be determined. As Naismith *et al.* (2011) warn, 'assessing collaborative activities within an institutional culture of individual achievement sends mixed messages about what is valued' (p. 241).

The dangers of introducing new technologies into the learning and teaching repertoire is that if they are used within existing individual-focused teaching approaches, rather than to challenge teachers and students to explore more participatory and collaborative models of learning, then they will not be transformative (Karasavvidis, 2010). If well designed, the collaborative potential of interactive tools, however, implicates teachers and students in new forms of learning in which students have a far greater role in the co-creation of knowledge and can exploit the opportunities for peer learning. Significantly, Lin and Kelsey (2009) found that student experiences of working with wikis were neither inevitably positive nor distinctively collaborative but went through a number of phases as users came to terms with the different learning relationships social media created. The first phase they describe as one of exploration and a crisis of authority. In this phase students did not use the tool to aid collaboration and, instead of co-writing, students used the tool to create content individually and present this in wiki format with little co-authorship or editing. The second phase is described as adaption or a crisis of relationship as students exploited discussion opportunities alongside the wiki (such as face-to-face meetings, email and discussion forums) to negotiate co-writing, editing decisions and the process of team-working. The final phase is described as a resolution of the crisis when students feel greater levels of confidence to co-write and edit the contributions of others. The implications of this phased engagement with wikis for collaborative learning is that the affordances of wiki software are increasingly exploited with use as students become more familiar with the technology and peer-learning relationships. Naismith *et al.* (2011) also identify a number of factors necessary for the successful implementation of wikis for collaboration. These include student familiarity with the technology, group dynamics, how the wiki is integrated with other elements of the design of the module and how it relates to individual and group assessment strategies.

Drawing on this research into effective use of wikis, social bookmarking and annotation tools, there are a number of practical considerations to ensure that social media technologies will enrich peer-to-peer interactions:

- It is not only necessary to familiarise and explore with students the technical functionality of the collaborative tools, but also to discuss the new peer and collaborative learning practices these tools make possible. Wiki software has an intuitive user interface that builds on students' basic word-processing and file-uploading skills. This means when introducing the activity it is possible to invest time in discussing the pedagogical implications of the task, the desired aims and learning outcomes as well as editing and co-writing skills.
- The 'social' aspects of editing, being edited, collaborating and co-writing are complicated and may be uncomfortable for students. Kear *et al.* (2010) recommend discussing with students the etiquette of co-writing, as well as modifying and reversing editorial actions. As part of the introduction to the wiki task, agree individual and group roles and the protocols for amending and commenting on the work of other students. Acknowledging the sensitivities, modelling how to critique peers' work and discussing how disputes will be resolved legitimises and relieves the negative emotional experience of collaboration while being the first step in building trust and rapport in the group.
- One of the most significant obstacles for effective use of collaborative tools is poor communication between students (Naismith *et al.*, 2011). Keep collaborative groups to a manageable size of four to five members and encourage

students to exploit opportunities to discuss, plan and make decisions about their group task outside the wiki or social annotation environment. Explicitly embedding collaborative activities into face-to-face contexts as well as directing students to use discussion forums, chat rooms or email to support writing and collating tasks will improve the communication skills necessary for collaboration (Lin and Kelsey, 2009).

- The implication of Lin and Kelsey's (2009) identification of the different phases of collaboration is that the quality of engagement improves with time. If a collaborative task is part of summative assessment, then it is important to introduce a practice wiki task earlier in the module to help students become familiar with the software as well as rehearse the critical skills of co-writing and peer feedback.

- Gao's (2013) evaluation of social annotation identified the need for teachers to ensure that the peer learning generated through collaboration is scaffolded with prompt questions and notes to help focus students on key issues and to consolidate student learning through synthesis and reflective activities at the end of the collaborative task. After collating and annotating resources, include a summary task to help students reflect on their learning and devise an action plan for putting the outcomes into practice.

Involving peers for learning

Higher education has traditionally rewarded individual learning and achievement but peers play a significant part in enhancing the learning experience of all students not only in group working, but also in assessment. Doctoral student supervision, in particular, is 'relentlessly individualized' (Boud and Lee, 2005: 512) and, while the potential of peer learning is becoming more established in undergraduate education, postgraduate supervisory practice continues to focus on the 'dyadic relationship' between supervisor and supervisee to the neglect of potential collaborative and reciprocal outcomes (Stracke, 2010: 2). Peer review and feedback, in which students give and receive qualitative feedback (though not necessarily grades) on individual assignments or their personal contribution to group tasks, provides important opportunities for students to calibrate their understanding of standards and assessment criteria as well as enhance their self-assessment skills. Although peer assessment, in which students themselves generate summative grades on work, has been found to be reliable when compared to teacher-led assessment, it remains contentious in higher education. The process of giving formative feedback through review and commentary, however, is more straightforward to introduce into existing teaching contexts.

Peer-assisted learning, also described as peer coaching or peer mentoring, is another strategy that can be used to support students to learn together to share learning experiences such as transition into university and building a sense of belonging to the wider learning community. Engaging with peers fosters learning that is 'extended from the private and individual domain to a more public (i.e. one or more peers) domain' (Liu and Carless, 2006: 281), emphasising the important social and interdependent nature of learning. In discussing the experiences and results of examinations and coursework, module content or working together in project groups, students already frequently participate informally in peer feedback and mentoring relationships (Ladyshewsky, 2013). Yet one of the challenges in facilitating collaborative learning experiences is that, although we might create environments or activities that require them to engage with their peers, students may not do so automatically or willingly. Students can be resistant to peer feedback or peer-assisted learning opportunities, believing their peers lack the expertise necessary for useful feedback (Hammond *et al.*, 2010). Collaborative learning, first and foremost, requires educators to pay full attention to the often overlooked interpersonal conditions that create trust, social interaction and individual accountability necessary for peer relationships to succeed (De Hei *et al.*, 2014).

Yet, despite these difficulties, there are several benefits to embedding peer learning into the curriculum. Building on the concept of 'sustainable feedback' we explored in Chapter 5, giving and receiving peer feedback:

- significantly increases the volume and frequency of feedback received by individual students in a timely way that enables them to respond directly to feedback they have received on a draft before the final submission of work (Nicol *et al.*, 2014);
- is more accessible for students in terms of language, with some students finding it more comfortable to take risks and receive feedback from peers than from their teacher or final assessor (Liu and Carless, 2006);
- gives students access to multiple viewpoints on work beyond that of their teacher that can increase their awareness of how the meaning of texts relates to different readers' perspectives (Nicol *et al.*, 2014);
- develops individual students' capacity to decode the feedback they receive from others, including teachers, and use this as the basis for undertaking complex self-appraisal of their own work (Sadler, 2010);
- provides opportunities for peer reviewers to revise, restate and explain key concepts to others as the basis for developing their own mastery of the subject matter (Nicol *et al.*, 2014).

Recognising the challenges of putting peer feedback processes into practice, it is important to consider the objectives for peer review (Ladyshewsky, 2013).

Will it be informally or formally structured within the curriculum? Will peer feedback involve single or multiple peer reviewers of the work on either a one-off or repeated basis? Are peers self-selecting, anonymous or assigned by the teacher? Will feedback be reciprocal or unilateral? Will it contribute to the final grades of students? Having made the decision about the purpose and intended outcomes of using peers to support learning, there are a number of ways to enhance the introduction of peer review, feedback and assessment to capitalise on the benefits outlined above:

- Always begin the process of peer review and feedback by discussing or working with students to define the assessment criteria against which work will be judged. This helps students to benchmark their understanding and reflect on how judgements are subsequently communicated through feedback (Bloxham and West, 2004). Recognising the importance of the interpersonal dimension for effective peer feedback processes, this initial discussion also helps students to reach agreement on shared values and develop their sense of the peer group as a safe space to learn, take risks and make mistakes.
- To help students engage seriously with the process of giving and receiving peer feedback it is important to show how this activity is valued within the curriculum. Bloxham and West (2004) included as part of assessment the quality of the peer feedback students gave others in an individual's final grade to signal how constructing meaningful feedback for others can inform a student's own learning as well as that of their peers.
- Providing quality feedback is difficult even for experienced assessors, so modelling effective feedback, using exemplars and giving opportunities for students to practice are important elements in embedding peer review and feedback into the curriculum. Peer review prompts or sentence openers help students to focus their feedback and organise their comments. For example, Gielen *et al.* (2010) suggest direct questions that peer reviewers respond to, such as 'Did the author cover all the relevant topics?' Sadler (2010) similarly outlines some basic answers that feedback needs to give as the basis for helping students structure their feedback: 'How well does the work achieve the purpose intended?'; 'What are the grounds for the judgement reached?'; 'How could the work be improved?' (p. 547).
- Translating peer feedback into meaningful learning requires students to use the feedback they give and receive in subsequent self-review and evaluation. Peer feedback interventions, therefore, should include opportunities for individual students to seek particular feedback from reviewers before peer feedback is undertaken, as well as reflective time after they have participated in peer review. In advance of peer review and feedback, learners can specify their own feedback needs and questions which the reviewer

must then respond to. The student then reflects on and replies to this feedback as part of a reflective dialogue (Gielen *et al.*, 2010). Students can also be encouraged to self-review their work using the same criteria as that used in peer review prior to submitting their own work for summative assessment (Nicol *et al.*, 2014).

Peer feedback can be integrated into a range of learning activities at different stages – not just on near-complete drafts of text-based assessments. Samball (2011) outlines several contexts for peer review as part of other collaborative learning opportunities including group peer feedback on group posters or verbal feedback on student presentations. Peer feedback can also be part of formative progress reports at key points in undergraduate and postgraduate research projects to assess research questions, research design and data analysis or student commentaries on blog posts. Case studies 11.1 and 11.2 demonstrate in more detail how peer review may form part of formal assessment and content generation.

 Case study 11.1   Peer assessment of group work in undergraduate nursing (Hunt and Hutchings, 2014)

Recognising that assessing group work may pose difficulties in relation to reaching fair and reliable outcomes for all students, Hunt and Hutchings at Bournemouth University developed several strategies to improve group assessment for a 20-credit undergraduate children's nursing unit. Students on the unit were assessed using an individual case study essay and a group presentation. For the group presentation students worked in groups of four. While the topic for the presentation was selected by the students, group membership was determined by the teacher on the basis of previous academic outcomes. Group presentations were assessed with a combined peer and teacher assessment as the basis for improving students' assessment skills and understanding of the learning outcomes and assessment criteria.

Peer assessment in this case was 'undertaken by groups, rather than individuals, on groups' (p. 26). Each group had to reach a consensus on the grade to be awarded to the other participating groups and the grades from all groups was combined to achieve a peer grade. These were added to assessor grades to reach a final grade for the presentation. To address concerns about 'free-riding' by some students, individual students were required to complete student contracts to explain their contribution to the group presentation. Evaluation of the initiative found that the teacher-determined groupings reduced the tensions of self-selection, although grouping by academic profile did lead to negative experiences for some students in lower-achieving groups and these groups required more teacher support. The group rather than individual peer assessment also relieved student anxieties about reaching independent assessment judgements, while the experience improved students' understanding of the assessment process.

Case study 11.2   Facilitating peer learning in sciences through peer review (Casey *et al.*, 2014)

To encourage student engagement and develop increased depth of understanding in undergraduate physics, chemistry and genetics modules in three universities (University of Edinburgh, University of Glasgow and University of Nottingham), Casey and colleagues used the tool PeerWise to create opportunities for student-generated content and peer learning. PeerWise (http://peerwise.cs.auckland.ac.nz/) is free software that enables students to anonymously author their own assessment questions, answer questions posed by other students and give feedback on their peers' learning. PeerWise was incorporated into the summative assessment strategy of five undergraduate modules and contributed between 2 and 5 per cent of the final grade. The peer-learning task replaced existing traditional assessments in the modules. An introductory 15-minute face-to-face scaffolding exercise with students prior to use of PeerWise introduced question exemplars to model how to write good-quality questions and how to provide feedback on answers. Students were encouraged to use the opportunity to take risks and make mistakes as part of their learning. The system was found to be self-regulating. Where there was debate about accuracy other students would quickly correct errors or identify plagiarised questions without intervention by staff and there was evidence that the peer task increased students' conceptual understanding of the topics. Where the peer-learning activity was utilised as a revision tool student engagement remained high throughout the module.

Supporting peer-assisted learning

The examples above demonstrate how collaboration can contribute to the quantity and quality of feedback available to students, but also how students might play significant roles in the process of learning, assessment decisions and the generation of module content. Peer-assisted learning has also been adopted as a strategy to support the development of study skills and increase understanding of content in different disciplines. For doctoral students, peer group learning is particularly valuable for countering isolation, maintaining motivation and facilitating the sense of belonging to a research community, as well as developing important research skills (Buissink-Smith *et al.*, 2013). The format of peer-assisted learning varies depending on the overall purpose of engaging peers in learning. It can be used for the purposes of peer coaching where student mentors and mentees are studying together and focuses on ongoing mutual formative feedback. Alternatively, a peer tutoring approach can be adopted based on exploiting differences in student level or experience. Peer mentors in these relationships focus explicitly on teaching content (Ladyshewsky, 2013). Peers can therefore be drawn from the same year group or, as is often the case in institutional mentoring schemes, from senior students with the aim to lead sessions to support first-year students during transition into university or to support commonly challenging modules. For postgraduate research students, peer groups can be either disciplinary or multidisciplinary and either student-led or supervisor-led in the form of group supervisions to complement one-to-one supervisions. Doctoral peer groups have been used for presenting ongoing research or practising conference paper presentations or function as a writing group for peer review and for sharing experiences of the research process such as reference management and using databases (Stracke, 2010).

At undergraduate level peer-assisted learning sessions are usually facilitated in small groups (five to 15 students) led by student tutors and sit alongside the curriculum, are optional and designed to complement the formal taught elements of the curriculum. The aim is to provide space for students to discuss questions, review module content and understanding of subject knowledge, problem-solve, develop study skills and familiarise themselves with the demands and expectations of higher-level study and assessment. Peer-assisted learning has been employed in a range of different disciplinary contexts including accountancy (Fox *et al.*, 2010), physiotherapy (Hammond *et al.*, 2010), creative writing (Batty and Sinclair, 2014), mathematics (case study 11.3) and law (case study 11.4). This demonstrates the applicability and utility of peer-assisted learning to support a breadth of learning outcomes and operate within curricula from different epistemological and pedagogical traditions. In putting peer-assisted learning into practice it is recommended that teachers consider the following points:

- Be clear about the purpose of sessions. Are you aiming to provide additional opportunities to discuss and debate content, solve problems, introduce new content, clarify module and assessment expectations, support academic skills such as research skills and essay writing or to support revision?

- Align sessions to the learning outcomes and content of other timetabled taught sessions in the module so that sessions are linked to the curriculum rather than additional work.
- Be explicit about who will be responsible for timetabling sessions, booking rooms and equipment and who will coordinate tutors' administrative and practical issues. As this is often extracurricular, how do you ensure it is inclusive for students with employment or caring responsibilities?
- Provide preparatory training for tutors to introduce them to how to structure active learning approaches, how to facilitate group discussion or support problem-solving and how to give effective feedback in inclusive contexts.
- Although sessions are usually student-directed, decide to what extent you will provide students with support to develop their resources and session plans or if you will make resources available to all tutors. Resources might include ice-breaking tasks, discussion prompts, case studies or problems to work through with additional guidance, quizzes or past examination papers and model answers.

 Case study 11.3   Peer-assisted learning in undergraduate mathematics (Duah *et al.*, 2014)

At Loughborough University, teachers noticed a 'cooling off' as some students became demotivated during the transition into university-level mathematics. Peer-assisted learning was trialled as one strategy for responding to this challenge in a second-year Vector Spaces module that was considered by students to be particularly difficult. The module was traditionally taught by a two-hour lecture and an hour tutorial per week. Thirteen peer mentors were recruited from third-year students who had successfully completed the module the previous year and 50-minute optional peer-assisted learning sessions were scheduled once a week for all current students on the module. A total of 57 second-year students took up the opportunity to attend at least one session. Credit for the peer mentoring was linked to a university employability award for mentors. All peer mentors received training from the central teaching unit on facilitating group learning, how to design resources and learning activities. Peer-assisted learning sessions would include a starter activity prepared by either peer mentors or the module teacher, as well as pair and small group activities based around discussion and questions. Problem-sheets, tests and previous exam papers were also used during

(Continued)

(Continued)

the sessions. While some students still preferred more teacher-led or didactic methods, evaluation of the initiative found a positive relationship between peer-assisted learning session attendance and the final module mark even if controlling for prior attainment and lecture attendance.

 Case study 11.4   Peer-assisted learning for first-year law students (Zacharopoulou and Turner, 2013)

Peer-assisted study sessions (PASS) were piloted as an optional supplement to the core first-year module Introduction to Law at the University of Ulster to improve student engagement and transition into university. Peer learning was seen as a response to high attrition rates, high failure rates in some modules and lack of student engagement. The sessions were aimed at supporting the social integration of students into university life, the development of study skills and to help students understand the requirements of independent study at university. Ten peer mentors were recruited from senior students to facilitate five small, informal groups comprised of 15 first-year law students. Peer mentors were not selected on the basis of their academic performance because the purpose of PASS was not to offer academic tuition but to provide support on shared experiences of study skills difficulties and dissatisfying examination results. PASS mentors were given training in peer facilitation techniques and had a regular debriefing with the module co-ordinator. Sessions were used to clarify readings, analyse topics and debate questions as well as support social induction of students into the university.

Collaborative learning in education for sustainable development (ESD)

In Chapter 3 we explored how ESD requires new ways of thinking about problems from interdisciplinary perspectives. ESD, however, also encapsulates other graduate outcomes related to understanding the processes of working in groups and achieving collective outcomes. In this context, collaborative learning creates opportunities to explore personal and collective values, beliefs and ethics, as well as knowledge and citizenship. The QAA (2014a) suggest outcomes related to collaboration include the ability to:

- 'evaluate the impacts and interconnections between the activities of different generations, demographic groups and cultures';
- 'demonstrate that the collective effect of actions is not necessarily just a simple sum of their individual effects but is likely to be more complex';
- 'identify the importance of empowering individuals and organisations to work together to create new knowledge';
- 'facilitate and mediate progressive discussions among interested parties (stakeholders) to help resolve dilemmas and conflicts' (pp. 10–12).

Sustainability pedagogies are likely to be participatory and inclusive, involve group work, engage students in small group discussion and encourage students to co-create knowledge and teach each other (Cotton and Sterling, 2012).

Table 11.1   Approaches to developing collaborative learning in sustainability education

Collaborative learning method	Strategies for supporting and reflecting on group learning
Role-play and simulations	Role-playing and simulations such as gaming, mock trials or press conferences based around real-world sustainability issues enable students to explore and empathise with different perspectives on contentious subjects, as well as to evaluate the process and impact of individual and collective decision-making
Group discussions	Facilitated group discussion is an important context for exploring multiple viewpoints and social values. By focusing on how arguments are constructed, developing listening skills and analysing discursive patterns, students can reflect on the processes of group interaction and communication
Debates	Preparing arguments to a brief for a debate requires students to work collaboratively and make decisions about the roles and responsibilities of different members of the group for research and developing an argument. Reflecting on the allocation of group roles, the construction of arguments and evaluating counter arguments enables students to consider point of view and how this influences the interpretation of evidence
Problem-based learning	Interrogating and working towards resolutions for a stated problem are seen by many as a key strategy for sustainability education because they involve student-led collaboration based around real-world complex problems. Problem-based learning is valuable for developing student team-working skills such as communication and interpersonal skills, leadership, project management and prioritisation, managing conflict and valuing alternative perspectives (Bessant et al., 2013)
Reflexive accounts	Encouraging students to reflect on their own views on a sustainability issue and identify individual action for change enables students to reflect on their personal values and their relationship to the values and actions of wider society

Learning experientially in relation to sustainability means being self-reflexive about the experience of collaboration and group work as well as of real-world or applied problems. Becoming sensitive to the issues, however, means students also recognise the interconnectedness of their experiences with that of their peers, value diversity of position and perspective and appreciate their individual and collective responsibility for social, economic and ecological conditions in the present and in the future. Fundamental to these outcomes is that students not only need to learn how to participate collaboratively in groups, but also to critically evaluate and enhance how individuals and groups work together. Teaching methods for sustainability deliberately create opportunities for experiencing collaborative group work (Cotton and Winter, 2010; Winter and Cotton, 2012). To enable students fully to achieve the graduate outcomes related to collaboration, however, the approaches also need to include space for students to reflect and evaluate the processes of working in groups. Some of the types of group activities and how to reflect on the experiences of collaborating are summarised in Table 11.1.

Introducing participatory sustainability pedagogies into the curriculum will inevitably draw on understanding of inclusive learning and teaching (Chapter 8) and internationalisation (Chapter 9). When implementing these activities as part of sustainability education it is important to include opportunities for students to pause and reflect on the process as well as the outcomes of learning collaboratively. Students might critically evaluate the group work in terms of participation, inclusion of all voices, roles and responsibilities, communication, conflict resolution and group norms. For example, assessment might include a reflective commentary on group processes using some of the following prompts:

- Did all members of the group contribute to the outcomes of the group? Did different members assume roles or were different roles allocated to individuals? How did the group agree individual roles in achieving the task?
- Did one or more members dominate the discussion or did all members contribute equally? Did all members of the group listen respectfully to each other? How was communication within the group organised and managed?
- How were different cultural, generational or political viewpoints of group members recognised and explored? How were shared values, positions and beliefs agreed? How were conflicts, dissent or different perspectives addressed, responded to and managed within the group?
- How did members determine the aims and objectives of the group in terms of task and process? How were decisions reached by the group?

> **Focus on practice**
>
> Review a module you currently teach and identify a place in the module where you can introduce one of the following:
>
> - formal collaborative writing or group project experience;
> - peer feedback or peer-assisted learning;
> - reflection on group work.
>
> How might these interventions enhance student learning in your context? What measures need to be put in place to ensure effective collaborative learning? What factors might hinder the successful embedding of collaborative learning?

Conclusion

In this chapter we have drawn together the ideas of employability, diversity, internationalisation and digital technologies as they coalesce around redefining the relationship between individual self-regulated learning and group collaborative learning. We have explored a number of ways in which collaborative learning can be embedded into the curriculum, giving students the opportunity to experience group work, peer learning and the challenges of team-work and task management in face-to-face and virtual contexts. Fundamental to fulfilling the learning potential of group activities, however, is the inclusion of space for students to reflect on group processes, to increase their awareness of the diversity of perspectives and the need to negotiate and challenge different viewpoints. Engaging in collaborative learning tasks and participating in peer feedback or peer tutoring also emphasise the importance of collaborative knowledge creation and decentralisation of authority and expertise in contemporary social, intellectual and employment contexts. The questions and case studies in this chapter demonstrate how collaborative and peer learning can be introduced into a range of disciplinary contexts while recognising the challenges and complexities of making collaborative learning meaningful for students. Ensuring learning and assessment tasks include explicit points for reflection will help students to develop and articulate their understanding of how groups work together more effectively. This capacity to reflect on group processes is increasingly regarded as an essential graduate outcome necessary not only for employment, but also global citizenship, sustainability literacy and the capacity to respond to the complexity of contemporary and future world problems.

Further reading

Brookfield, Stephen and Preskill, Stephen (1999) *Discussion as a Way of Teaching: Tools and Techniques for University Teachers*. Buckingham: Open University Press.
This book conceptualises discussion and group work as democratic and emancipatory practices and includes practical suggestions for facilitating discussion and collaborative working.

Gibbs, Graham (2009) 'The assessment of group work: lessons from the literature' (http://www.brookes.ac.uk/aske/documents/Brookes%20groupwork%20Gibbs%20Dec%2009.pdf).
This literature review provides an overview of the issues involved in assessing individual and group contributions as an outcome of group work.

Nicol, David, Thomson, Avril and Breslin, Caroline (2014) 'Rethinking feedback practices in higher education: a peer review perspective', *Assessment & Evaluation in Higher Education*, 39(1): 102–22.
This paper explores how peer review might be integrated into assessment practice to improve students' capacity to give quality feedback as an important graduate outcome.

PART III

FROM DISCIPLINARY TEACHER TO SCHOLARLY TEACHER

CHAPTER 12

UNDERTAKING ENQUIRY INTO LEARNING AND TEACHING

Learning objectives

This chapter will support you to:

- Develop a critical understanding of how enquiry into learning and teaching informs the professional practice of teachers in higher education;
- Consider the different aims and methods for investigating learning and teaching as a teacher-as-researcher;
- Plan and undertake a scholarly enquiry into a specific question, problem or issue in your own context.

Introduction

In the preceding chapters we have explored the challenges and opportunities of undertaking teaching in the context of expanding student numbers and increased diversity while preparing our students for global employment and lives, as well as engaging with technologies that have the potential to transform both educational and workplace practice. What these shifting demands on higher education mean for educators is that maintaining and updating disciplinary expertise alone is not sufficient for effective learning and teaching in universities. The complexities of the experience of learning, the realities of the interactions of teachers with students, students with their peers, and teachers and students with the curriculum content, mean that we cannot fully predict how learners will respond to our teaching in a particular time or place. Hunches, intuitions or assumptions about learning might reflect our professional experience and may be proved correct, but, equally, the outcomes of learning experiences we facilitate might be shaped by many confounding and unexpected factors. Christensen Hughes (2007) warns that educators may 'routinely make decisions about their teaching and service activities that are not evidence-based (a standard they would not accept in their research activity)' (p. 109). Research by education researchers or academic developers into learning and teaching in higher education may provide insights or suggest enhancements to put into practice. Yet, ultimately, a situated and contextualised understanding of learning in a specific lecture or supervision, module or degree programme empowers teachers to make informed judgements about their own teaching as professionals. To achieve this as teachers we also need to be a 'teacher-as-researcher' of our own practice by enquiring into the learning experiences we plan for our students and using an evidence-informed approach that helps us to test our instincts or our hypotheses about learning (Stenhouse, 1975).

While we may begin our teaching careers as researchers or professionals with expertise and knowledge that we need to recontextualise for our students through the curriculum, becoming scholarly in our approach means we need to relook at our teaching through the lens of pedagogic enquiry. Bass (1999) highlights the way we often differentiate between research and teaching around the construction of the 'problem'. On the one hand, in research, 'having a "problem" is at the heart of the investigative process; it is the compound of the generative question around which all creative and productive activity revolves'. In teaching, on the other hand, and in the context of public university key information sets, we often seek to resolve a 'problem' as quickly and discretely as possible. How then, Bass asks, might 'we think of teaching practice, and the evidence of student learning, as problems to be investigated, analysed, represented, and debated'? Being a scholarly teacher means using teaching problems to drive our enquiry into our own practice, to learn from that enquiry and to generate new questions. Sometimes these investigations will be for us alone, to evaluate and develop our individual teaching and knowledge about how we support learning. Alternatively, these investigations may be enquiries that we want to share with others, to make public our findings and further our wider knowledge as a community about learning and teaching in higher education.

Building on Boyer's (1990) idea of a 'scholarship of teaching' in which teaching and research are comparable acts of knowledge-making, when we approach our teaching from this perspective of enquiry as 'teacher-as-researcher' with the aim to share this with a wider audience, we are engaging in learning and teaching research. It is underpinned by a commitment to asking questions about student learning that are contextually grounded, and making that enquiry systematic, public, open to critique by others and, where possible, undertaken in collaboration with our students (Felten, 2013).

This form of enquiry is often referred to, especially in the US context, as a 'scholarship of teaching and learning' or 'SoTL'. In the UK context, Cleaver *et al.* (2014) suggest that the concept of 'scholarship' is understood in a more constricted way. As such, we tend to use the terms 'educational' or 'pedagogic research' when we talk about this type of enquiry. The distinctive features of the type of investigation that we will be exploring in this chapter are that it is systematic enquiry that is undertaken by teachers into their own learning and teaching practice. It is predominantly 'insider' research by those directly implicated in the outcomes and is undertaken for the purposes of extending the personal learning of the teacher or students and to improve practice. It may be that we choose to share the outcomes publicly with others – for example, to enable peer scrutiny of our conclusions or to disseminate effective practice – but it may be equally for our own understanding and decision-making as professionals. Hence, here we will use the terms 'enquiry' and 'teacher-as-researcher' to convey this scholarly approach to teaching as the basis for the professional engagement of teachers in higher education.

As well as enacting one form of distinctly disciplinary enquiry, enquiry into learning and teaching will often also be a process of engaging with people, methodologies and concepts that lie outside of a teacher-as-researcher's disciplinary context. Planning, undertaking and sharing a systematic enquiry into learning and teaching may involve working in multidisciplinary teams with experts from other disciplines or with input from academic developers, education researchers or education technologists (Cousin, 2009). Because of the nature of teaching as a social phenomenon, researching teaching practice also draws predominantly on social science epistemologies, methodologies and language that can make those working in other disciplinary communities feel 'a stranger in a strange land' (Stierer, 2008: 35). Engaging in enquiry into learning and teaching in our own context, therefore, can become interdisciplinary, potentially drawing on a breadth of educational methodologies as well as more familiar disciplinary research perspectives to understand our students' learning (Potter, 2009; Cleaver *et al.*, 2014). As such, undertaking systematic, critically informed and potentially public enquiry into our teaching and learning, is a challenging but central feature of our professional identity as teachers.

In this chapter we will begin by exploring what it means to be a teacher-as-researcher and the type of questions we might want to ask about our own teaching practice. We will then look at how we embark on rigorous enquiry into our practice as scholarly teachers through two modes of enquiry: evaluation and action research. We can use these ways of enquiring into our practice to increase our understanding of learning and teaching, for changing and evaluating our practice and for disseminating our findings to our colleagues. Many of the case studies included throughout this book are not conducted by education researchers but are the outcome of teachers researching their own practice and sharing this with others through publication. We will conclude by revisiting what we might want to investigate in our practice as scholarly teachers and agents for change in response to some of the new priorities for higher education we have explored in previous chapters.

Asking questions about learning and teaching

Hutchings and Shulman (1999) contend that 'a scholarship of teaching is *not* synonymous with excellent teaching' but 'requires a kind of "going meta," in which faculty frame and systematically investigate questions related to student learning' with 'an eye not only to improving their own classroom but to advance practice beyond it' (p. 13, emphasis original). Aside from this necessity for 'going public', however, scholarly teaching is inherently entwined with what it means to be a professional university teacher (Potter and Kustra, 2011). All forms of knowledge creation about teaching require the capacity for teachers-as-researchers to be systematic, to be critical and to locate their practice in their context while drawing on a wider literature about learning and teaching to inform their understanding and decision-making. Drawing on work by Ashwin and Trigwell (2004), McEwen and Mason O' Connor (2014) distinguish between three different purposes for investigating practice:

- to develop our personal knowledge through reflective practice, evaluation and engagement with relevant literature;
- to develop local knowledge that will inform the understanding and work of a group through, for example, evaluation of a module, programme or new strategy;
- to develop public knowledge that will inform the understanding and work of a wider audience beyond the teacher-as-researcher's own context.

Ashwin and Trigwell (2004) argue that these different purposes for generating practice knowledge will call on different types of evidence that is validated in different ways and that the outcomes of these investigations will have different implications. Nevertheless, enquiry that is undertaken, in the first instance, to inform personal learning can become part of the evidence for a wider audience and, similarly, enquiry aimed at contributing to public knowledge will inevitably result in both personal knowledge and local enhancement. All these forms of enquiry are driven by 'problems' or questions that arise out of the experience of teaching, out of new demands or pressures or out of engagement with new perspectives or ideas from peers or the wider pedagogic debates. Hutchings (2000) suggests that these questions take different forms. The first type of question that we ask about teaching relates to 'what works'. These are questions that seek to determine how effective specific teaching interventions are for learning. The second type of question we could explore relates to 'what is'. These are exploratory and will enable us to describe the characteristics of a particular teaching and learning experience or setting. The third type of question we might pursue relates to 'what could be'. These questions are concerned with challenging our assumptions or routines and openness to change; these might emerge out of our exploration of a particular incident or activity, leading us to something new we might want to achieve or do in our teaching. For example, we might want to improve student engagement in a seminar or introduce a more inclusive assessment strategy. A 'what could be' question would enable us to understand and reflect on existing circumstances, plan an intervention or change and examine the outcomes (Robson, 2011).

These different types of questions drive ongoing evaluation of existing teaching as well as informing curriculum development or pedagogic enhancement work. In the UK the National Student Survey and Postgraduate Taught and Research Experience Surveys often sit alongside institutional module evaluations and form one set of data that informs our understanding of our students' learning experience. The focus on student satisfaction and the 'what works' orientation of these survey tools, however, mean that if we want to explore other aspects of how our teaching is enhancing our students' learning or to imagine future possibilities we must deliberately ask other questions and turn to other sources of evidence. Importantly, we also need to recognise the form of evidence we will generate out of our enquiry. The danger of 'what works' questions is that they imply that we can collect sufficient evidence to correct all failings in a teaching system and, ultimately, identify the correct actions that will lead consistently to the same desirable and predictable learning outcomes for all students. While operating on hunch or simply ignoring the impact of our pedagogic decisions is not defensible, overestimating the nature of the evidence that we might draw on when trying to understand or improve our teaching is also problematic.

When we talk about teaching being evidence-informed we need, Biesta (2010) warns, to recognise that education settings are not closed systems that can be controlled or isolated from the environment as is possible in randomised control trials in scientific experimental research. Unlike the cause and effect relationships we might identify in a closed system, any claims we make about education settings are likely to be 'probabilistic' at best. Evidence-informed teaching, therefore, does not assume a 'mechanistic connection between evidence and truth', but still requires teachers to operate a professional value 'judgement about the relative weight of what is being submitted as evidence for a particular belief or proposition' and how we might use that evidence to inform our understanding of our practice (p. 493). When we engage in collecting evidence about our teaching we should do so with the aim to use the data we gather not to tell us definitive facts about teaching but to help us understand the experience and make expert critical judgements about how we enable student learning.

If 'what works' questions are problematic, enquiring into our practice using 'what is' and 'what could be' questions enables us to gain insight into the experiences of our students. We can use enquiry to identify the possible enablers and barriers for student learning and our values and biases as teachers, as well as to support us to make and evaluate changes to our practice. We can do this in many ways, but we are going to focus on two different forms of enquiry, evaluation and action research, as the basis for gaining knowledge about our learning and teaching practice. What drives any enquiry will always be the types of questions we bring to our investigation. It may be that we are seeking to understand a particular activity or context that is achieving effective outcomes. The aim is not necessarily to make any changes to practice but to get a better insight into the activity; an evaluation will enable us to learn more and potentially share this with others. If, however, a particular learning task or assessment leads to unequal or unsuccessful experiences for students, we might use an action research approach to review the situation, identify a possible way to improve it, intervene and then evaluate the outcome. Where evaluation alone can be undertaken to be predominantly 'informative', the intention behind action research is to be deliberately 'transformative' (Cousin, 2009: 152).

Using evaluation to understand the experience of student learning

While evaluation of the student experience using national and institutional programme and module surveys is widespread and gives us benchmarked information about our institutions and programmes, it does not always help educators make fully informed and thoughtful judgements about the learning experience of their students or how it might be improved. Over a period of time we may also find that regular end-of-module surveys become a ritual, positioning students as passive and giving them little opportunity to see any impact on their own learning experiences as an outcome of evaluation. These approaches to student evaluation position the teacher simply as a receiver of feedback, often focusing on summative assessment of a teaching performance rather than formative feedback that can be used to enhance their students' learning or contribute to an educators' own professional knowledge. As Nygaard and Belluigi (2011) argue, standardised surveys de-contextualise the learning experience and fail to take account of the fact that every cohort of students and every iteration of a lecture or module is a complex and 'unique ongoing system of social relations' (p. 659). The motives, questions, audience and outcomes for evaluation should therefore be specific to that context and, as such, evaluation is best understood as a situated 'social practice' within that learning and teaching system (Saunders *et al.*, 2011). Asking students to do more than rate the quality of teaching and, instead, soliciting their feedback on their learning experiences in discursive and collaborative ways, especially on an ongoing basis during a module or programme rather than as an end-of-module evaluation, is a powerful tool for engaging students and teachers in collaborative reflection about their own approaches to learning. Drawing on the idea of assessment for, rather than of, learning that we discussed in Chapter 5, Freeman and Dobbins (2013) argue that dialogue-based evaluation is formative *for* student and teacher learning rather than summative end-of-module evaluation *of* teaching.

When planning an evaluation it is useful to clarify the aims and planned out-comes for an evaluation (Nygaard and Belluigi, 2011; Saunders, 2000), such as:

- purpose of the evaluation: why are you evaluating and what are the aims of the activity or module you are wanting to evaluate? Is it to inform you or your students' learning or is it for accountability?
- focus of the evaluation: for example, do you want to focus on the quality of learning resources, student engagement, perceptions of the learning experience, teaching methods used or the content of the module?
- use of the evaluation: are the results of the evaluation going to be used for enhancing student learning, informing teacher personal or group knowl-edge, to find evidence of effective practice or for assuring the quality of individual teachers or modules? Who is the audience for the evaluation? Will the outcomes be shared with students and why?
- methods that will be used: who will you collect evidence from and when? For instance, will it be current or exiting students or alumni, future employ-ers or colleagues or a number of sources? What type of data do you want to collect? Will it be numerical, such as quantitative surveys or virtual learning environment analytics, or qualitative data, such as closed or open questions and observational data, or a mixture of different types of data? What is the timing of the data collection?

In this approach to evaluation the decisions about what methods to use to collect the data, from whom and when, are made only after we have decided why we are doing the evaluation and what our intended outcomes will be. Fundamentally, before we evaluate we need to be clear about the criteria against which we will be judging practice. These criteria articulate what we believe constitutes effective learning and teaching. If we believe effective teaching is concerned with efficient transmission of information then our focus will be very different to if we believe effective teaching is about student engagement. The important thing is that we do not need to wait until the end of a module to do an evaluation and we can draw on a range of sources and types of evidence to inform our critical judgements about teaching.

Case study 12.1   Investigating student perceptions of mooting in an undergraduate law module (Jones and Field, 2014)

Mooting is a well-established mode of legal education providing law students with the opportunity to develop their analysis, problem-solving and oral communication skills. Colleagues at the University of Brighton wanted to explore student perceptions of a compulsory 20-credit independent study module 'Law in Practice: Moot' in the Law LLB programme. The module teachers undertook a small-scale study of the module with the aim to collect qualitative and quantitative data from students to evaluate their perception of the module. Participating students were fully briefed on the aims of the research, the use of the data and issues of confidentiality before the collection of the data. The module teachers invited 58 students to participate in 15-minute semi-structured interviews in groups of three or four to respond to open-ended questions about their perspectives on the module. In addition to this qualitative data, they also asked students to complete an anonymous online quantitative questionnaire. Some of the questions gave students a positive or negative choice of response while other questions asked students to rate their response on a five-point Likert scale measured from totally agree to totally disagree. The two teachers-as-researchers then analysed the qualitative and quantitative data to identify the themes in the students' responses. The two forms of data enabled them to build up a picture of the student experience of the module and to relate this to relevant literature on student self-regulated and active learning. They concluded that the module does encourage students to adopt active learning strategies and develop relevant critical thinking skills as an important part of their law degree.

We can evaluate teaching and learning throughout a module, including through informal discussion with our students and our colleagues during teaching, short polls, student assessment outcomes, peer teaching observations, student focus groups and individual interviews, as well as the standard institutional end-of-module surveys. However, if we want to conduct evaluation *for* learning we can use dialogue-based and collaborative methods that are embedded into the learning process that help students use evaluation of teaching to make sense and reflect on their learning.

Reaction cards

Like the 'minute paper' (see Chapter 4), 'reaction cards' (Costello *et al.*, 2002) create opportunities for evaluation to take the form of an ongoing dialogue between students and the teacher about the module and give feedback on student understanding and engagement with content as well as the learning processes. Reaction cards are a low-technology tool manageable with medium-sized groups that are seen regularly. Students are asked to write a response, or 'reaction', at some point during a lecture or seminar. It might include a response to something challenging, unintuitive or surprising. Alternatively, they can be asked to respond to specific questions about the content or learning activity posed by the teacher or write down their own questions. The reaction cards include the student's name and are returned to the teacher at the end of the session. The teacher then responds individually to each comment by writing a brief answer, question or comment on the card. The students collect their card at the next lecture or seminar and can read and respond again to their teacher's comments.

Twitter

A digital alternative to the 'minute paper' or 'reaction card' is to use microblogging tools such as Twitter (https://twitter.com) as an instant feedback tool during, or after, teaching. Students are asked to post short comments, questions or responses to the content. To use microblogging, students need a mobile device and either to follow the teacher on Twitter or use a hashtag. They can live tweet their questions or comments during the lecture and teachers can choose to stream them alongside the presentation or, more manageably, review them at key revision points in the lecture and respond. This tool enables teachers to pose specific questions about a particular activity as well as evaluate their students' understanding in real-time. It is possible to respond to and extend student questions or comments by retweeting key points for the whole group after a lecture or to encourage student-to-student interaction in ways that are not always possible in large enrolment cohorts (Kassens-Noor, 2012; Prestridge, 2014).

Nominal group technique

This is a technique that is useful for group problem-solving and decision-making and can be used to generate, categorise and test out ideas in the context of learning, but it is also adaptable to evaluating practice. The first stage in the process is to ask students to respond to a question individually and silently. For example, they can be asked to identify the strengths and weaknesses of an activity or module or suggest ways in which it might be improved. The questions posed might have emerged out of the results of a student survey. The next stage is to collate all the responses from all group members and list these concisely on a flipchart or board. In large groups, small sub-groups of five or six students can compile composite lists instead and feed these back into the group to keep the number of ideas manageable. When all the ideas have been generated the group discusses each idea to clarify the meaning and collaboratively cluster or categorise the list of responses. This is then followed by a vote whereby individual students identify the five most important ideas to them and rank these by allocating a score of one to five. This can be done quickly using polling tools or collated manually. This identifies the ranking for the group as a whole and is fed back to the group to discuss or problem-solve. The benefits of this method include capturing a breadth of student views and priorities and, through collaborative problem-solving of issues this raises, enabling them to take greater ownership of the learning experience (Chapple and Murphy, 1996).

Students as consultants in the enhancement of teaching

Collaborating with students to better understand how learning and teaching are experienced by learners provides unique insights that are unavailable to teachers in any other ways while helping students to reflect on their learning. This can be taken beyond 'consulting students' about their experience to viewing 'students as consultants' in their learning (Cook-Sather, 2009: 232). One way to do this is to ask students to take an active role in gathering and interpreting student evaluations of a module at the mid-term or mid-module point. Volunteer student consultants co-construct with their teacher a series of questions about the learning experience to ask students in the class. After speaking to students, the student consultants summarise the feedback and collaborate with the teacher to interpret the collected data and determine how the feedback and the solutions or clarifications might be shared with students. Undertaking this at a mid-point in the module rather than after teaching has finished allows the teacher to respond in ways that have a direct impact on the students who have provided the feedback. Working with student consultants in the process also gives teachers access to insights, experiences and interpretations that might not be available in staff-led evaluation. For example, the University of Exeter's 'Students as Change Agents' scheme invites students to undertake projects to investigate and propose improvements to their university experience and the University of Lincoln's 'Students Consulting on Teaching' (SCOTs) scheme enables students to observe and give feedback on teaching practice outside their discipline.

Case study 12.2   Student–teacher engagement in appreciative enquiry to improve inclusivity (Kadi-Hanifi et al., 2014)

As part of a commitment to enhancing inclusion in the Institute of Education at the University of Worcester, three students (two postgraduate and one first-year undergraduate) were recruited to participate in an appreciative enquiry into inclusivity. Appreciative enquiry is an approach that focuses on identifying the successes and opportunities rather than deficits or failings of a context. The students collected data from their peers by asking them to write positive adjectives about their learning experience and elicited 58 different adjectives from 176 students from which they identified the 12 most popular comments. The students then conducted face-to-face, phone or email interviews with nine students that had declared a disability, focusing on their perceptions of how inclusive the learning environment was and what university facilities supported their learning. These were developed into statements that demonstrated the university was inclusive when, for instance, 'cultural diversity is embraced', or 'it sets high expectations and supports students in achieving them' (p. 590). These statements were presented by students to staff members at a professional development day. The staff then worked collaboratively to understand when practice was inclusive and visualise how an inclusive environment would look in the future. This has led to increased engagement with inclusivity, including recognition of diversity as a resource in teaching, increased explicitness about inclusion in practice and listening to the student voice.

Enquiry into learning and teaching using action research

The enriched, collaborative outcomes of evaluation described above will begin to provide us with answers to 'what is' questions that give us insight into the experiences of our students, their expectations, the challenges or the interventions that help their learning. If we want to explore 'what could be' questions, however, we need to conduct investigations into learning and teaching that enable us not only to find out the effects of our existing curriculum or teaching decisions, but also help us plan and investigate changes to improve learning and teaching. The purpose of action research is to carry out an enquiry into a change in practice that has been instigated to enhance any aspect of teaching, learning, assessment or the context within which it takes place. As McNiff (2013) explains, 'the "action" of action research refers to what you do' and 'the "research" of action research refers to how you find out about what you do' (p. 25). Action research, therefore, allows us to identify a question, concern or issue we want to explore in our teaching, review the current situation and, drawing on our experience as well as suggestions and ideas from students, colleagues or the educational literature, to 'imagine a way forward' (p. 90). We then try out our proposed change and evaluate the outcome. Action research is, therefore, a cyclical process of review, planning for change, action and ensuing enquiry that results in both concrete problem-solving and greater understanding about a learning and teaching situation. As such, evaluation may become a central component of action research. Likewise, the outcomes of an evaluation of teaching can illuminate a problem that we want to resolve and this will lead to the planning and implementation of a change in practice and follow-up evaluation. These two approaches to understanding our teaching, therefore, are not discrete activities but usefully connected (Robson, 2011).

As we explored above, when evaluation is based on dialogue and collaboration with students, it can become part of the mutual learning of students and their teachers rather than external to the process. Likewise, action research is a participative and emancipatory form of research that leads to mutual knowledge outcomes for students and their teachers-as-researchers. It is a type of enquiry that is usually done with the subjects of the research rather than on them or to them, so enquiry is not a separate activity to our practice but is a 'lived experience' at the heart of what it means to be a teacher in higher education (McNiff, 2013: 24). This means that teachers-as-researchers 'position themselves as learners throughout the process, expecting to be transformed as well as transform' (Cousin, 2009: 155). Embedding action research into our educational practice, therefore, means we reinvigorate and reintegrate our identities as teachers, researchers and learners in higher education and that we are as critical and systematic in our approach to teaching as we are in our disciplinary research.

Case study 12.3   An action research study of a 'feedback on request' intervention in undergraduate business programmes (Jones and Gorra, 2013)

Colleagues in the Business School at Leeds Beckett University, formerly Leeds Metropolitan University, wanted to investigate how many students accessed summative feedback provided by teachers and their reasons for doing so. The study examined student engagement with teacher feedback following the introduction of a new way of giving feedback to second-year students in two undergraduate business programmes. The problem the teachers wanted to investigate was that, despite the provision of detailed feedback to over 250 students on the programmes, they had noted a lack of student engagement with the assessment feedback. The change that they wanted to evaluate involved offering students different levels of feedback. All students would receive generic cohort feedback from the assessors as well as an individual marking matrix using the assessment criteria to indicate how they had performed and a short commentary. Students could access this feedback through the module virtual learning environment. Finally, students could opt to request further, more detailed individual feedback from their marker in the form of an audio podcast within a week of receiving their original feedback. This placed the emphasis on the students to seek the type of feedback that they wanted. Data on student feedback engagement behaviour following this change included an online survey before students submitted their assignment which asked them to enter the percentage grade they expected for the work and the likelihood they would seek the audio podcast additional feedback. After submission and marking, virtual learning environment tracking data enabled the researchers to monitor student access of the different levels of feedback. All the students who requested individual feedback were asked to complete an online survey to indicate the level of feedback they had accessed and how valuable they had found each of them. A general survey of student experience of feedback was also distributed to all students on several modules including those students involved in the action research study. What the teachers found was that when there was a discrepancy between expected and received grade students were more likely to actually seek further detailed feedback. The implications for the teachers are that the study demonstrated that the selective provision of comments on request rather than detailed feedback to all students was a viable option given the finite resources of staff time when giving feedback to large student cohorts.

Action research involves progressing through a series of stages and may include using some of the evaluation tools described above to inform your understanding of a situation and monitoring a change in practice:

- Planning: What is the problem or issue? What are you trying to achieve? What do you know about the current situation? How and from whom can you collect data that will help you understand the situation better? What does other research in this area tell you about the issue? What change might you introduce as an outcome of this analysis that will improve the situation?
- Acting: How will you introduce the change? What is the timescale for the change? What resources do you need? Will you involve colleagues and students?
- Observing: How will you monitor the impact of the change, for instance, using surveys, observation, interviews, assessment outcomes, reflective diaries? Who will you collect this from?
- Reflecting: What does the information you have collected tell you about the change? What do you know about the new situation? Did the change achieve what you planned? Were there other outcomes? Is the change sustainable in the future? Do you need to do something else?

Focus on practice

Identify a question related to an activity or module you teach or support and consider how you might investigate it. Does it involve developing a better understanding of the situation or might you want to make a change and evaluate it? What data sources (such as students, teachers, assessors, peers, employers) and types of data will you need to draw on in your enquiry? What research is available to inform your understanding? How might you involve students in the enquiry?

Conclusion

Investigating our educational practice as a teacher-as-researcher is as essential to our professional identity as maintaining our disciplinary or practice expertise. Higher education has the potential to transform individual lives as well as our collective endeavours as we seek to understand and respond to the complex challenges of the contemporary world. We cannot predict with certainty how or where knowledge will be generated or to what purpose we or future generations will need to apply it. As de-contextualised institutional and national surveys place increasing pressure on universities to be accountable for the learning experiences they provide, the evaluative and action research approaches to enquiry introduced in this chapter remind us that the data we collect about teaching and learning is not objective truth. It offers us evidence that we must interpret and weigh up using our professional judgement. Undertaking systematic enquiry into learning and teaching is a fundamental facet of our professional identity that empowers us to challenge inappropriate policy or practice decisions as informed members of the university community. It challenges us to test our own prejudices and assumptions and work in collaboration with our students to explore our academic practice as an ongoing, creative and inspiring process of learning that can be personally transformational for teachers and their students. This book began from the question of how we recontextualise our disciplinary or professional expertise in ways that are meaningful for our students. Trying to answer that question has meant rethinking the responsibilities of teaching as part of our own ongoing learning not about teaching but through teaching as an act of enquiry. We are inspiring teachers only if we are inspiring learners willing to challenge ourselves, destabilise what we already know and draw on the knowledge and expertise of those we teach and those we teach with. Being enquiring university teachers enables us to live this in our practice.

Further reading

Cleaver, Elizabeth, Lintern, Maxine and McLinden, Mike (2014) *Teaching and Learning in Higher Education: Disciplinary Approaches to Educational Enquiry*. London: SAGE.
This book is an accessible introduction to educational literature, types of data that can be collected and how to disseminate the outcomes of learning and teaching enquiry. The authors also usefully look at ways in which educational enquiry might be undertaken using research approaches already familiar to teachers wanting to investigate their own practice from, for example, sciences, art, humanities, mathematics and engineering perspectives.

Nygaard, Claus and Belluigi, Dina Zoe (2011) 'A proposed methodology for contextualised evaluation in higher education', *Assessment & Evaluation in Higher Education*, 36(6): 657–71.
This paper outlines a structured approach to planning evaluation of teaching in relation to purpose, content, usage and method with the aim to integrate the process into both student and teaching reflection on learning. It includes ten prompt questions to help individuals and module teams make decisions about why and how they will evaluate.

BIBLIOGRAPHY

Abasi, Ali R. and Graves, Barbara (2008) 'Academic literacy and plagiarism: conversations with international graduate students and disciplinary professors', *Journal of English for Academic Purposes*, 7: 221–33.

Ackermann, Sanne, Van den Bossche, Piet, Admiraal, Wilfried, Gijselaers, Wim, Segers Mien, Simons, Robert-Jan and Kirschner, Paul (2007) 'Reconsidering group cognition: from conceptual confusion to a boundary area between cognitive and socio-cultural perspectives?', *Educational Research Review*, 2: 39–63.

Åkerlind, Gerlese S. (2008) 'An academic perspective on research and being a researcher: an integration of the literature', *Studies in Higher Education*, 33(1): 17–31.

Anderson, Charles and Hounsell, Dai (2007) 'Knowledge practices: "doing the subject" in undergraduate courses', *The Curriculum Journal*, 18(4): 463–78.

Anderson, Kirsteen (2010) 'The whole learner: the role of imagination in developing disciplinary understanding', *Arts and Humanities in Higher Education*, 9(2): 205–21.

Angelo, Thomas A. and Cross, K. Patricia (1993) *Classroom Assessment Techniques: A Handbook for College Teachers*. 2nd edn. San Francisco: Jossey-Bass.

Archer, Louise (2008) 'Younger academics' constructions of "authenticity", "success" and professional identity', *Studies in Higher Education*, 33(4): 385–403.

Arkoudis, Sophie, Watty, Kim, Baik, Chi, Yu, Xin, Borland, Helen, Chang, Shanton, Lang, Ian, Lang, Josephine and Pearce, Amanda (2012) 'Finding common ground: enhancing interaction between domestic and international students in higher education', *Teaching in Higher Education*, 18(3): 222–35.

Arnold, Lydia, Williams, Tim and Thompson, Kevin (2009) 'Advancing the patchwork text: the development of patchwork media approaches', *International Journal of Learning*, 16(5): 151–66.

Ashwin, Paul and Trigwell, Keith (2004) 'Investigating staff and educational development', in D. Baume and P. Kahn (eds), *Enhancing Staff and Educational Development*. London: Routledge. pp. 117–31.

Bache, Ian and Hayton, Richard (2012) 'Inquiry-based learning and the international student', *Teaching in Higher Education*, 17(4): 411–23.

Baepler, Paul, Walker, J.D. and Driessen, Michelle (2014) 'It's not about seat time: blending, flipping, and efficiency in active learning classrooms', *Computers & Education*, 78: 227–36.

Baillie, Caroline (2006) 'Enhancing students' creativity through creative-thinking techniques', in N. Jackson, M. Oliver, M. Shaw and J. Wisdom (eds), *Developing Creativity in Higher Education: An Imaginative Curriculum*. London: Routledge. pp. 142–55.

Baillie, Sarah, Crossan, Andrew, Brewster, May, Stephen and Mellor, Dominic (2010) 'Evaluating an automated haptic simulator designed for veterinary students to learn bovine rectal palpation', *Simulation in Healthcare*, 5(5): 261–66.

Barkley, Elizabeth F. (2010) *Student Engagement Techniques: A Handbook for College Faculty*. San Francisco: Jossey-Bass.

Barnes, E., Goldring, L., Bestwick, A. and Wood, J. (2010) 'A collaborative evaluation of student–staff partnership in inquiry-based educational development', in S. Little (ed.), *Staff-Student Partnerships in Higher Education*. London: Continuum. pp. 16–30.

Barnett, Heather and Smith, John R.A. (2013) 'Broad vision: the art & science of looking', *The STEAM Journal*, 1(1) (http://scholarship.claremont.edu/steam/vol1/iss1/21).

Barnett, Ronald (1997) *Higher Education: A Critical Business*. Buckingham: SRHE/ Open University Press.

Barnett, Ronald (2000) *Realizing the University in an Age of Supercomplexity*. Buckingham: Open University Press.

Barnett, Ronald (2009) 'Knowing and becoming in the higher education curriculum', *Studies in Higher Education*, 34(4): 429–40.

Barnett, Ronald (2012) 'Learning for an unknown future', *Higher Education Research & Development*, 31(1): 65–77.

Barnett, Ronald and Coate, Kelly (2005) *Engaging the Curriculum in Higher Education*. Maidenhead: Open University Press.

Baron, Paula and Corbin, Lillian (2012) 'Student engagement: rhetoric and reality', *Higher Education Research & Development*, 31(6): 759–72.

Barrow, Rosemary, Behr, Charlotte, Deacy, Susan, McHardy, Fiona and Tempest, Kathryn (2010) 'Embedding employability into a classics curriculum: the classical civilisation Bachelor of Arts programme at Roehampton University', *Arts and Humanities in Higher Education*, 9(3): 339–52.

Barton, Georgina and Ryan, Mary (2014) 'Multimodal approaches to reflective teaching and assessment in higher education', *Higher Education Research & Development*, 33(3): 409–24.

Bass, Randy (1999) 'The scholarship of teaching: what's the problem?', *Invention*, 1(1).

Bates, Simon and Galloway, Ross (2012) 'The inverted classroom in a large enrolment introductory physics course: a case study', *Proceedings of the HEA STEM Learning and Teaching Conference*. DOI: 10.11120/stem.hea.2012.071.

Batty, Craig and Sinclair, Jennifer (2014) 'Peer-to-peer learning in the higher degree by research context: a creative writing case study', *New Writing: The International Journal for the Practice and Theory of Creative Writing*, 11(3): 335–46.

Baxter-Magolda, Marcia B. (2001) *Making their Own Way: Narratives for Transforming Higher Education to Promote Self-Development*. Sterling, VA: Stylus.

Baynham, Mike (2000) 'Academic writing in new and emergent discipline areas', in M. Lea and B. Stierer (eds), *Student Writing in Higher Education: New Contexts*. Buckingham: Open University Press. pp. 17–31.

Beetham, Helen (2013) 'Designing for active learning in technology-rich contexts', in H. Beetham and R. Sharpe (eds), *Rethinking Pedagogy for a Digital Age: Designing for 21st Century Learning*. 2nd edn. New York: Routledge. pp. 31–48.

Beetham, Helen (2014) 'Post-digital provocations #4: "in recovery from" the digital', HelenB's e-learning blog, 12 November (http://design-4-learning.blogspot.co.uk/2014/11/post-digital-provocations-4-in-recovery.html?m=1).

Bernstein, Basil (2000) *Pedagogy, Symbolic Control and Identity: Theory, Research, Critique*. Lanham: Rowman and Littlefield.

Bessant, Sophie, Bailey Patrick, Robinson, Zoe, Tomkinson, C. Bland, Tomkinson, Rosemary, Ormerod, R. Mark and Boast, Rob (2013) *Problem-based Learning: A Case Study of Sustainability Education* (http://www.keele.ac.uk/media/keeleuniversity/group/hybridpbl/PBL_ESD_Case%20Study_Bessant,%20et%20al.%202013.pdf).

Bhagat, Dipti and O'Neill, Peter (2011) 'Thinking about the canon', in D. Bhagat and P. O'Neill (eds), *Inclusive Practices, Inclusive Pedagogies: Learning from Widening Participation Research in Art and Design Higher Education* (http://ukadia.ac.uk/wp-content/uploads/sites/3/2013/11/Inclusive_Practices_Inclusive_Pedagogies.pdf). pp. 224–28.

Bianchini, Julie, Whitney, David, Breton, Therese and Hilton-Brown, Bryan (2002) 'Towards inclusive science education: university scientists' views of students, instructional practices and the nature of science', *Science Education*, 86(1): 47–78.

Biesta, Gert J.J. (2010) 'Why "what works" still won't work: from evidence-based education to value-based education', *Studies in Philosophy and Education*, 29: 491–503.

Biggs, John (2003) *Teaching for Quality Learning at University*. 2nd edn. Buckingham: Open University Press.

Biggs, John and Tang, Catherine (2011) *Teaching for Quality Learning at University*. 4th edn. Buckingham: Open University Press.

Biglan, Antony (1973) 'The characteristics of subject matter in different academic areas', *Journal of Applied Psychology*, 57(3): 195–203.

Blake, Joanna, Sterling, Stephen and Kagawa, Fumiyo (2013) *Getting it Together: Interdisciplinarity and Sustainability in the Higher Education Institution*. Plymouth: Pedagogic Research Institute and Observatory. PedRIO Occasional Paper 4. (https://www1.plymouth.ac.uk/research/pedrio/Documents/PedRIO%20Paper%204.pdf).

Blair, Bernadette (2011) 'Elastic minds? Is the interdisciplinary/multidisciplinary curriculum equipping our students for the future: a case study', *Art, Design and Communication in Higher Education*, 10(1): 33–50.

Bloom, Benjamin S. (1956) *Taxonomy of Educational Objectives*. New York: Longmans, Green & Co.

Bloxham, Sue and Boyd, Pete (2007) *Developing Effective Assessment in Higher Education: A Practical Guide*. Maidenhead: Open University Press.

Bloxham, Sue and Campbell, Liz (2010) 'Generating dialogue in assessment feedback: exploring the use of interactive cover sheets', *Assessment & Evaluation in Higher Education*, 35(3): 291–300.

Bloxham, Sue and West, Amanda (2004) 'Understanding the rules of the game: marking peer assessment as a medium for developing students' conceptions of assessment', *Assessment & Evaluation in Higher Education*, 29(6): 721–33.

Bourdieu, Pierre (1973) 'Cultural reproduction and social reproduction', in R. Brown (ed.), *Knowledge, Education and Social Change: Papers in the Sociology of Education*. London: Tavistock. pp. 71–112.

Boud, David and Lee, Alison (2005) '"Peer learning" as pedagogic discourse for research education', *Studies in Higher Education*, 30(5): 501–16.

Boud, David and Molloy, Elizabeth (2013) 'Rethinking models of feedback for learning: the challenge of design', *Assessment & Evaluation in Higher Education*, 38(6): 698–712.

Bovill, Catherine (2011) 'Sharing responsibility for learning through formative evaluation: moving to evaluation as learning', *Practice and Evidence of Scholarship of Teaching and Learning in Higher Education*, 6(2): 96–109.

Bovill, Catherine (2014) 'An investigation of co-created curricula within higher education in the UK, Ireland and the USA', *Innovations in Education and Teaching International*, 51(4): 15–25.

Bovill, Catherine and Bulley Cathy J. (2011) 'A model of active student participation in curriculum design: exploring desirability and possibility', in C. Rust (ed.), *Improving Student Learning 18: Global Theories and Local Practices: Institutional, Disciplinary and Cultural Variations*. Oxford: Oxford Brookes University. pp. 176–88.

Boyer, Ernest (1990) *Scholarship Reconsidered: Priorities of the Professoriate*. San Francisco: Jossey-Bass.

Brennan, John and Osborne, Mike (2008) 'Higher education's many diversities: of students, institutions and experiences; and outcomes?', *Research Papers in Education*, 23(2): 179–90.

Brew, Angela (2001) 'Conceptions of research: a phenomenographic study', *Studies in Higher Education*, 26(3): 271–85.

Brew, Angela (2010) 'Imperatives and challenges in integrating teaching and research', *Higher Education Research & Development*, 29(2): 139–50.

Brew, Angela (2012) 'Teaching and research: new relationships and their implications for inquiry-based teaching and learning in higher education', *Higher Education Research & Development*, 31(1): 101–14.

Bridgstock, Ruth (2009) 'The graduate attributes we've overlooked: enhancing graduate employability through career management skills', *Higher Education Research & Development*, 28(1): 31–44.

Brint, Steven, Cantwell, Allison M. and Hanneman, Robert A. (2008) 'The two cultures of undergraduate academic engagement', *Research in Higher Education*, 49: 383–402.

Brookfield, Stephen and Preskill, Stephen (1999) *Discussion as a Way of Teaching: Tools and Techniques for University Teachers*. Buckingham: Open University Press.

Brooman, S., Darwent, S. and Pimor, A. (2014) 'The student voice in higher education curriculum design: is there value in listening?', *Innovations in Education and Teaching International*. DOI: 10.1080/14703297.2014.910128.

Brown, Sally (2012) 'Diverse and innovative assessment at Masters level: alternatives to conventional written assignments', *All Ireland Journal of Teaching and Learning in Higher Education*, 4(2): 85.

Bruce, Christine and Stoodley, Ian (2013) 'Experiencing higher degree research supervision as teaching', *Studies in Higher Education*, 38(2): 226–41.

Bryson, Colin and Hand, Len (2008) 'An introduction to student engagement', in L. Hand and C. Bryson (eds), *Student Engagement*. London: SEDA. pp. 7–12.

Buissink-Smith, Nell, Hart, Simon and van der Meer, Jacques (2013) '"There are other people out there!" Successful postgraduate peer groups and research communities at a New Zealand university', *Higher Education Research & Development*, 32(5): 695–705.

Cadman, Kate (2000) '"Voices in the air": evaluations of the learning experiences of international postgraduates and their supervisors', *Teaching in Higher Education*, 5(4): 475–91.

Caple, Helen and Bogle, Mike (2013) 'Making group assessment transparent: what wikis can contribute to collaborative projects', *Assessment & Evaluation in Higher Education*, 38(2): 198–210.

Carless, David (2013) 'Sustainable feedback and the development of student self-evaluative capacities', in S. Merry, M. Price, D. Carless and M. Taras (eds), *Reconceptualising Feedback in Higher Education: Developing Dialogue with Students*. London: Routledge. pp. 113–22.

Carless, David, Salter, Diane, Yang, Min and Lam, Joy (2011) 'Developing sustainable feedback practices', *Studies in Higher Education*, 36(4): 395–407.

Carrington, Michael, Chen, Richard, Davies, Martin, Kaur, Jagjit and Neville, Benjamin (2011) 'The effectiveness of a single intervention of computer-aided argument mapping in a marketing and a financial accounting subject', *Higher Education Research & Development*, 30(3): 387–403.

Casanovas-Rubio, Maria del Mar, Ahearn, Alison, Ramos, Gonazalo and Popo-Ala, Sunday (2014) 'The research–teaching nexus: using a construction teaching event as a research tool', *Innovations in Education and Teaching International*, DOI: 10.1080/14703297.2014.943787.

Casey, M.M., Bates, S.P., Galloway, K.W., Hardy, J.A., Kay, A.E., Kirsop, P. and McQueen, H.A. (2014) 'Scaffolding student engagement via online peer learning', *European Journal of Physics*, 35(4): 045002. DOI: 10.1088/0143-0807/35/4/045002.

CBI (2013) *Changing the Pace: CBI/Pearson Education and Skills Survey 2013* (http://www.cbi.org.uk/media/2119176/education_and_skills_survey_2013.pdf).

CBI (2014) *Gateway to Growth: CBI/Pearson Education and Skills Survey 2014* (http://www.cbi.org.uk/media/2807987/gateway-to-growth.pdf).

CBI/UUK (2009) *Future Fit: Preparing Students for the World of Work* (http://www.cbi.org.uk/media/1121435/cbi_uuk_future_fit.pdf).

Chapple, Mary and Murphy, Roger (1996) 'The nominal group technique: extending the evaluation of students' teaching and learning experiences', *Assessment & Evaluation in Higher Education*, 21(2): 147–60.

Chettiparamb, Angelique (2007) *Interdisciplinarity: A Literature Review*. Southampton: Subject Centre for Languages, Linguistics and Area Studies (https://www.llas.ac.uk/resourcedownloads/2892/interdisciplinarity_literature_review.pdf).

Ching, Yu-Hui and Hsu, Yu-Chang (2011) 'Design-grounded assessment: a framework and a case study of Web 2.0 practices in higher education', *Australasian Journal of Educational Technology*, 27(5): 781–97.

Christensen Hughes, Julia (2007) 'Supporting curriculum assessment and development: implications for the faculty role and institutional support', *New Directions for Teaching and Learning*, 112: 107–10.

Cleaver, Elizabeth, Lintern, Maxine and McLinden, Mike (2014) *Teaching and Learning in Higher Education: Disciplinary Approaches to Educational Enquiry*. London: SAGE.

Clegg, Sue (2008) 'Academic identities under threat?', *British Educational Research Journal*, 34(3): 329–45.

Clegg, Sue (2011) 'Cultural capital and agency: connecting critique and curriculum in higher education', *British Journal of Sociology of Education*, 32(1): 93–108.

Clifford, Valerie Anne (2009) 'Engaging the disciplines in the curriculum', *International Journal for Academic Development*, 14(2): 133–43.

Coates, Hamish (2007) 'A model of online and general campus-based student engagement', *Assessment & Evaluation in Higher Education*, 32(2): 121–41.

Collini, Stefan (2012) *What are Universities For?* London: Penguin.

Cook-Sather, Alison (2009) 'From traditional accountability to shared responsibility: the benefits and challenges of student consultants gathering midcourse feedback in college classrooms', *Assessment & Evaluation in Higher Education*, 34(2): 231–41.

Cooper, James L. and Robinson, Pamela (2000a) 'The argument for making large groups seem small', *New Directions for Teaching and Learning*, 81: 5–16.

Cooper, James L. and Robinson, Pamela (2000b) 'Getting started: informal small group strategies in large classes', *New Directions for Teaching and Learning*, 81: 17–24.

Cormier, Dave (2008) 'Rhizomatic education: community as curriculum', Dave's Educational Blog (http://davecormier.com/edblog/2008/06/03/rhizomatic-education-community-as-curriculum/).

Cormier, Dave (2010) 'Community as curriculum and open learning', Dave's Educational Blog (http://davecormier.com/edblog/2010/06/17/community-as-curriculum-and-open-learning/).

Cortazzi, Martin and Jin, Lixian (1997) 'Communication for learning across cultures', in D. McNamara and R. Harris (eds), *Overseas Students in Higher Education: Issues in Teaching and Learning*. London: Routledge. pp. 76–90.

Costello, Melinda L., Weldon, Alice and Brunner, Penelope (2002) 'Reaction cards as a formative evaluation tool: students' perceptions of how their use impacted classes', *Assessment & Evaluation in Higher Education*, 27(1): 23–33.

Cotton, Debby and Sterling, Stephen (2012) 'Introduction', in D. Cotton, S. Sterling, V. Neal and J. Winter (eds), *Putting the 'S' into ED: Education for Sustainable Development in Educational Development*. London: Staff and Educational Development Association.

Cotton, Debby and Winter, Jennie (2010) '"It's not just bits of paper and light bulbs": a review of sustainability pedagogies and their potential for use in higher education', in P. Jones, D. Selby and S. Sterling (eds), *Sustainability Education: Perspectives and Practices across Higher Education*. London: Earthscan. pp. 39–54.

Cotton, Debby, Bailey, Ian, Warren, Martyn and Bissell, Susie (2009) 'Revolutions and second-best solutions: education for sustainable development in higher education', *Studies in Higher Education*, 34(7): 719–33.

Cotton, Debby, Winter, Jennie and Bailey, Ian (2013) 'Researching the hidden curriculum: intentional and unintended messages', *Journal of Geography in Higher Education*, 37(2): 192–203.

Cotton, D.R.E., Joyner, M., George, R. and Cotton, P.A. (2015) 'Understanding the gender and ethnicity attainment gap in UK higher education', *Innovations in Education and Teaching International*, DOI: 10.1080/14703297.2015.1013145.

Cowan, John and Harding, Alan G. (1986) 'A logical model for curriculum development', *British Journal of Educational Technology*, 17(2): 103–9.

Cousin, Glynis (2006) 'An introduction to threshold concepts', *Planet*, 17: 4–5.

Cousin, Glynis (2009) *Researching Learning in Higher Education: An Introduction to Contemporary Methods and Approaches*. New York: Routledge.

Cox, Andrew, Levy, Philippa, Stordy, Peter and Webber, Sheila (2008) 'Inquiry-based learning in the first-year information management curriculum', *Innovation in Teaching and Learning in Information and Computer Sciences*, 7(1): 3–21.

Crozier, Gill, Reay, Diane, Clayton, John, Colliander, Lori and Grinsted, Jan (2008) 'Different strokes for different folks: diverse students in diverse institutions – experiences of higher education', *Research Papers in Education*, 23(2): 167–77.

Crozier, Gill, Reay, Dianne and Clayton, John (2010) 'Access, participation and diversity questions in relation to different forms of post-compulsory further and higher education: the socio-cultural and learning experiences of working class students in higher education', in M. David (ed.), *Improving Learning by Widening Participation in Higher Education*. Abingdon: Routledge. pp. 62–74.

Cruickshank, Ken, Chen, Honglin and Warren, Stan (2012) 'Increasing international and domestic student interaction through group work: a case study from the humanities', *Higher Education Research & Development*, 31(6): 797–810.

Cunningham, Sheila (2013) 'Teaching a diverse student body: a proposed tool for lecturers to self-evaluate their approach to inclusive teaching', *Practice and Evidence of Scholarship of Teaching and Learning in Higher Education*, 8(1): 3–27.

Davies, John and Rutherford, Ursula (2012) 'Learning from fellow engineering students who have current professional experience', *European Journal of Engineering Education*, 37(4): 354–65.

Davies, Martin (2011) 'Concept mapping, mind mapping and argument mapping: what are the differences and do they matter?', *Higher Education*, 62: 279–301.

Davies, Martin and Devlin, Marcia (2007) *Interdisciplinary Higher Education: Implications for Teaching and Learning*. Melbourne: Centre for the Study of Higher Education (http://www.cshe.unimelb.edu.au/resources_teach/curriculum_design/docs/InterdisciplinaryHEd.pdf).

Davis, Kathryn Simons and Minifie, J. Roberta (2013) 'Ensuring Gen Y students come prepared for class: then leveraging active learning techniques to most effectively engage them', *American Journal of Business and Management*, 2(1): 13–19.

De Hei, Miranda, Strijbos, Jan-Willem, Sjoer, Ellen and Admiraal, Wilfried (2014) 'Collaborative learning in higher education: lecturers' practices and beliefs', *Research Papers in Education*. DOI 10.1080/02671522.2014.908407.

De Vita, Glauco (2000) 'Inclusive approaches to effective communication and active participation in the multicultural classroom: an international business management context', *Active Learning in Higher Education*, 1(2): 168–80.

De Vita, Glauco (2005) 'Fostering intercultural learning through multicultural group work', in J. Carroll and J. Ryan (eds), *Teaching International Students: Improving Learning for All*. London: Routledge. pp. 75–83.

De Vita, Glauco (2007) 'Taking stock: an appraisal of the literature on internationalising higher education learning', in E. Jones and S. Brown (eds), *Internationalising Higher Education*. London: Routledge. pp. 154–67.

de Wever, Bram, Van Keer, Hilde, Schellens, Tammy and Valcke, Martin (2011) 'Assessing collaboration in a wiki: the reliability of university students' peer assessment', *Internet and Higher Education*, 14: 201–6.

Delpish, Ayesha, Darby, Alexa, Holmes, Ashley, Knight-McKenna, Mary, Mihans, Richard, King, Catherine and Felten, Peter (2010) 'Equalizing voices: student–faculty partnership in course design', in C. Werder and M. Otis (eds), *Engaging Student Voices in the Study of Teaching and Learning*. Stylus: Sterling, VA. pp. 96–114.

Devereux, Linda and Wilson, Kate (2008) 'Scaffolding literacies across the Bachelor of Education program: an argument for a course-wide approach', *Asia-Pacific Journal of Teacher Education*, 36(2): 121–34.

Devlin, Marcia (2013) 'Bridging socio-cultural incongruity: conceptualising the success of students from low socio-economic status backgrounds in Australian higher education', *Studies in Higher Education*, 38(6): 939–49.

DiCarlo, Stephen E. (2009) 'Too much content, not enough thinking, and too little FUN', Claude Bernard Distinguished Lecture, *Advanced Physiology Education*, 33: 257–64.

Dobson, Helen and Tomkinson, C. Bland (2012) 'Creating sustainable development change agents through problem-based learning: designing appropriate students PBL projects', *International Journal of Sustainability*, 13(3): 263–78.

Dobson, Helen and Tomkinson, C. Bland (2013) 'Practical education for sustainable development through interdisciplinary problem-based learning', in R. Atfield and P. Kemp (eds), *Enhancing Education for Sustainable Development in Business, Management, Hospitality, Leisure, Marketing, Tourism*. York: HEA (http://www.heacademy.ac.uk/sites/default/files/ESD_Dobson_final_0.pdf).

Downes, Stephen (2007) 'What connectivism is', *Half an Hour* (http://halfanhour. blogspot.co.uk/2007/02/what-connectivism-is.html).

Drayson, Rachel, Bone, Elizabeth, Agombar, Jamie and Kemp, Simon (2014) *Student Attitudes Towards and Skills for Sustainable Development.* York: HEA (https://www. heacademy.ac.uk/sites/default/files/resources/Student%20attitudes%20towards%20 and%20skills%20for%20sustainable%20development.pdf).

Duah, Francis, Croft, Tony and Inglis, Matthew (2014) 'Can peer assisted learning be effective in undergraduate mathematics?', *International Journal of Mathematical Education in Science and Technology,* 45(4): 552–65.

Duhs, Rosalind (2013) 'Assessment and the student experience', in C.B. Kandiko and M. Weyers (eds), *The Global Student Experience: An International and Comparative Analysis.* London: Routledge. pp. 98–116.

Dunn, Lee and Wallace, Michelle (2006) 'Australian academics and transnational teaching: an exploratory study of their preparedness and experiences', *Higher Education Research & Development,* 25(4): 357–69.

Dunne, Ciarán (2011) 'Developing intercultural curriculum within the context of the internationalisation of higher education: terminology, typologies and power', *Higher Education Research & Development,* 30(5): 609–22.

Dwyer, Claire (2001) 'Linking research and teaching: a staff–student interview project', *Journal of Geography in Higher Education,* 25(3): 357–66.

Ecclestone, Kathryn (1999) 'Empowering or ensnaring? The implications of outcome-based assessment in higher education', *Higher Education Quarterly,* 53(1): 29–48.

The Economist (2014) 'The digital degree: the staid higher-education business is about to experience a welcome earthquake', 28 June (http://www.economist.com/news/ briefing/21605899-staid-higher-education-business-about-experience-welcome-earthquake-digital).

ECU (Equality Challenge Unit) (2014) *Equality in Higher Education: Statistical Report 2014* (http://www.ecu.ac.uk/publications/equality-higher-education-statistical-report-2014).

Eden, Sally (2014) 'Out of the comfort zone: enhancing work-based learning about student employability through student reflection on work placements', *Journal of Geography in Higher Education,* 38(2): 266–76.

Edmead, Christine (2013) 'Capitalising on a multicultural learning environment: using group work as a mechanism for student integration', in J. Ryan (ed.), *Cross-Cultural Teaching and Learning for Home and International Students: Internationalisation of Pedagogy and Curriculum in Higher Education.* London: Routledge. pp. 15–26.

Efstathiou, Nikolaos and Bailey, Cara (2012) 'Promoting active learning using Audience Response System in large bioscience classes', *Nurse Education Today,* 32: 91–5.

European Commission (2013) *The Bologna Process: Towards the Higher Education Area* (http://ec.europa.eu/education/policy/higher-education/bologna-process_en.htm).

Farwell, Tricia M. and Waters, Richard D. (2010) 'Exploring the use of social bookmarking technology in education: an analysis of students' experiences using a course-specific Delicious.com account', *Journal of Online Learning and Teaching,* 6(2) (http://jolt. merlot.org/vol6no2/waters_0610.htm?utm_source=twitterfeed&utm_medium=twitter).

Felten, Peter (2013) 'Principles of good practice in SoTL', *Teaching & Learning Inquiry,* 1(1): 121–5.

Fernsten, Linda and Reda, Mary (2011) 'Helping students meet the challenges of academic writing', *Teaching in Higher Education*, 16(2): 171–82.

Fox, Alison, Stevenson, Lorna, Connelly, Patricia, Duff, Angus and Dunlop, Angela (2010) 'Peer-mentoring undergraduate accounting students: the influence on approaches to learning and academic performance', *Active Learning in Higher Education*, 11(2): 145–56.

Fraser, Sharon P. and Bosanquet, Agnes M. (2006) 'The curriculum? That's just a unit outline, isn't it?', *Studies in Higher Education*, 31(3): 269–84.

Freeman, Rebecca and Dobbins, Kerry (2013) 'Are we serious about enhancing courses? Using the principles of assessment for learning to enhance course evaluation', *Assessment & Evaluation in Higher Education*, 38(2): 142–51.

Freire, Paulo (1970[1996]) *Pedagogy of the Oppressed*. London: Penguin.

Frost, Alan (1999) 'Supervision of NESB postgraduate students in science-based disciplines', in Y. Ryan and O. Zuber-Skerrit (eds), *Supervising Postgraduates from Non-English Speaking Backgrounds*. Buckingham: Open University Press. pp. 101–9.

Gao, Fei (2013) 'A case study of using a social annotation tool to support collaboratively learning', *Internet and Higher Education*, 17: 76–83.

Garrison, D. Randy and Kanuka, Heather (2004) 'Blended learning: uncovering its transformative potential in higher education', *Internet and Higher Education*, 7: 95–105.

Gibbs, Graham (2009) 'The assessment of group work: lessons from the literature' (http://www.brookes.ac.uk/aske/documents/Brookes%20groupwork%20Gibbs%20 Dec%2009.pdf).

Gibbs, Graham (2010) *Dimensions of Quality*. York: HEA.

Gibbs, Graham and Simpson, Claire (2004) 'Conditions under which assessment supports students' learning', *Learning and Teaching in Higher Education*, 1: 3–31.

Gielen, Sarah, Peeters, Elien, Dochy, Filip, Onghena, Patrick and Struyven, Katrien (2010) 'Improving the effectiveness of peer feedback for learning', *Learning and Instruction*, 20(4): 304–15.

Gordon, Sue, Reid, Anna and Petocz, Peter (2010) 'Educators' conceptions of student diversity in their classes', *Studies in Higher Education*, 35(8): 961–74.

Grace, Sue and Gravestock, Phil (2009) *Inclusion and Diversity: Meeting the Needs of All Students*. New York: Routledge.

Grant, Peter, MacPherson, Ewen, Harrison, Gareth, Brunson, Kevin, Hyde, Robert and Williams, David (2010) 'Teaching integrated system design with interdisciplinary group design exercises', *Engineering Education*, 5(1): 30–41.

Gray, Kathleen, Thompson, Celia, Sheard, Judithe, Clerehan, Rosemary and Hamilton, Margaret (2010) 'Students as Web 2.0 authors: implications for assessment design and conduct', *Australasian Journal of Educational Technology*, 26(1): 105–22.

Green Lister, Pam and Crisp, Beth R. (2007) 'Critical incident analyses: a practice tool for students and practitioners', *Practice: Social Work in Action*, 19(1): 47–60.

Gribble, Kate and Ziguras, Christopher (2003) 'Learning to teach offshore: pre-departure training for lecturers in transnational programs', *Higher Education Research & Development*, 22(2): 205–16.

Griffiths, Ron (2004) 'Knowledge production and the research-teaching nexus: the case of the built environment disciplines', *Studies in Higher Education*, 29(6): 709–26.

Griffiths, Sandra (2010) *Teaching for Inclusion in Higher Education: A Guide to Practice* (http://www.qub.ac.uk/directorates/AcademicStudentAffairs/CentreforEducational Development/CurriculumDevelopment/Inclusion/).

Guertin, Laura A. (2010) 'Creating and using podcasts across the disciplines', *Currents in Teaching and Learning*, 2(1): 4–11.

Gurlitt, Johannes, Dummel, Sebastian, Schuster, Silvia and Nückles, Matthias (2012) 'Differently structured advance organizers lead to different initial schemata and learning outcomes', *Instructional Science*, 40: 351–69.

Hadi-Kanifi, Karima, Dagman, Ozlem, Peter, John, Snell, Ellen, Tutton, Caroline and Wright, Trevor (2014) 'Engaging students and staff with educational development through appreciative inquiry', *Innovations in Education and Teaching International*, 51(6): 584–94.

Hagel, Pauline, Carr, Rodney and Devlin, Marcia (2012) 'Conceptualising and measuring student engagement through the Australasian Survey of Student Engagement (AUSSE): a critique', *Assessment & Evaluation in Higher Education*, 37(4): 475–86.

Haggis, Tamsin (2006) 'Pedagogies for diversity: retaining critical challenge amidst fears of "dumbing down"', *Studies in Higher Education*, 31(5): 521–35.

Haigh, Martin J. (2002) 'Internationalisation of the curriculum: designing inclusive education for a small world', *Journal of Geography in Higher Education*, 26(1): 49–66.

Hajdarpasic, Ademir, Brew, Angela and Popenici, Stefan (2013) 'The contribution of academic's engagement in research to undergraduate education', *Studies in Higher Education*, DOI: 10.1080/03075079.2013.842215.

Hammer, Sara Jeanne and Green, Wendy (2011) 'Critical thinking in a first-year management unit: the relationship between disciplinary learning, academic literacy and learning progression', *Higher Education Research & Development*, 30(3): 303–15.

Hammond, John A., Bithell, Christine P., Jones, Lester and Bidgood, Penelope (2010) 'A first year experience of student-directed peer-assisted learning', *Active Learning in Higher Education*, 11(3): 201–12.

Hardy, Christine and Bryson, Colin (2009) 'Student engagement: paradigm change or political expediency' (www.adm.heacademy.ac.uk/resources/features/student-engagement-paradigm-change-or-political-expediency/).

Hassanien, Ahmed (2006) 'Using Webquest to support learning with technology in higher education', *Journal of Hospitality, Leisure, Sport and Tourism Education*, 5(1): 41–9.

Hattie, John and Marsh, H.W. (1996) 'The relationship between research and teaching: a meta-analysis', *Review of Educational Research*, 66(4): 507–42.

Hay, David, Kinchin, Ian and Lygo-Baker, Simon (2008) 'Making learning visible: the role of concept mapping in higher education', *Studies in Higher Education*, 33(3): 295–311.

Haythornthwaite, Caroline (2013) 'Emergent practices for literacy, e-learners, and the digital university', in R. Goodfellow and M. Lea (eds), *Literacy in the Digital University: Critical Perspectives on Learning, Scholarship, and Technology*. London: Routledge. pp. 56–66.

Healey, Mick (2005) 'Linking research and teaching: exploring disciplinary spaces and the role of inquiry-based learning', in R. Barnett (ed.), *Reshaping the University:*

New Relationships between Research, Scholarship and Teaching. Maidenhead: Open University Press. pp. 67–78.

Healey, Mick and Jenkins, Alan (2009) *Developing Undergraduate Research and Inquiry*. York: HEA (https://www.heacademy.ac.uk/sites/default/files/developingundergraduate_final.pdf).

Healey, Mick, Flint, Abbi and Harrington, Kathy (2014) *Engagement through Partnership: Students as Partners in Learning and Teaching in Higher Education*. York: HEA (https://www.heacademy.ac.uk/sites/default/files/resources/Engagement_through_partnership.pdf).

Hendry, Graham (2013) 'Integrating feedback with classroom teaching: using exemplars to scaffold learning', in S. Merry, M. Price, D. Carless and M. Taras (eds), *Reconceptualising Feedback in Higher Education: Developing Dialogue with Students*. London: Routledge. pp. 133–41.

Higher Education Academy (HEA) (2006) *Student Employability Profiles: A Guide for Higher Education Practitioners*. York: HEA.

Higher Education Funding Council for England (HEFCE) (2009) *Enhancing Learning and Teaching through the Use of Technology: A Revised Approach to HEFCE's Strategy for e-Learning* (http://www.hefce.ac.uk/media/hefce1/pubs/hefce/2009/0912/09_12.pdf).

Higher Education Funding Council for Wales (HEFCW) (2014) *Partnership for Higher Education in Wales* (http://www.hefcw.ac.uk/documents/policy_areas/learning_and_teaching/wise_eng2.pdf).

Hills, J.M, Robertson, G., Walker, R, Adey, M.A. and Nixon, I. (2003) 'Bridging the gap between degree programme curricula and employability: through implementation of work-related learning', *Teaching in Higher Education*, 8(2): 211–31.

Hilton III, John, Wiley, David, Stein, Jared and Johnson, Aaron (2010) 'The four "R"s of openness and ALMS analysis: frameworks for open educational resources', *Open Learning: The Journal of Open, Distance and e-Learning*, 25(1): 37–44.

Hinchcliffe, Geoffrey William and Jolly, Adrienne (2011) 'Graduate identity and employability', *British Educational Research Journal*, 37(4): 563–84.

Hmelo-Silver, Cindy, Duncan, Ravit Golan, Chinn and Clark A. (2007) 'Scaffolding and achievement in problem-based and inquiry learning: a response to Kirschner, Sweller and Clark (2006)', *Educational Psychologist*, 42(2): 99–107.

Hockings, Christine (2010) *Inclusive Learning and Teaching in Higher Education: A Synthesis of Research*. York: HEA (https://www.heacademy.ac.uk/sites/default/files/inclusive_teaching_and_learning_in_he_synthesis_200410_0.pdf).

Hockings, Christine, Brett, Paul and Terentjevs, Mat (2012) 'Making a difference: inclusive learning and teaching in higher education through open educational resources', *Distance Education*, 33(2): 237–52.

Holmes, Leonard (2013) 'Competing perspectives on graduate employability: possession, position or process?', *Studies in Higher Education*, 38(4): 538–54.

Honeychurch, Sarah (2012) 'Taking forward the jigsaw classroom: the development and implementation of a method of collaborative learning for first year philosophy tutorials', *Discourse*, 11(2): 40–52.

hooks, bell (1994) *Teaching to Transgress: Education as the Practice of Freedom*. New York: Routledge.

Hughes, Mark (2005) 'The mythology of research and teaching relationships in universities', in R. Barnett (ed.), *Reshaping the University: New Relationships between Research, Scholarship and Teaching*. Maidenhead: Open University Press. pp. 14–26.

Hunt, Jane A. and Hutchings, Maggie (2014) 'Innovative group-facilitated peer and educator assessment of nursing students' group presentations', *Health Science Journal*, 8(1): 22–31.

Hussey, Trevor and Smith, Patrick (2002) 'The trouble with learning outcomes', *Active Learning in Higher Education*, 3(3): 220–33.

Hussey, Trevor and Smith, Patrick (2003) 'The uses of learning outcomes', *Teaching in Higher Education*, 8(3): 357–68.

Hutchings, Bill and O'Rourke, Karen (2002) 'Problem-based learning in literary studies', *Arts and Humanities in Higher Education*, 1(1): 73–83.

Hutchings, Pat (2000) 'Approaching the scholarship of teaching and learning', in P. Hutchings (ed.), *Opening Lines: Approaches to the Scholarship of Teaching and Learning*. Menlo Park, CA: Carnegie. pp. 1–10.

Hutchings, Pat and Shulman, Lee (1999) 'The scholarship of teaching: new elaborations, new developments', *Change: The Magazine of Higher Learning*, 31(5): 10–15.

Huxham, Mark (2005) 'Learning in lectures: do "interactive windows" help?', *Active Learning in Higher Education*, 6(1): 17–31.

IET (2014) *Engineering and Technology: Skills and Demand in Industry. Annual Survey 2014*. London: IET. (http://www.theiet.org/factfiles/education/skills2014-page.cfm).

Imran, Muhammad Ali and Arshad, Kamran (2013) 'Increasing the interaction time in a lecture by integrating flipped classroom and just-in-time teaching concepts', *Compass: The Journal of Learning and Teaching at the University of Greenwich*, 7: 1–12.

Ireland, Chris and English, John (2011) 'Let them plagiarise: developing academic writing in a safe environment', *Journal of Academic Writing*, 1(1): 165–72.

Ivanič, Roz, Clark, Ronny and Rimmershaw, Rachel (2000) 'What am I supposed to make of this? The messages conveyed to students by tutors' written comments', in M. Lea and B. Stierer (eds), *Student Writing in Higher Education: New Contexts*. Buckingham: Open University Press. pp. 47–65.

Jackson, Denise (2015) 'Employability skills development in work-integrated learning: barriers and best practice', *Studies in Higher Education*, 40(2): 350–67.

James, Alison (2013) 'Lego Serious Play: a three-dimensional approach to learning development', *Journal of Learning Development in Higher Education*, 6: 1–18.

James, Alison and Brookfield, Stephen (2014) *Engaging Imagination: Helping Students to Become Creative and Reflective Thinkers*. San Francisco: Jossey-Bass.

Jay, Joelle K. and Johnson, Kerri L. (2002) 'Capturing complexity: a typology of reflective practice for teacher education', *Teaching and Teacher Education*, 18: 73–85.

Jisc (2008) *Effective Practice with e-Portfolios: Supporting 21st Century Learning*. Bristol: Jisc (http://www.jisc.ac.uk/media/documents/publications/effectivepractice eportfolios.pdf).

Jisc (2009) *Effective Practice in a Digital Age: A Guide to Technology-Enhanced Learning and Teaching*. Bristol: Jisc (http://www.webarchive.org.uk/wayback/archive/20140615094835/http://www.jisc.ac.uk/media/documents/publications/effectivepracticedigitalage.pdf).

Jisc (2015) 'Jisc Digital Student' (http://digitalstudent.jiscinvolve.org/wp/exemplars/).

Johnson, David W. and Johnson, Roger T. (1999) *Learning Together and Alone: Cooperative, Competitive and Individualistic Learning*. 5th edn. Boston: Allyn and Bacon.

Jones, Lucy and Field, Sarah (2014) 'Mooting within the curriculum as a vehicle for learning', *Practice and Evidence of Scholarship of Teaching and Learning in Higher Education*, 9(1): 33–45.

Jones, Ollie and Gorra, Andrea (2013) 'Assessment feedback only on demand: supporting the few not supplying the many', *Active Learning in Higher Education*, 14(2): 149–61.

Jones, Paula, Selby, David and Sterling, Stephen (2010) 'More than the sum of their parts? Interdisciplinarity and sustainability', in P. Jones, D. Selby and S. Sterling (eds), *Sustainability Education: Perspectives and Practices across Higher Education*. London: Earthscan. pp.17–37.

Justice, Christopher, Rice, James, Warry, Wayne, Inglis, Sue, Miller, Stefania and Sammon, Sheila (2007) 'Inquiry in higher education: reflections and directions on course design and teaching methods', *Innovative Higher Education*, 31(4): 201–14.

Kadi-Hanifi, Karima, Dagman, Ozlem, Peters, John, Snell, Ellen, Tutton, Caroline and Wright, Trevor (2014) 'Engaging students and staff with educational development through appreciative inquiry', *Innovations in Education and Teaching International*, 51(6): 584–94.

Kahn, Peter and O'Rourke, Karen (2005) 'Understanding enquiry-based learning', in T. Barrett, I. Mac Labhrainn and I. Fallon (eds), *Handbook of Enquiry & Problem Based Learning*. Galway: CELT. pp. 1–12.

Kahu, Ella R. (2013) 'Framing student engagement in higher education', *Studies in Higher Education*, 38(5): 758–73.

Kamler, Barbara and Thomson, Pat (2006) *Helping Doctoral Students Write: Pedagogies for Supervision*. Abingdon: Routledge.

Kandiko, Camille B. (2013a) 'Students in a global market', in C.B. Kandiko and M. Weyers (eds), *The Global Student Experience: An International and Comparative Analysis*. Abingdon: Routledge. pp. 13–26.

Kandiko, Camille B. (2013b) 'Globalised undergraduate curriculum', in C.B. Kandiko and M. Weyers (eds), *The Global Student Experience: An International and Comparative Analysis*. Abingdon: Routledge. pp. 117–31.

Kandiko, Camille B. and Blackmore, Paul (2012a) 'The networked curriculum', in P. Blackmore and C.B. Kandiko, *Strategic Curriculum Change: Global Trends in Universities*. Abingdon: Routledge. pp. 3–20.

Kandiko, Camille B. and Blackmore, Paul (2012b) 'Shaping the curriculum: a characteristics approach', in P. Blackmore and C.B. Kandiko, *Strategic Curriculum Change: Global Trends in Universities*. Abingdon: Routledge. pp. 73–91.

Karasavvidis, Ilias (2010) 'Wiki use in higher education: exploring barriers to successful implementation', *Interactive Learning Environments*, 18(3): 219–31.

Kassens-Noor, Eva (2012) 'Twitter as a teaching practice to enhance active and informal learning in higher education: the case of sustainable tweets', *Active Learning in Higher Education*, 13(1): 9–21.

Kear, Karen, Woodthorpe, John, Robertson, Sandy and Hutchison, Mike (2010) 'From forums to wikis: perspectives on tools for collaboration', *Internet and Higher Education*, 13: 218–25.

Kehrwald, Benjamin (2010) 'Being online: social presence as subjectivity in online learning', *London Review of Education*, 8(1): 39–50.

Kiley, Margaret and Mullins, Gerry (2005) 'Supervisors' conceptions of research: what are they?', *Scandinavian Journal of Educational Research*, 49(3): 245–62.

Kim, Min Kyu, Kim, So Min, Khera, Otto and Getman, Joan (2014) 'The experience of three flipped classrooms in an urban university: an exploration of design principles', *Internet and Higher Education*, 22: 37–50.

Kirkwood, Adrian and Price, Linda (2013) 'Missing: evidence of a scholarly approach to teaching and learning with technology in higher education', *Teaching in Higher Education*, 18(3): 327–37.

Kirkwood, Adrian and Price, Linda (2014) 'Technology-enhanced learning and teaching in higher education: what is "enhanced" and how do we know? A critical literature review', *Learning, Media and Technology*, 39(1): 6–36.

Klein, Julie (2004) 'Interdisciplinarity and complexity: an evolving relationship', *E:CO*, 6(1–2): 2–10.

Klein, Julie (2010) 'A taxonomy of interdisciplinarity', in R. Frodeman and J.T. Klein (eds), *The Oxford Handbook of Interdisciplinarity*. New York: Oxford University Press. pp. 15–30.

Knight, Jane (2004) 'Internationalization remodelled: definition, approaches, and rationales', *Journal of Studies in International Education*, 8(1): 5–31.

Knight, Nick (1999) 'Responsibilities and limits in the supervision of NESB research students in the social sciences and humanities', in Y. Ryan and O. Zuber-Skerrit (eds), *Supervising Postgraduates from Non-English Speaking Backgrounds*. Buckingham: Open University Press. pp. 93–100.

Knight, Peter (2001) 'Complexity and curriculum: a process approach to curriculum-making', *Teaching in Higher Education*, 6(3): 369–81.

Knight, Peter (2005) 'Unsustainable developments', *Guardian*, 8 February (http://www.theguardian.com/education/2005/feb/08/highereducation.administration).

Koehne, Norma (2006) '(Be)coming, (be)longing: ways in which international students talk about themselves', *Discourse: Studies in the Cultural Politics of Education*, 27(2): 241–57.

Kolb, David (1984) *Experiential Learning: Experience as the Source of Learning and Development*. New Jersey: Prentice Hall.

Krathwohl, David R. (2002) 'A revision of Bloom's Taxonomy: an overview', *Theory into Practice*, 41(4): 212–18.

Krause, Kerri-Lee (2005) 'Understanding and promoting student engagement in university learning communities', paper presented as keynote address 'Engaged, inert or otherwise occupied: deconstructing the 21st century undergraduate student'. James Cook University Symposium 2005, *Sharing Scholarship in Learning and Teaching: Engaging Students*, James Cook University, Townsville/Cairns, Australia, 21–22 September (https://cshe.unimelb.edu.au/resources_teach/teaching_in_practice/docs/Stud_eng.pdf).

Kreber, Carolin (2009) 'Supporting student learning in the context of diversity, complexity and uncertainty', in C. Kreber (ed.), *The University and its Disciplines: Teaching and Learning Within and Beyond Disciplinary Boundaries*. New York: Routledge. pp. 3–18.

Kuh, George D. (2009) 'The National Survey of Student Engagement: conceptual and empirical foundations', *New Directions in Institutional Research*, 141: 5–20.

Ladyshewsky, Richard K. (2013) 'The role of peers in feedback processes', in D. Boud and E. Molloy (eds), *Feedback in Higher and Professional Education: Understanding It and Doing It Well*. London: Routledge. pp. 174–89.

Lan, Li, Liu, Xiongyi and Steckelberg, Allen L. (2009) 'Assessor or assessee: how student learning improves by giving and receiving peer feedback', *British Journal of Educational Technology*, 41(3): 525–36.

Lancaster, Simon (2013) 'The flipped lecture', *New Directions*, 9(1): 28–32.

Largent, David L. (2012) 'A tale of two courses: an experience report about student engagement related to the use of an electronic student response system and pre-lecture videos', *Journal of Computing Sciences in Colleges*, 28(1): 47–54.

Laru, Jari, Näykki, Piia and Järvelä, Sanna (2012) 'Supporting small-group learning using multiple Web 2.0 tools: a case study in the higher education context', *Internet and Higher Education*, 15: 29–38.

Laycock, Mike (2011) *Learner Engagement: A Guide to Negotiated Work-based Learning*. SEDA Special 29. London: Staff and Educational Development.

Lea, Mary (2013) 'Reclaiming literacies: competing textual practices in a digital higher education', *Teaching in Higher Education*, 18(1): 106–18.

Lea, Mary R. and Jones, Sylvia (2011) 'Digital literacies in higher education: exploring textual and technological practice', *Studies in Higher Education*, 36(4): 377–93.

Lea, Mary and Street, Brian (1998) 'Student writing in higher education: an academic literacies approach', *Studies in Higher Education*, 23(2): 157–71.

Lea, Mary and Street, Brian (2000) 'Student writing in higher education: an academic literacies approach', in M. Lea and B. Stierer (eds), *Student Writing in Higher Education: New Contexts*. Buckingham: Open University Press. pp. 32–46.

Lea, Mary and Street, Brian (2006) 'The "academic literacies" model: theory and applications', *Theory and Practice*, 45(4): 368–77.

Leach, Linda (2011) '"I treat all students as equal": further and higher education teachers' responses to diversity', *Journal of Further and Higher Education*, 35(2): 247–63.

Leach, Linda and Zepke, Nick (2011) 'Engaging students in learning: a review of a conceptual organiser', *Higher Education Research & Development*, 30(2): 193–204.

Leask, Betty (2006) 'Plagiarism, cultural diversity and metaphor: implications for academic staff development', *Assessment & Evaluation in Higher Education*, 31(2): 183–99.

Leask, Betty (2007) 'International teachers and international learning', in E. Jones and S. Brown (eds), *Internationalising Higher Education*. London: Routledge. pp. 86–94.

Leask, Betty (2009) 'Using formal and informal curricula to improve interactions between home and international students', *Journal of Studies in International Education*, 13(2): 205–21.

Leask, Betty (2013) 'Internationalizing the curriculum in the disciplines: imagining new possibilities', *Journal of Studies in International Education*, 17(2): 103–18.

Leask, Betty and Carroll, Jude (2011) 'Moving beyond "wishing and hoping": internationalisation and student experiences of inclusion and engagement', *Higher Education Research & Development*, 30(5): 647–59.

Leathwood, Carole and O'Connell, Paul (2003) '"It's a struggle": the construction of the "new student" in higher education', *Journal of Education Policy*, 18(6): 597–615.

Levin, Daniel, Brennan, Keith, Hurlstone, Adam and Hentges, Kathryn E. (2014) 'Implementing and evaluating a set of online virtual experimental scenarios for teaching developmental biology', *Journal of Learning Development in Higher Education*, Special Edition Digital Technologies in Higher Education.

Levy, Philippa and Petrulis, Robert (2012) 'How do first-year university students experience inquiry and research, and what are the implications for the practice of inquiry-based learning?', *Studies in Higher Education*, 37(1): 85–101.

Li, Linda Y. and Vandermensbrugghe, Joelle (2011) 'Supporting the thesis writing process of international research students through an ongoing writing group', *Innovations in Education and Teaching International*, 48(2): 195–205.

Lillis, Theresa (2006) 'Moving towards an "academic literacies" pedagogy: dialogues of participation', in L. Ganobcsik-Williams (ed.), *Teaching Academic Writing in UK Higher Education: Theories, Practices and Models*. Basingstoke: Palgrave Macmillan. pp. 30–45.

Lillis, Theresa and Scott, Mary (2007) 'Defining academic literacies research: issues of epistemology, ideology and strategy', *Journal of Applied Linguistics*, 4(1): 5–32.

Lin, Hong and Kelsey, Kathleen D. (2009) 'Building a networked environment in wikis: the evolving phases of collaborative learning in a wikibook project', *Journal of Educational Computing Research*, 40(2): 145–69.

Liu, Ngar-Fun and Carless, David (2006) 'Peer feedback: the learning element of peer assessment', *Teaching in Higher Education*, 11(3): 279–90.

Livingstone, Larry (2010) 'Teaching creativity in higher education', *Arts Education Policy Review*, 111: 59–62.

Lucas, Timothy and Rowley, Natalie (2011) 'Enquiry-based learning: experiences of first year chemistry students learning spectroscopy', *Chemistry Education Research and Practice*, 12: 478–86.

Luxon, Tony and Peelo, Moira (2009) 'Internationalisation: its implications for curriculum design and course development in UK higher education', *Innovations in Education and Teaching International*, 46(1): 51–60.

Macfarlane, Bruce (2010) 'The morphing of academic practice: unbundling and the rise of the para-academic', *Higher Education Quarterly*, 65(1): 59–73.

Mackinnon, Dolly and Manathunga, Catherine (2003) 'Going global with assessment: what to do when the dominant culture's literacy drives assessment', *Higher Education Research & Development*, 22(2): 131–44.

McAlpine, Lynn and Åkerlind, Gerlese (2010) 'Academic practice in a changing international landscape', in L. McAlpine and G. Åkerlind (eds), *Becoming an Academic: International Perspectives*. Basingstoke: Palgrave Macmillan. pp. 1–17.

McCartney, Mark, Bradshaw, Noel-Ann and Mann, Tony (2011) 'Mathematical motivators: using the history of mathematics to enrich the curriculum', *MSOR Connections*, 11(2): 14–16.

McCulloch, Alistair (2009) 'The student as co-producer: learning from public administration about the student–university relationship', *Studies in Higher Education*, 34(2): 171–83.

McCune, Velda and Hounsell, Dai (2005) 'The development of students' ways of thinking and practising in three final-year biology courses', *Higher Education*, 49: 255–89.

McDrury, Janice and Alterio, Maxine (2002) *Learning through Storytelling in Higher Education: Using Reflection and Experience to Improve Learning*. London: Kogan Page.

McEwen, Lindsay and Mason O'Connor, Kristine (2014) 'Developing pedagogic research in higher education', in L. McEwen and K. Mason O'Connor (eds), *Developing Pedagogic Research in Higher Education*. SEDA Special 37. London: Staff and Educational Development. pp. 7–14.

McKenna, Colleen and Hughes, Jane (2013) 'Values, digital texts, and open practices: a changing scholarly landscape in higher education', in R. Goodfellow and M. Lea (eds), *Literacy in the Digital University: Critical Perspectives on Learning, Scholarship, and Technology*. London: Routledge. pp. 15–26.

McLean, Patricia and Ransom, Laurie (2005) 'Building intercultural competencies: implications for academic skills development', in J. Carroll and J. Ryan (eds), *Teaching International Students: Improving Learning for All*. London: Routledge. pp. 45–62.

McNiff, Jean (2013) *Action Research: Principles and Practices*. 3rd edn. Abingdon: Routledge.

Mann, Sarah J. (2001) 'Alternative perspectives on the student experience: alienation and engagement', *Studies in Higher Education*, 26(1): 7–19.

Matthews, Nicole (2009) 'Teaching the "invisible" disabled students in the classroom: disclosure, inclusion and the social model of disability', *Teaching in Higher Education*, 14(3): 229–39.

Mayes, Terry and de Freitas, Sara (2013) 'Technology-enhanced learning: the role of theory', in H. Beetham and R. Sharpe (eds), *Rethinking Pedagogy for a Digital Age: Designing for 21st Century Learning*. 2nd edn. New York: Routledge. pp. 17–30.

Maxwell, Amanda, Curtis, Guy J. and Vardanega, Lucia (2008) 'Does culture influence understanding and perceived seriousness of plagiarism?', *The International Journal for Educational Integrity*, 4(2): 25–40.

Meishar-Tal, Hagit and Gorsky, Paul (2010) 'Wikis: what students do and do not do when writing collaboratively', *Open Learning: The Journal of Open, Distance and e-Learning*, 25(1): 25–35.

Meyer, Jan and Land, Ray (2003) *Threshold Concepts and Troublesome Knowledge: Linkages to Ways of Thinking and Practising within the Disciplines*. Occasional Report 4 (http://www.etl.tla.ed.ac.uk/docs/ETLreport4.pdf).

Meyer, Jan and Land, Ray (2005) 'Threshold concepts and troublesome knowledge (2): epistemological considerations and a conceptual framework for teaching and learning', *Higher Education*, 49: 373–88.

Middendorf, Joan and Pace, David (2004) 'Decoding the disciplines: a model for helping students learn disciplinary ways of thinking', *New Directions for Teaching and Learning*, 98: 1–12.

Miles, Melissa and Rainbird, Sarah (2014) 'Evaluating interdisciplinary collaborative learning and assessment in the creative arts and humanities', *Arts and Humanities in Higher Education*. DOI: 10.1177/1474022214561759.

Molesworth, Mike, Nixon, Elizabeth and Scullion, Richard (2009) 'Having, being and higher education: the marketisation of the university and the transformation of the student into consumer', *Teaching in Higher Education*, 14(3): 277–87.

Montgomery, Catherine (2010) *Understanding the International Student Experience*. Basingstoke: Palgrave Macmillan.

Moon, Jenny (2002) *The Module and Programme Development Handbook: A Practical Guide to Linking Levels, Outcomes and Assessment Criteria*. London: Kogan Page.

Moon, Jennifer (2010) *Using Story in Higher Education and Professional Development*. London: Routledge.

Moon, Jenny and Gosling, David (2002) *How to Use Learning Outcomes and Assessment Criteria*. 3rd edn. London: Southern Consortium for Credit Accumulation and Transfer.

Morris, Dick and Martin, Stephen (2009) 'Complexity, systems thinking and practice', in A. Stibbe (ed.), *The Handbook of Sustainable Literature: Skills for a Changing World*. Place: Green Books (http://www.sustainability-literacy.org).

Mutch, Alistair (2003) 'Exploring the practice of feedback to students', *Active Learning in Higher Education*, 4(1): 24–38.

Naismith, N., Lee, B.H. and Pilkington, R.M. (2011) 'Collaborative learning with a wiki: differences in perceived usefulness in two contexts of use', *Journal of Computer Assisted Learning*, 27: 228–42.

Nerantzi, Chrissi and Beckingham, Sue (2014) 'BYOD4L: our magical open box to enhance individuals' learning ecologies', in N. Jackson and J. Willis (eds), *Lifewide Learning & Education in Universities and Colleges* (http://learninglives.co.uk/e-book.html).

Neumann, Ruth (1992) 'Perceptions of the teaching–research nexus: a framework for analysis', *Higher Education*, 23: 159–71.

Neumann, Ruth, Parry, Sharon and Becher, Tony (2002) 'Teaching and learning in their disciplinary context: a conceptual analysis', *Studies in Higher Education*, 27(4): 405–17.

Ni Raghallaigh, M. and Cunniffe, R. (2013) 'Creating a safe climate for active learning and student engagement: an example from an introductory social work module', *Teaching in Higher Education*, 18(1): 93–105.

Nicholson, Dawn (2011) 'Embedding research in a field-based module through peer review and assessment for learning', *Journal of Geography in Higher Education*, 35(4): 529–49.

Nicol, David (2010) 'From monologue to dialogue: improving written feedback processes in mass higher education', *Assessment & Evaluation in Higher Education*, 35(5): 501–17.

Nicol, David and Macfarlane-Dick, Debra (2006) 'Formative assessment and self-regulated learning: a model and seven principles of good feedback practice', *Studies in Higher Education*, 31(2): 199–218.

Nicol, David, Thomson, Avril and Breslin, Caroline (2014) 'Rethinking feedback practices in higher education: a peer review perspective', *Assessment & Evaluation in Higher Education*, 39(1): 102–22.

Nikitina, Svetlana (2006) 'Three strategies for interdisciplinary teaching: contextualising, conceptualizing and problem-centring', *Journal of Curriculum Studies*, 38(3): 251–71.

Northedge, Andrew (2003) 'Enabling participation in academic discourse', *Teaching in Higher Education*, 8(2):169–80.

Nunan, Ted, George, Rigmor and McCausland, Holly (2000) 'Inclusive education in universities: why it is important and how it might be achieved', *International Journal of Inclusive Education*, 4(1): 63–88.

NUS (National Union of Students) (2012) *A Manifesto for Partnership* (http://www.nusconnect.org.uk/campaigns/highereducation/partnership/a-manifesto-for-partnerships/).

Nutbeam, Ron (2013) 'Students can be interdisciplinary too', *Guardian*, 12 August (http://www.theguardian.com/higher-education-network/blog/2013/aug/12/students-interdisciplinary-teaching-research-university).

Nygaard, Claus and Belluigi, Dina Zoe (2011) 'A proposed methodology for contextualised evaluation in higher education', *Assessment & Evaluation in Higher Education*, 36(6): 657–71.

O'Brien, Stephen and Brancaleone, David (2011) 'Evaluating learning outcomes: in search of lost knowledge', *Irish Educational Studies*, 30(1): 5–21.

O'Donovan, Berry, Price, Margaret and Rust, Chris (2008) 'Developing student understanding of assessment standards: a nested hierarchy of approaches', *Teaching in Higher Education*, 13(2): 205–17.

Oliver, Martin (2011) 'Technological determinism in educational technology research: some alternative ways of thinking about the relationship between learning and technology', *Journal of Computer Assisted Learning*, 27: 373–84.

Otter, Dorron (2007) 'Globalisation and sustainability: global perspectives and education for sustainable development in higher education', in E. Jones and S. Brown (eds), *Internationalising Higher Education*. London: Routledge. pp. 42–53.

Overton, Tina L. and Bradley, John S. (2010) 'Internationalisation of the chemistry curriculum: two problem-based learning activities for undergraduate chemists', *Chemistry Education Research and Practice*, 11: 124–8.

Ozay, Samuary B. (2012) 'The dimensions of research in undergraduate learning', *Teaching in Higher Education*, 17(4): 453–64.

Pan, W., Cotton, D. and Murray, P. (2014) 'Linking research and teaching: context, conflict and complementarity', *Innovations in Education and Teaching International*, 51(1): 3–14.

Parker, Jan (2002) 'A new disciplinarity: communities of knowledge, learning and practice', *Teaching in Higher Education*, 7(4): 373–86.

Parker, Jan (2003) 'Reconceptualising the curriculum: from commodification to transformation', *Teaching in Higher Education*, 8(4): 529–43.

Parker, Jenneth (2010) 'Competencies for interdisciplinarity in higher education', *International Journal for Sustainability in Higher Education*, 11(4): 325–38.

Parker, Kevin R. and Chao, Joseph, T. (2007) 'Wiki as a teaching tool', *Interdisciplinary Journal of Knowledge and Learning Objects*, 3: 57–72.

Pearce, Nick and Learmonth, Sarah (2013) 'Learning beyond the classroom: evaluating the use of Pinterest in learning and teaching in an introductory anthropology class', *Journal of Interactive Media in Education* (http://jime.open.ac.uk/2013/12).

Pecorari, Diane (2003) 'Good and original: plagiarism and patchwriting in academic second-language writing', *Journal of Second Language Writing*, 12: 317–45.

Pegg, Ann, Waldock, Jeff, Hendy-Isaac, Sonia and Lawton, Ruth (2012) *Pedagogy for Employability*. York: HEA (https://www.heacademy.ac.uk/sites/default/files/pedagogy_for_employability_update_2012.pdf).

Pharo, E.J., Davison, S., Warr, K., Nursey-Bray, M. Beswick, K., Wapstra, E. and Jones, C. (2012) 'Can teacher collaboration overcome barriers to interdisciplinary learning in a disciplinary university? A case study using climate change', *Teaching in Higher Education*, 17(5): 497–507.

Pitcher, Rod and Åkerlind, Gerlese S. (2009) 'Post-doctoral researchers' conceptions of research: a metaphor analysis', *International Journal for Researcher Development*, 1(2): 160–72.

Popovic, Celia and Green, David (2012) *Understanding Undergraduates: Challenging our Preconceptions of Student Success*. Abingdon: Routledge.

Portelli, John P. (1993) 'Exposing the hidden curriculum', *Journal of Curriculum Studies*, 25(4): 343–58.

Potter, Jacqueline (2009) 'Starting with the discipline', in R. Murray (ed.), *The Scholarship of Teaching and Learning in Higher Education*. Maidenhead: Open University Press. pp. 58–68.

Potter, Michael K. and Kustra, Erika D.H. (2011) 'The relationship between scholarly teaching and SoTL: models, distinctions, and clarifications', *International Journal for the Scholarship of Teaching and Learning*, 5(1), Article 23.

Prensky, Marc (2001) 'Digital natures, digital immigrants part 1', *On the Horizon*, 9(5): 2–6.

Prestridge, Sarah (2014) 'A focus on students' use of Twitter: their interactions with each other, content and interface', *Active Learning in Higher Education*, 15(2): 101–15.

Price, Margaret, Handley, Karen and Millar, Jill (2011) 'Feedback: focusing attention on engagement', *Studies in Higher Education*, 36(8): 879–96.

Prosser, Michael and Trigwell, Keith (1999) *Understanding Learning and Teaching: The Experience in Higher Education*. Buckingham: Open University Press.

Prosser, Michael, Martin, Elaine, Trigwell, Keith, Ramsden, Paul and Middleton, Heather (2008) 'University academics' experience of research and its relationship to their experience of teaching', *Instructional Science*, 36(3): 3–16.

QAA (Quality Assurance Agency for Higher Education) (2001) *Framework for Qualifications of Higher Education Institutions in Scotland*. Gloucester: QAA.

QAA (2014a) *Education for Sustainable Development: Guidance for UK Higher Education Providers*. Gloucester: QAA.

QAA (2014b) *UK Quality Code for Higher Education*. Gloucester: QAA.

Quinton, Sarah and Smallbone, Teresa (2010) 'Feeding forward: using feedback to promote student reflection and learning – a teaching model', *Innovations in Education and Teaching International*, 47(1): 125–35.

Reay, Diane, Crozier, Gill and Clayton, John (2010) '"Fitting in" or "standing out": working class students in UK higher education', *British Educational Research Journal*, 36(1): 107–24.

Richardson, John (2015) 'The under-attainment of ethnic minority students in UK higher education: what we know and what we don't know', *Journal of Further and Higher Education*, 39(2): 278–91.

Roberts, Carolyn and Roberts, Jane (2010) *Greener by Degrees: Exploring Sustainability through Higher Education Curricula* (http://insight.glos.ac.uk/tli/resources/toolkit/resources/pages/greenerbydegrees.aspx).

Robertson, Jane and Blackler, Gillian (2006) 'Students' experiences of learning in a research environment', *Higher Education Research & Development*, 25(3): 215–29.

Robertson, Jane and Bond, Carol H., (2001) 'Experiences of the relation between teaching and research: what do academics value?', *Higher Education Research & Development*, 20(1): 5–19.

Robinson, Ken (2001) *Out of our Minds: Learning to be Creative*. Chichester: Capstone.

Robinson-Pant, Anna (2009) 'Changing academies: exploring international PhD students' perspectives on "host" and "home" universities', *Higher Education Research & Development*, 28(4): 417–29.

Robinson-Pant, Anna (2010) 'Internationalisation of higher education: challenges for the doctoral supervisor', in M. Walker and P. Thomson (eds), *The Routledge Doctoral Supervisor's Companion: Supporting Effective Research in Education and the Social Sciences*. Abingdon: Routledge. pp. 147–57.

Robson, Colin (2011) *Real World Research*. 3rd edn. Chichester: John Wiley & Sons.

Robson, Sue, Leat, David, Wall, Kate and Lofthouse, Rachel (2013) 'Feedback or feed forward? Supporting Masters students through effective assessment to enhance future learning', in J. Ryan (ed.), *Cross-Cultural Teaching and Learning for Home and International Students: Internationalisation of Pedagogy and Curriculum in Higher Education*. London: Routledge. pp. 53–68.

Roddam, Hazel, McCandless, Paula, Thewlis, Dominic and McDonald, Kateryna (2009) 'Judging the evidence with confidence: the student experience of an undergraduate journal club', *UCLan Journal of Pedagogic Research*, 1(1): 29–33.

Rodriguez-Falcon, Elena, Hodzic, Alma and Symington, Anna (2011) 'Learning from each other: engaging engineering students through their cultural capital', *Engineering Education*, 6(2): 29–38.

Rust, Chris, Price, Margaret and O'Donovan, Berry (2003) 'Improving students' learning by developing their understanding of assessment criteria and processes', *Assessment & Evaluation in Higher Education*, 28(2): 147–64.

Ryan, Janette (2005) 'Improving teaching and learning practices for international students: implications for curriculum, pedagogy and assessment', in J. Carroll and J. Ryan (eds), *Teaching International Students: Improving Learning for All*. London: Routledge. pp. 92–100.

Ryan, Janette and Carroll, Jude (2005) '"Canaries in the coalmine": international students in Western universities', in J. Carroll and J. Ryan (eds), *Teaching International Students: Improving Learning for All*. London: Routledge. pp. 3–10.

Ryan, Janette and Viete, Rosemary (2009) 'Respectful interactions: learning with international students in the English-speaking academy', *Teaching in Higher Education*, 14(3): 303–14.

Ryan, Mary and Ryan, Michael (2013) 'Theorising a model for teaching and assessing reflective learning in higher education', *Higher Education Research & Development*, 32(2): 244–57.

Sabou, Marta, Bontcheva, Kalina and Scharl, Arno (2012) 'Crowdsourcing research opportunities: lessons from natural language processing', *i-Know '12*, Proceedings of the 12th International Conference on Knowledge Management and Knowledge Technologies, Graz, Austria, 5–7 July.

Sadler, D. Royce (2009) 'Transforming holistic assessment and grading into a vehicle for complex learning', in G. Joughin (ed.), *Assessment, Learning and Judgement in Higher Education*. Dordrecht: Springer. pp. 49–64.

Sadler, D. Royce (2010) 'Beyond feedback: developing student capability in complex appraisal', *Assessment & Evaluation in Higher Education*, 35(5): 535–50.

Said, Edward W. (1978[2003]) *Orientalism*. London: Penguin.

Salmon, Gilly (2013) *E-tivities: The Key to Active Online Learning*. 2nd edn. New York: Routledge.

Samball, Kay (2011) *Rethinking Feedback in Higher Education: An Assessment for Learning Perspective*. Bristol: ESCalate.

Samball, Kay, McDowell, Liz and Montgomery, Catherine (2013) *Assessment for Learning in Higher Education*. London: Routledge.

Sanders, John and Rose-Adams, John (2014) 'Black and minority ethnic student attainment: a survey of research and exploration of the importance of teacher and student expectations', *Widening Participation and Lifelong Learning*, 16(2): 5–27.

Saunders, Murray (2000) 'Beginning an evaluation with RUFDATA: theorizing a practical approach to evaluation planning', *Evaluation*, 6(1): 7–21.

Saunders, Murray, Trowler, Paul and Bamber, Veronica (2011) *Reconceptualising Evaluation in Higher Education: The Practice Turn*. Maidenhead: Open University Press.

Sawir, Erlenawati (2011) 'Academic staff response to international students and internationalising the curriculum: the impact of disciplinary differences', *International Journal for Academic Development*, 16(1): 45–57.

Scott, Peter (2005) 'Divergence of convergence? The links between teaching and research in mass higher education', in R. Barnett (ed.), *Reshaping the University: New Relationships between Research, Scholarship and Teaching*. Maidenhead: Open University Press. pp. 53–66.

Scudamore, Rachel (2013) *Engaging Home and International Students: A Guide for New Lecturers*. York: HEA (https://www.heacademy.ac.uk/sites/default/files/RachelScudamoreReportFeb2013.pdf).

Selby, David (2006) 'The catalyst that is sustainability: bringing permeability to disciplinary boundaries', *Planet*, 17: 57–9.

Sharpe, Rhona and Oliver, Martin (2007) 'Designing courses for e-learning', in H. Beetham and R. Sharpe (eds), *Rethinking Pedagogy for a Digital Age: Designing and Delivering e-Learning*. London: Routledge. pp. 41–51.

Short, Edmund C. (2002) 'Knowledge and the educative functions of a university: designing the curriculum of higher education', *Journal of Curriculum Studies*, 34(2): 139–48.

Siemens, George (2005) 'Connectivism: a learning theory for the digital age', *International Journal of Instructional Technology and Distance Learning*, 2(1) (http://itdl.org/journal/jan_05/article01.htm).

Singh, Gurnam (2011) *Black and Minority Ethnic (BME) Students' Participation in Higher Education: Improving Retention and Success. A Synthesis of Research Evidence*. York: HEA (http://www.heacademy.ac.uk/sites/default/files/BME_synthesis_FINAL.pdf).

Slade, Sharon, Galpin, Fenella and Prinsloo, Paul (2012) 'Exploring stakeholder perspectives regarding a "global" curriculum: a case study', in J. Ryan (ed.), *Cross-Cultural Teaching and Learning for Home and International Students: Internationalisation of Pedagogy and Curriculum in Higher Education*. London: Routledge. pp. 141–55.

Smith, Elizabeth (2011) 'Teaching critical reflection', *Teaching in Higher Education*, 16(2): 211–23.

Smith, Jan (2010) 'Forging identities: the experiences of probationary lecturers in the UK', *Studies in Higher Education*, 35(5): 577–91.

Smith, Karen (2009) 'Transnational teaching experiences: an under-explored territory for transformative professional development', *International Journal for Academic Development*, 14(2): 111–22.

Smith, Karen (2014) 'Exploring flying faculty teaching experiences: motivations, challenges and opportunities', *Studies in Higher Education*, 39(1): 117–34.

Smith, Karl A. (2000) 'Going deeper: formal small-group learning in large classes', *New Directions for Teaching and Learning*, 81: 25–46.

Smith, Mark (2012) 'Improving student engagement with employability: the project pitch assessment', *Planet*, 26: 2–6.

Soilemetzidis, Ioannis, Bennett, Paul, Buckley, Alex, Hillman, Nick and Sotakes, Geoff (2014) *The HEPI–HEA Student Academic Experience Survey 2014*. York: HEA.

Solomonides, Ian and Martin, Phillipa (2008) '"All this talk of engagement is making me itch": an investigation into the conceptions of engagement held by students and tutors', in L. Hand and C. Bryson (eds), *Student Engagement*. London: SEDA. pp. 13–17.

Spelt, Elizabeth, Biemans, Harm, Tobi, Hilde, Luning, Pieternal and Mulder, Martin (2009) 'Teaching and learning in interdisciplinary higher education: a systematic review', *Educational Psychology Review*, 21(4): 365–78.

Spronken-Smith, Rachel and Walker, Rebecca (2010) 'Can inquiry-based learning strengthen the links between teaching and disciplinary research?', *Studies in Higher Education*, 35(6): 723–40.

Stead, David (2005) 'A review of the one-minute paper', *Active Learning in Higher Education*, 6(2): 118–31.

Stefani, Lorraine (2008) 'Assessment in interdisciplinary and interprofessional programs: shifting paradigms', in B. Chandramohan and S. Fallows (eds), *Interdisciplinary Learning and Teaching in Higher Education: Theory and Practice*. Abingdon: Routledge. pp. 44–57.

Stenhouse, Lawrence (1975) *An Introduction to Curriculum Research and Development*. Oxford: Heinemann Educational.

Sterling, Stephen (2012) *The Future Fit Framework: An Introductory Guide to Teaching and Learning for Sustainability in HE*. York: HEA (http://www.heacademy.ac.uk/sites/default/files/Future_Fit_270412_1435.pdf).

Stevenson, Jacqueline (2012) *Black and Minority Ethnic Student Degree Retention and Attainment*. York: HEA (http://www.heacademy.ac.uk/sites/default/files/bme_summit_final_report.pdf).

Stibbe, Arran (2013) 'Work-based learning in the humanities: a welcome stranger?', *Practice and Evidence of Scholarship of Teaching and Learning in Higher Education*, 8(3): 241–55.

Stierer, Barry (2008) 'Learning to write about teaching: understanding the demands of lecturer development programmes in higher education', in R. Murray (ed.), *The Scholarship of Teaching and Learning in Higher Education*. Maidenhead: Open University Press. pp. 34–45.

Stone, Bethany B. (2012) 'Flip your classroom to increase active learning and student engagement', paper presented at 28th Annual Conference on Distance Teaching and Learning, 8–10 August, Madison, Wisconsin. (http://www.uwex.edu/disted/conference/Resource_library/proceedings/56511_2012.pdf).

Stott, Tim, Litherland Kate, Carmichael, Patrick and Nuthall, Anne-Marie (2014) 'Using interactive virtual field guides and linked data in geoscience teaching and learning', in V. Tong (ed.), *Geoscience Research and Education: Teaching at Universities*. Innovations in Science Education and Technology. Vol. 20. Heidelberg: Springer Dordrecht. pp. 163–88.

Stracke, Elke (2010) 'Undertaking the journey together: peer learning for a successful and enjoyable PhD experience', *Journal of University Teaching & Learning Practice*, 7(1): 1–12.

Stubbs, Wendy and Schapper, Jan (2011) 'Two approaches to curriculum development for educating for sustainability and CSR', *International Journal of Sustainability in Higher Education*, 12(3): 259–68.

Summers, Mark and Volet, Simone (2008) 'Students' attitudes towards culturally mixed groups on international campuses: impact of participation in diverse and non-diverse groups', *Studies in Higher Education*, 33(4): 357–70.

Sung, Eunmo and Mayer, Richard (2012) 'Five facets of social presence in online distance education', *Computers in Human Behavior*, 28: 1738–47.

Sykes, Janine (2012) 'Locating the value and opportunities for online collaborative creativity within advertising', *Art, Design and Communication in Higher Education*, 11(2): 91–109.

Tange, Hanne and Kastberg, Peter (2013) 'Coming to terms with "double knowing": an inclusive approach to international education', *International Journal of Inclusive Education*, 17(1): 1–14.

Tennant, Mark, McMullen, Cathi and Kaczynski, Dan (2010) *Teaching, Learning and Research in Higher Education: A Critical Approach*. New York: Routledge.

Tian, Mei and Lowe, John (2013) 'The role of feedback in cross-cultural learning: a case study of Chinese taught postgraduate students in a UK university', *Assessment & Evaluation in Higher Education*, 38(5): 580–98.

Toohey, Susan (1999) *Designing Courses for Higher Education*. Buckingham: Open University Press.

Tremonte, Colleen M. (2011) 'Window shopping: fashioning a scholarship of interdisciplinary teaching and learning', *International Journal for the Scholarship of Teaching and Learning*, 5(1): Article 26 (1–12).

Trevelyan, Rose and Wilson, Ann (2012) 'Using patchwork texts in assessment: clarifying and categorising choices in their use', *Assessment & Evaluation in Higher Education*, 37(4): 487–98.

Trowler, Paul (2012) 'Disciplines and interdisciplinarity: conceptual groundwork', in P. Trowler, M. Saunders and V. Bamber (eds), *Tribes and Territories in the 21st Century*. London: Routledge. pp. 5–29.

Trowler, Paul (2014) 'Depicting and researching disciplines: strong and moderate essentialist approaches', *Studies in Higher Education*, 39(10): 1720–31.

Trowler, Paul and Wareham, Terry (2007) 'Re-conceptualising the teaching–research nexus', *Enhancing Higher Education, Theory and Scholarship*, Proceedings of the 30th HERDSA Annual Conference, Adelaide, Australia, 8–11 July (http://www.herdsa.org.au/wp-content/uploads/conference/2007/papers/p53.pdf).

Uchiyama, Kay Pippin and Radin, Jean L. (2009) 'Curriculum mapping in higher education: a vehicle for collaboration', *Innovative Higher Education*, 33: 271–80.

UKCES (2014) *UK Commission's Employer Skills Survey 2013: UK Results* (https://www.gov.uk/government/uploads/system/uploads/attachment_data/file/327492/evidence-report-81-ukces-employer-skills-survey-13-full-report-final.pdf).

UKCISA (UK Council for Student International Affairs) (2009) *Discussing Difference, Discovering Similarities: A Toolkit of Learning Activities to Improve Cross-Cultural Exchange between Students of Different Cultural Backgrounds for Academic and Support Staff/Students*. London: UKCISA (www.ukcisa.org.uk/resources_download.aspx?resourceid=35&documentid=33).

UKCISA (2015) *International Student Statistics: UK Higher Education* (www.ukcisa.org.uk/Info-for-universities-colleges--schools/Policy-research--statistics/Research--statistics/International-students-in-UK-HE/#International-(non-UK)-students-in-UK-HE-in-2013-14).

UNESCO (United Nations Educational, Scientific and Cultural Organisation) (2014) *Shaping the Future We Want: UN Decade of Education for Sustainable Development*

(2005–2014) Final Report. Paris: UNESCO (http://www.unesco.org/new/en/unesco-world-conference-on-esd-2014/esd-after-2014/desd-final-report/).

University of Hertfordshire (2015) *Graduate Attributes* (http://www.herts.ac.uk/about-us/student-charter/graduate-attributes).

University of Sheffield (2011–16) *The Sheffield Graduate Attributes* (first developed in 2005) (http://www.sheffield.ac.uk/sheffieldgraduate/studentattributes).

UUK (Universities UK) (2014) *Patterns and Trends in UK Higher Education 2014*. London: UUK.

Visser-Wijnveen, Gerda J., Van Driel, Jan H., Van der Rijst, Roeland M., Verloop, Nico and Visser, Anthonya (2010) 'The ideal research–teaching nexus in the eyes of academics: building profiles', *Higher Education Research & Development*, 29(2): 195–210.

Walden, Kim and Peacock, Alan (2006) 'The i-Map: a process-centred response to plagiarism', *Assessment & Evaluation in Higher Education*, 31(2): 201–14.

Walker, Richard, Voce, Julie, Nicholls, Joe, Swift, Elaine, Ahmed, Jebar, Horrigan, Sarah and Vincent, Phil (2014) *UCISA 2014 Survey of Technology Enhanced Learning for Higher Education in the UK*. Oxford: UCISA.

Wang, Ting and Li, Linda Y. (2011) '"Tell me what to do" vs "guide me through it": feedback experiences of international doctoral students', *Active Learning in Higher Education*, 12(2): 101–12.

Warburton, Natalie and Volet, Simone (2013) 'Enhancing self-directed learning through a content quiz group learning assignment', *Active Learning in Higher Education*, 14(1): 9–22.

Waterfield, Judith and West, Bob (2006) *Inclusive Assessment in Higher Education: A Resource for Change*. Plymouth: University of Plymouth.

Welikala, Thushari (2011) *Rethinking International Higher Education Curriculum: Mapping the Research Landscape* (www.universitas21.com/relatedfile/download/217).

Weller, Martin (2009) 'Using learning environments as a metaphor for educational change', *On the Horizon*, 17(3): 181–9.

Weller, Saranne (2010) 'Comparing lecturer and student accounts of reading in the humanities', *Arts and Humanities in Higher Education*, 9(1): 87–106.

Weller, Saranne (2011) 'New lecturers' accounts of reading higher education research', *Studies in Continuing Education*, 33(1): 93–106.

Weller, Saranne (2012) 'Achieving curriculum coherence: curriculum design and delivery as social practice', in P. Blackmore and C.B. Kandiko, *Strategic Curriculum Change: Global Trends in Universities*. Abingdon: Routledge. pp. 21–33.

Whalley, W. Brian, Saunders, Angharad, Lewis, Robin A., Buenemann, Michaela and Sutton, Paul C. (2011) 'Curriculum development: producing geographers for the 21st century', *Journal of Geography in Higher Education*, 35(3): 379–93.

White, David and Le Cornu, A. (2011) 'Visitors and residents: a new typology for online engagement', *First Monday*, 16(9) (http://firstmonday.org/article/view/3171/3049).

Willison, John and O'Regan, Kerry (2007) 'Commonly known, commonly not known, totally unknown: a framework for students becoming researchers', *Higher Education Research & Development*, 26(4): 393–409.

Wingate, Ursula and Dreiss, Cécile A., (2009) 'Developing students' academic literacy: an online approach', *Journal of Academic Language and Learning*, 3(1): 14–25.

Wingate, Ursula, Andon, Nick and Cogo, Alessia (2011) 'Embedding academic writing instruction into subject teaching: a case study', *Active Learning in Higher Education*, 12(1): 69–81.

Winter, Richard (2003) 'Contextualising the patchwork text: addressing problems of coursework assessment in higher education', *Innovations in Education and Teaching International*, 40(2): 112–22.

Winter, Jennie and Cotton, Debby (2012) 'Making the hidden curriculum visible: sustainability literacy in higher education', *Environmental Education Research*, 18(6): 783–96.

Witney, Debbie and Smallbone, Teresa (2011) 'Wiki work: can using wikis enhance student collaboration for group assignment tasks?', *Innovations in Education and Teaching International*, 48(1): 101–10.

Wood, Jamie (2011) 'Helping students to become disciplinary researchers using questioning, social bookmarking and inquiry-based learning', *Practice and Evidence of Scholarship of Teaching and Learning in Higher Education*, 6(1): 3–26.

Woods, Charlotte (2007) 'Researching and developing interdisciplinary teaching: towards a conceptual framework for classroom communication', *Higher Education*, 54: 853–66.

Woods, Peter, Barker, Michelle and Hibbins, Raymond (2011) 'Tapping the benefits of multicultural group work: an exploratory study of postgraduate management students', *International Journal of Management Education*, 9(2): 59–70.

Wrigglesworth, John and McKeever, Mary (2010) 'Writing history: a genre-based, interdisciplinary approach linking disciplines, language and academic skills', *Arts and Humanities in Higher Education*, 9(1): 107–26.

Yocom, Ken, Proksch, Gundula, Born, Branden and Tyman, Shannon K. (2012) 'The built environments laboratory: an interdisciplinary framework for studio education in the planning and design disciplines', *Journal for Education in the Built Environment*, 7(2): 8–25.

Yorke, Mantz (2006) *Employability in Higher Education: What it is – What it is not.* Learning and Employability Series One. York: HEA.

Yorke, Mantz (2013) 'Surveys of the "student experience" and the politics of feedback', in S. Merry, M. Price, D. Carless and M. Taras (eds), *Reconceptualising Feedback in Higher Education: Developing Dialogue with Students*. London: Routledge. pp. 6–18.

Yorke, Mantz and Knight, Peter (2006) *Embedding Employability into the Curriculum.* Learning and Employability Series One. York: HEA.

Zacharopoulou, Amanda and Turner, Catherine (2013) 'Peer assisted learning and the creation of a "learning community" for first year law students', *The Law Teacher*, 47(2): 192–214.

Zepke, Nick and Leach, Linda (2007) 'Improving student outcomes in higher education: New Zealand teachers' views on teaching students from diverse backgrounds', *Teaching in Higher Education*, 12(5–6): 655–68.

Zepke, Nick and Leach, Linda (2010) 'Improving student engagement: ten proposals for action', *Active Learning in Higher Education*, 11(3): 167–77.

INDEX